FREE Test Taking Tips DVD Offer

To help us better serve you, we have developed a Test Taking Tips DVD that we would like to give you for FREE. **This DVD covers world-class test taking tips that you can use to be even more successful when you are taking your test.**

All that we ask is that you email us your feedback about your study guide. Please let us know what you thought about it – whether that is good, bad or indifferent.

To get your **FREE Test Taking Tips DVD**, email freedvd@studyguideteam.com with "FREE DVD" in the subject line and the following information in the body of the email:

    a. The title of your study guide.

    b. Your product rating on a scale of 1-5, with 5 being the highest rating.

    c. Your feedback about the study guide. What did you think of it?

    d. Your full name and shipping address to send your free DVD.

If you have any questions or concerns, please don't hesitate to contact us at freedvd@studyguideteam.com.

Thanks again!

NCMHCE Study Guide

NCMHCE Exam Prep and Practice Test Questions for the National Clinical Mental Health Counseling Examination [2nd Edition]

TPB Publishing

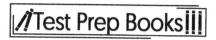

Written and edited by TPB Publishing.

Interested in buying more than 10 copies of our product? Contact us about bulk discounts:
bulkorders@studyguideteam.com

ISBN 13: 9781628455991
ISBN 10: 1628455993

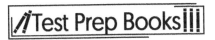

Table of Contents

Test Prep Books!!!

Test Prep Books!!!

Quick Overview

As you draw closer to taking your exam, effective preparation becomes more and more important. Thankfully, you have this study guide to help you get ready. Use this guide to help keep your studying on track and refer to it often.

This study guide contains several key sections that will help you be successful on your exam. The guide contains tips for what you should do the night before and the day of the test. Also included are test-taking tips. Knowing the right information is not always enough. Many well-prepared test takers struggle with exams. These tips will help equip you to accurately read, assess, and answer test questions.

A large part of the guide is devoted to showing you what content to expect on the exam and to helping you better understand that content. In this guide are practice test questions so that you can see how well you have grasped the content. Then, answer explanations are provided so that you can understand why you missed certain questions.

Don't try to cram the night before you take your exam. This is not a wise strategy for a few reasons. First, your retention of the information will be low. Your time would be better used by reviewing information you already know rather than trying to learn a lot of new information. Second, you will likely become stressed as you try to gain a large amount of knowledge in a short amount of time. Third, you will be depriving yourself of sleep. So be sure to go to bed at a reasonable time the night before. Being well-rested helps you focus and remain calm.

Be sure to eat a substantial breakfast the morning of the exam. If you are taking the exam in the afternoon, be sure to have a good lunch as well. Being hungry is distracting and can make it difficult to focus. You have hopefully spent lots of time preparing for the exam. Don't let an empty stomach get in the way of success!

When travelling to the testing center, leave earlier than needed. That way, you have a buffer in case you experience any delays. This will help you remain calm and will keep you from missing your appointment time at the testing center.

Be sure to pace yourself during the exam. Don't try to rush through the exam. There is no need to risk performing poorly on the exam just so you can leave the testing center early. Allow yourself to use all of the allotted time if needed.

Remain positive while taking the exam even if you feel like you are performing poorly. Thinking about the content you should have mastered will not help you perform better on the exam.

Once the exam is complete, take some time to relax. Even if you feel that you need to take the exam again, you will be well served by some down time before you begin studying again. It's often easier to convince yourself to study if you know that it will come with a reward!

Test-Taking Strategies

1. Predicting the Answer

When you feel confident in your preparation for a multiple-choice test, try predicting the answer before reading the answer choices. This is especially useful on questions that test objective factual knowledge. By predicting the answer before reading the available choices, you eliminate the possibility that you will be distracted or led astray by an incorrect answer choice. You will feel more confident in your selection if you read the question, predict the answer, and then find your prediction among the answer choices. After using this strategy, be sure to still read all of the answer choices carefully and completely. If you feel unprepared, you should not attempt to predict the answers. This would be a waste of time and an opportunity for your mind to wander in the wrong direction.

2. Reading the Whole Question

Too often, test takers scan a multiple-choice question, recognize a few familiar words, and immediately jump to the answer choices. Test authors are aware of this common impatience, and they will sometimes prey upon it. For instance, a test author might subtly turn the question into a negative, or he or she might redirect the focus of the question right at the end. The only way to avoid falling into these traps is to read the entirety of the question carefully before reading the answer choices.

3. Looking for Wrong Answers

Long and complicated multiple-choice questions can be intimidating. One way to simplify a difficult multiple-choice question is to eliminate all of the answer choices that are clearly wrong. In most sets of answers, there will be at least one selection that can be dismissed right away. If the test is administered on paper, the test taker could draw a line through it to indicate that it may be ignored; otherwise, the test taker will have to perform this operation mentally or on scratch paper. In either case, once the obviously incorrect answers have been eliminated, the remaining choices may be considered. Sometimes identifying the clearly wrong answers will give the test taker some information about the correct answer. For instance, if one of the remaining answer choices is a direct opposite of one of the eliminated answer choices, it may well be the correct answer. The opposite of obviously wrong is obviously right! Of course, this is not always the case. Some answers are obviously incorrect simply because they are irrelevant to the question being asked. Still, identifying and eliminating some incorrect answer choices is a good way to simplify a multiple-choice question.

4. Don't Overanalyze

Anxious test takers often overanalyze questions. When you are nervous, your brain will often run wild, causing you to make associations and discover clues that don't actually exist. If you feel that this may be a problem for you, do whatever you can to slow down during the test. Try taking a deep breath or counting to ten. As you read and consider the question, restrict yourself to the particular words used by the author. Avoid thought tangents about what the author *really* meant, or what he or she was *trying* to say. The only things that matter on a multiple-choice test are the words that are actually in the question. You must avoid reading too much into a multiple-choice question, or supposing that the writer meant something other than what he or she wrote.

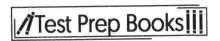

5. No Need for Panic

It is wise to learn as many strategies as possible before taking a multiple-choice test, but it is likely that you will come across a few questions for which you simply don't know the answer. In this situation, avoid panicking. Because most multiple-choice tests include dozens of questions, the relative value of a single wrong answer is small. As much as possible, you should compartmentalize each question on a multiple-choice test. In other words, you should not allow your feelings about one question to affect your success on the others. When you find a question that you either don't understand or don't know how to answer, just take a deep breath and do your best. Read the entire question slowly and carefully. Try rephrasing the question a couple of different ways. Then, read all of the answer choices carefully. After eliminating obviously wrong answers, make a selection and move on to the next question.

6. Confusing Answer Choices

When working on a difficult multiple-choice question, there may be a tendency to focus on the answer choices that are the easiest to understand. Many people, whether consciously or not, gravitate to the answer choices that require the least concentration, knowledge, and memory. This is a mistake. When you come across an answer choice that is confusing, you should give it extra attention. A question might be confusing because you do not know the subject matter to which it refers. If this is the case, don't eliminate the answer before you have affirmatively settled on another. When you come across an answer choice of this type, set it aside as you look at the remaining choices. If you can confidently assert that one of the other choices is correct, you can leave the confusing answer aside. Otherwise, you will need to take a moment to try to better understand the confusing answer choice. Rephrasing is one way to tease out the sense of a confusing answer choice.

7. Your First Instinct

Many people struggle with multiple-choice tests because they overthink the questions. If you have studied sufficiently for the test, you should be prepared to trust your first instinct once you have carefully and completely read the question and all of the answer choices. There is a great deal of research suggesting that the mind can come to the correct conclusion very quickly once it has obtained all of the relevant information. At times, it may seem to you as if your intuition is working faster even than your reasoning mind. This may in fact be true. The knowledge you obtain while studying may be retrieved from your subconscious before you have a chance to work out the associations that support it. Verify your instinct by working out the reasons that it should be trusted.

8. Key Words

Many test takers struggle with multiple-choice questions because they have poor reading comprehension skills. Quickly reading and understanding a multiple-choice question requires a mixture of skill and experience. To help with this, try jotting down a few key words and phrases on a piece of scrap paper. Doing this concentrates the process of reading and forces the mind to weigh the relative importance of the question's parts. In selecting words and phrases to write down, the test taker thinks about the question more deeply and carefully. This is especially true for multiple-choice questions that are preceded by a long prompt.

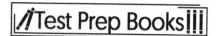

9. Subtle Negatives

One of the oldest tricks in the multiple-choice test writer's book is to subtly reverse the meaning of a question with a word like *not* or *except*. If you are not paying attention to each word in the question, you can easily be led astray by this trick. For instance, a common question format is, "Which of the following is...?" Obviously, if the question instead is, "Which of the following is not...?," then the answer will be quite different. Even worse, the test makers are aware of the potential for this mistake and will include one answer choice that would be correct if the question were not negated or reversed. A test taker who misses the reversal will find what he or she believes to be a correct answer and will be so confident that he or she will fail to reread the question and discover the original error. The only way to avoid this is to practice a wide variety of multiple-choice questions and to pay close attention to each and every word.

10. Reading Every Answer Choice

It may seem obvious, but you should always read every one of the answer choices! Too many test takers fall into the habit of scanning the question and assuming that they understand the question because they recognize a few key words. From there, they pick the first answer choice that answers the question they believe they have read. Test takers who read all of the answer choices might discover that one of the latter answer choices is actually *more* correct. Moreover, reading all of the answer choices can remind you of facts related to the question that can help you arrive at the correct answer. Sometimes, a misstatement or incorrect detail in one of the latter answer choices will trigger your memory of the subject and will enable you to find the right answer. Failing to read all of the answer choices is like not reading all of the items on a restaurant menu: you might miss out on the perfect choice.

11. Spot the Hedges

One of the keys to success on multiple-choice tests is paying close attention to every word. This is never truer than with words like almost, most, some, and sometimes. These words are called "hedges" because they indicate that a statement is not totally true or not true in every place and time. An absolute statement will contain no hedges, but in many subjects, the answers are not always straightforward or absolute. There are always exceptions to the rules in these subjects. For this reason, you should favor those multiple-choice questions that contain hedging language. The presence of qualifying words indicates that the author is taking special care with his or her words, which is certainly important when composing the right answer. After all, there are many ways to be wrong, but there is only one way to be right! For this reason, it is wise to avoid answers that are absolute when taking a multiple-choice test. An absolute answer is one that says things are either all one way or all another. They often include words like every, always, best, and never. If you are taking a multiple-choice test in a subject that doesn't lend itself to absolute answers, be on your guard if you see any of these words.

12. Long Answers

In many subject areas, the answers are not simple. As already mentioned, the right answer often requires hedges. Another common feature of the answers to a complex or subjective question are qualifying clauses, which are groups of words that subtly modify the meaning of the sentence. If the question or answer choice describes a rule to which there are exceptions or the subject matter is complicated, ambiguous, or confusing, the correct answer will require many words in order to be expressed clearly and accurately. In essence, you should not be deterred by answer choices that seem excessively long. Oftentimes, the author of the text will not be able to write the correct answer without

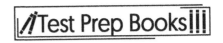

offering some qualifications and modifications. Your job is to read the answer choices thoroughly and completely and to select the one that most accurately and precisely answers the question.

13. Restating to Understand

Sometimes, a question on a multiple-choice test is difficult not because of what it asks but because of how it is written. If this is the case, restate the question or answer choice in different words. This process serves a couple of important purposes. First, it forces you to concentrate on the core of the question. In order to rephrase the question accurately, you have to understand it well. Rephrasing the question will concentrate your mind on the key words and ideas. Second, it will present the information to your mind in a fresh way. This process may trigger your memory and render some useful scrap of information picked up while studying.

14. True Statements

Sometimes an answer choice will be true in itself, but it does not answer the question. This is one of the main reasons why it is essential to read the question carefully and completely before proceeding to the answer choices. Too often, test takers skip ahead to the answer choices and look for true statements. Having found one of these, they are content to select it without reference to the question above. Obviously, this provides an easy way for test makers to play tricks. The savvy test taker will always read the entire question before turning to the answer choices. Then, having settled on a correct answer choice, he or she will refer to the original question and ensure that the selected answer is relevant. The mistake of choosing a correct-but-irrelevant answer choice is especially common on questions related to specific pieces of objective knowledge. A prepared test taker will have a wealth of factual knowledge at his or her disposal, and should not be careless in its application.

15. No Patterns

One of the more dangerous ideas that circulates about multiple-choice tests is that the correct answers tend to fall into patterns. These erroneous ideas range from a belief that B and C are the most common right answers, to the idea that an unprepared test-taker should answer "A-B-A-C-A-D-A-B-A." It cannot be emphasized enough that pattern-seeking of this type is exactly the WRONG way to approach a multiple-choice test. To begin with, it is highly unlikely that the test maker will plot the correct answers according to some predetermined pattern. The questions are scrambled and delivered in a random order. Furthermore, even if the test maker was following a pattern in the assignation of correct answers, there is no reason why the test taker would know which pattern he or she was using. Any attempt to discern a pattern in the answer choices is a waste of time and a distraction from the real work of taking the test. A test taker would be much better served by extra preparation before the test than by reliance on a pattern in the answers.

FREE DVD OFFER

Don't forget that doing well on your exam includes both understanding the test content and understanding how to use what you know to do well on the test. We offer a completely FREE Test Taking Tips DVD that covers world class test taking tips that you can use to be even more successful when you are taking your test.

All that we ask is that you email us your feedback about your study guide. To get your **FREE Test Taking Tips DVD**, email freedvd@studyguideteam.com with "FREE DVD" in the subject line and the following information in the body of the email:

- The title of your study guide.
- Your product rating on a scale of 1-5, with 5 being the highest rating.
- Your feedback about the study guide. What did you think of it?
- Your full name and shipping address to send your free DVD.

Introduction to the NCMHCE Exam

Function of the Test

The National Clinical Mental Health Counseling Examination (NCMHCE) is a nationwide exam taken by industry professionals or recent graduates in order to fulfill the requirement for counselor licensure by receiving a certificate of the Certified Clinical Mental Health Counselor (CCMHC). The exam consists of ten simulations, each giving a scenario relatable to a client/counselor relationship. The test taker must go through each simulation and choose the best answers indicated for each question under the simulation. The indicators range from a -3 to a +3. In order to take the NCMHCE, candidates must have a master's degree in counseling or another related field along with 60 credit hours of counseling coursework.

Test Administration

In order to register for and schedule an examination for the NCMHCE, test candidates must first apply as the first step of the process in the national certification application, and the application must be approved by the NBCC. Once the application is approved, Pearson VUE will notify applicants via email with information on scheduling. The NCMHCE is given twice a year (April and October) through approximately 900 Pearson VUE testing centers. Options for test times are from 8 a.m. to 5:30 p.m. Monday through Saturday by appointment only. You can schedule for the exam (after being approved) and find test centers on the Pearson VUE website. If you receive a failing score, you can register through ProCounselor to retake the exam on the next date available. Using a single application, you can retake the exam three times within a two-year period.

Test Format

The NCMHCE is administered through a computer at a testing center. You will be provided with a dry-erase board during check-in for note-taking. Note that you should not ask any questions dealing with the actual content of the exam, and that no additional time is given for breaks. You may not bring any food or drink into the examination room.

The ten simulation scenarios on the exam each have sections that are considered either Information Gathering (IG) or Decision Making (DM). Each of these sections will be introduced by a single question asking the test taker to choose one or multiple answers that may be relevant to the case. The exam is meant to test a general knowledge of counseling areas, including assessment and diagnosis; counseling and psychotherapy; and administration, consultation, and supervision.

For the test structure and content, you will be presented with ten separate scenarios depicting a client and their introductory information, including presenting problems, age, and gender. For the Information Gathering (IG) questions, the test taker is expected to choose the answers that are necessary in order to gather relevant information about the client and their presenting problem. For Decision Making (DM) sections, test takers are asked to make decisions regarding ethical judgments or clinical decisions. If any of the Decision Making sections are labeled with "Single Best Option," choose only one answer choice out of that section. In the sections labeled "Multiple Options," you are to choose as many options as you see fit.

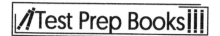

Scoring

The passing score for the NCMHCE will be given to the test taker on a printed score report. The Angoff method is used to determine pass or fail for the Information Gathering and Decision Making sections, and the set score may vary depending on the examination. IG and DM sections have separate scores, so that the test taker can determine their knowledge of each area. Test takers must pass both sections in order to pass the examination as a whole. Nine of the ten simulations will be scored. The tenth simulation is used for research purposes.

Recent/Future Developments

Starting in 2022, the NBCC has decided to change the educational requirements for national certification, stating that applicants must obtain a master's degree from a CACREP-accredited program. Note that this does not affect current NCCs or their certification.

Assessment and Diagnosis

Client Assessment and Observational Data

Obtaining a Biological, Psychological, Social, and Spiritual History

In order for an assessment to be comprehensive, the practitioner must gather information and assess the individual holistically, which includes examining systems related to the biological, psychological, and social or sociocultural factors of functioning. In some cases, a spiritual component may be included. This process is based on the **biopsychosocial framework**, which describes the interaction between biological, psychological, and social factors. The key components of the biopsychosocial assessment can be broken down into five parts: identification, chief complaint, social/environmental issues, history, and mental status exam.

Identification

Identification consists of the details or demographic information about the client that can be seen with the eye and documented accordingly. Some examples of identification information are age, gender, height, weight, and clothing.

Chief Complaint

A chief complaint is the client's version of what the overarching problem is. The client's description of the chief complaint may include factors from the past that the client views as an obstacle to optimal functioning. It could also be an issue that was previously resolved but reoccurs, thus requiring the client to develop additional coping skills.

Social/Environmental Issues

The social and environmental issue component evaluates social development and physical settings. **Social development** is critical to understanding the types of support systems the client has and includes information about the client's primary family group, including parents, siblings, and extended family members.

The client's peers and social networks should also be examined. There should be a clear distinction between peers available online (such as through online social networks) and peers the client interacts with face-to-face, as online systems may provide different forms of support than in-person systems.

The client's work environment and school or vocational settings should also be noted in this portion of the assessment. The client's current housing situation and view of financial status are also included to determine the type of resources the client has. Legal issues may also be included.

History

The history component includes events in the client's past. Clients may need to be interviewed several times in order to get a thorough picture of their history. Some information in a client's history, such as events that occurred during the stages of infancy and early childhood, may need to be gathered from collateral sources. Obtaining the client's historical information is usually a multi-stage process and can involve the following methods of data collection:

Presenting Problem

Clients should be asked to describe what brings them in for treatment. Although a client may attempt to delve into information that is well in the past, the practitioner should redirect the client to emphasize the past week or two. Emphasis is placed on the client's current situation when assessing the presenting problem.

Past Personal

When reviewing a client's history, noting biological development may determine whether or not the client hit milestones and the ensuing impact it had on their health. In reviewing biological development, other physical factors should also be assessed for impact on current emotional wellbeing, including those that may no longer persist, like a childhood illness. As much information as possible regarding the client's entire lifespan (birth to present) should be gathered, with attention paid to sexual development.

Medical

During the medical component of the assessment process, information should be obtained on the client's previous or current physiological diagnoses. These diagnoses can contribute to the client's current situation.

For example, a client with frequent headaches and back pain may be unable to sleep well and therefore may be experiencing the physical and psychosocial effects of sleep deprivation. Additional information on other conditions, such as pregnancy, surgeries, or disabilities, should also be explored during this time.

Mental Health

Previous mental health diagnoses, symptoms, and/or evaluations should be discussed. If a client discloses prior diagnoses or evaluations, the practitioner should determine the following:

- Whether or not the client has been hospitalized (inpatient)
- If the client has received supervised treatment in an outpatient setting (to include psychotherapeutic intervention)
- Whether the client has been prescribed medications
- If the client has undertaken other treatments related to mental health diagnoses

The client's psychological development should also be reviewed. It is important to gather details on how clients view their emotional development, including their general affect.

The client's cognitive development, in relation to information previously obtained regarding the biological development, should also be reviewed.

Substance Use

Without demonstrating judgment, practitioners should encourage clients to disclose whether or not they have used controlled substances. It is important that thorough information is gathered and symptoms related to substance abuse are assessed BEFORE rendering a primary mental health disorder diagnosis.

Should a client disclose that they have engaged in the use of substances, information as to the type of substance, frequency of use, and duration of exposure to the lifestyle should be gathered. Additionally, information on what the client perceives as the positive and negative aspects of substance use should

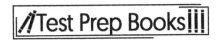

be gathered, noting whether or not the client perceives any consequences of substance abuse, such as job loss, decreased contact with family and friends, and effects on physical appearance.

Mental Status Exam

A mental status exam is a concise, complete evaluation of the client's current mental functioning level regarding **cognitive and behavioral aspects** (rapport-building, mood, thought content, hygiene). There are mini mental status examinations available that allow practitioners to provide a snapshot of the client's overall level of functioning with limited resources and time available. Mental status examinations are usually conducted regularly and discreetly through questioning and noting nonverbal indicators (such as appearance) in order for the practitioner to best guide the session.

Obtaining and Evaluating Collateral Information

Collateral sources are persons other than the client, such as family members, police officers, friends, or other medical providers, who can provide information related to the client's levels of functioning, life events, and other potential areas of significance in the client's treatment.

Prior to obtaining collateral information from any source, a signed **Release of Information** (**ROI**) form should be obtained from the client (or from a parent or guardian if the client is a minor). The necessity for an ROI may be waived if there is explicit legal consent granting access to collateral sources. This is most commonly seen during forensic interviews. It is important to explain the purpose behind collecting an ROI to the client. Relatedly, it is also important to make the collateral source aware of the reason behind the request for information on the client.

Information from collateral sources is useful in cases when the client is unable to provide reliable information. The inability to provide reliable information could be due to a number of factors, like substance abuse issues, severe cognitive impairment, or severe mental illness/disorder. Based on the client's background, there could be a number of collateral resources from which to solicit information. Thus, it is important to filter these resources based on those who have had regular or recent contact with the client.

It is important to select collateral resources that can provide information about significant experiences and events relating to the client's presenting problem. Collateral sources can provide a level of objectivity when discussing the client's situation. Additional examples of collateral sources include physician reports, police reports, reports from other medical professionals or mental health agencies, school reports, and employment records.

Information Available from Employment, Medical, Psychological, Psychiatric, and Educational Records

While the privacy and confidentiality of the client must always be protected, with proper permission it can be beneficial for the counselor to access and view records from others who have played a significant role in the client's life and treatment. This helps to establish a more holistic view of the client and gives a comprehensive perspective of the client's strengths and difficulties. Medical records can provide information about some of the physical and medical reasons behind the client's behaviors, as well as information about the medications the client is taking. Educational and employment records can shed light on how the client functions within the milieus of school and work, providing insight into areas that may need to be addressed with the client. Employment information can also assist the counselor in determining the client's financial eligibility for services. Psychological assessments and psychiatric diagnoses can also help the counselor provide more efficient and knowledgeable treatment. Although the counselor should never depend primarily on secondhand reports, these records can provide a complete picture that may assist in effectively meeting the needs of the client.

Common Prescription Medications

Seventy percent of Americans take at least one prescription medication. Taking note of prescription medication history and current usage may provide valuable insight into the cause and treatment of an individual's presenting issues.

One of the most common reasons for taking prescription medications is to reduce risk factors for heart attack and stroke, such as high cholesterol, hypertension, and triglyceride levels (Crestor, Diovan, Lipitor, Prinivil, Toprol, and Zestril are often prescribed). Other common conditions treated with prescription medication include thyroid disorders (Synthroid was the most prescribed drug in 2015), arthritis (commonly treated by Humira), gastroesophageal reflux (Nexium), and asthma and chronic obstructive pulmonary disease (ADVAIR). The combination of hydrocodone and acetaminophen is the most common prescription painkiller for moderate to severe pain.

Types of Reliability

Reliability in testing is the degree to which the assessment tool produces consistent and stable results. There are four types of reliability:

- **Test-Retest Reliability** involves administering the same test twice to a group of individuals, then correlating the scores to evaluate stability.

- **Parallel-Forms Reliability** (also referred to as **equivalence**) involves administering two different versions of an assessment that measure the same set of skills or knowledge and then correlating the results. A test can be written and split into two parts, thus creating parallel versions.

- **Inter-Rater Reliability** (also referred to as **inter-observer**) checks to see that raters—those administering, grading, or judging a measure—do so in agreement. Each rater should value the same measures and at the same degree to ensure consistency. Inter-rater reliability prevents overly subjective ratings, since each rater is measuring on the same terms.

- **Internal Consistency** refers to how well a test or assessment measures what it's intended to measure, while producing similar results each time. Questions on an assessment should be similar and in agreement, but not repetitive. High internal consistency indicates that a measure is reliable.

  - **Average Inter-Item Correlation** is used to determine if scores on one item relate to the scores on all of the other items in that scale.

  - **Split-Half Reliability** is the random division of questions into two sets. Results of both halves are compared to ensure correlation.

Validity

Validity refers to how well a test or assessment measures what it's intended to measure. For example, an assessment on depression should only measure the degree to which an individual meets the

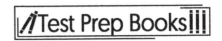

diagnostic criteria for depression. Though validity does indicate reliability, a test can be reliable but not be valid. There are four major types of validity, with subtypes:

- **Content Validity** ensures that the test questions align with the content or study area. This can be measured by two subtypes of validation:

    o **Face Validity** refers to a commonsense view that a test measures what it should and looks accurate from a non-professional viewpoint.

    o **Curricular Validity** is evaluated by experts and measures that a test aligns with the curriculum being tested. For example, a high school exit exam measures the information taught in the high school curriculum.

- **Criterion Validity** measures success and the relationship between a test score and an outcome, such as scores on the SAT and success in college. It's two subtypes are:

    o **Predictive Validity** refers to how useful test scores are at predicting future performance.

    o **Concurrent Validity** is used to determine if measures can be substituted, such as taking an exam in place of a class. Measures must take place concurrently to accurately test for validity.

- **Construct Validity** refers to a test that measures abstract traits or theories and isn't inadvertently testing another variable. For example, a math test with complex word problems may be assessing reading skills. Two subtypes of validation are needed to assess construct validity:

    o **Convergent Validity** uses two sets of tests to determine that the same attributes are being measured and correlated. For example, two separate tests can measure students similarly.

    o **Discriminant Validity** refers to using tests that measure differently and results that don't correlate.

- **Consequential Validity** refers to the social consequences of testing. Though not all researchers feel it's a true measure of validity, some believe a test must benefit society in order to be considered valid.

Administering Tests to Clients

As part of the counseling process, it can be necessary for the counselor to administer tests or assessments to measure and evaluate the client. Tests are a more formalized means to quantify information, guide treatment options, and develop goals. Assessments are more informal. They can include surveys, interviews, and observations.

There are a variety of reasons a counselor can choose to administer a test or assessment, such as to:

- Help the client gain a better understanding of themselves
- Provide counselors with concrete data
- Ensure a client's needs are within the counselor's scope of practice
- Assist in decision-making and goal-setting for the counseling process

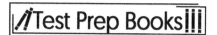

- Provide insight to both the client and the counselor
- Assist in setting clear expectations for clients
- Help the counselor gain a deeper understanding of their client's needs
- Set benchmarks to ensure client and counselor are making progress toward their goals
- Evaluate the effectiveness of counseling interventions

Interpreting Test Scores

To begin, any test or assessment should be given under controlled circumstances. The counselor should follow any instructions provided in the test manual. Once completed, the counselor and client can discuss the results.

Some best practices for interpreting results are listed below:

- Counselor must thoroughly understand the results
- Counselor should explain results in easily understood terms and be able to provide supporting details and norms as needed
- Counselor should explain and understand average scores and the meanings of results
- Counselor should allow the client to ask questions and review aspects of the test to ensure understanding
- Counselor must explain the ramifications and limitations of any data obtained through testing

Major Types of Tests and Inventories

Achievement tests measure knowledge of a specific subject and are primarily used in education. Examples include exit exams for high school diplomas and tests used in the Common Core for educational standards. The General Education Development (GED) and the California Achievement Test are both achievement tests that measure learning.

Aptitude tests measure the capacity for learning and can be used as part of a job application. These tests can measure abstract/conceptual reasoning, verbal reasoning, and/or numerical reasoning. Examples include the Wonderlic Cognitive Ability Test, the Differential Aptitude Test (DAT), the Minnesota Clerical Test, and the Career Ability Placement Survey (CAPS).

Intelligence tests measure mental capability and potential. One example is the Wechsler Adult Intelligence Scale (WAIS-IV), currently in its fourth edition. The Wechsler Intelligence Scale for Children (WISC-IV), also in its fourth edition, is used for children six years of age to sixteen years eleven months of age and can be completed without reading or writing. There's a separate version of the test for children aged two years six months to seven years seven months, known as the Wechsler Preschool and Primary Scale of Intelligence (WPPSI-III). Examples of other intelligence tests are the Stanford-Binet Intelligence Scale, the Woodcock-Johnson Tests of Cognitive Abilities, and the Kaufman Assessment Battery for Children.

Occupational tests can assess skills, values, or interests as they relate to vocational and occupational choices. Examples include the Strong Interest Inventory, the Self-Directed Search, the O*Net Interest Profiler, the Career Assessment Inventory, and the Kuder Career Interests Assessment.

Personality tests can be objective (rating-scale based) or projective (self-reporting based) and help the counselor and client understand personality traits and underlying beliefs and behaviors. The Myers-Briggs Type Inventory (MBTI) provides a specific psychological type, reflecting the work of Carl Jung. It's often used as part of the career development process. Other rating scale personality tests include the

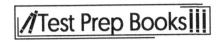

Minnesota Multiphasic Personality Inventory (MMPI-2), the Beck Depression Inventory, and the Tennessee Self-Concept Scale. The Rorschach (inkblot) Test and the Thematic Apperception Test are both projective tests, designed to reveal unconscious thoughts, motives, and views.

Ethical Issues in Testing

A variety of ethical issues must be considered before, during, and after any test or assessment is administered. To begin, the counselor must be adequately trained and earn any certifications and have the supervision necessary to administer and interpret the test. Tests must be appropriate for the needs of the specific client. Next, the client must provide informed consent, and they must understand the purpose and scope of any test. Test results must remain confidential, which includes access to any virtual information. Finally, tests must be validated for the specific client and be unbiased toward the race, ethnicity, and gender of the client.

Key Contributors in the Field of Intelligence Testing

Sir Francis Galton, an English anthropologist and explorer, was one of the first individuals to study intelligence in the late 1800s. A cousin of Charles Darwin, Galton coined the term **eugenics** and believed that intelligence was genetically determined and could be promoted through selective parenting.

American psychologist **J.P. Guilford** conducted psychometric studies of human intelligence and creativity in the early 1900s. He believed intelligence tests were limited, one-dimensional, and didn't factor in the diversity of human abilities, thought, and creativity.

English psychologist **Charles Spearman** was responsible for bringing statistical analysis to intelligence testing. In the early 1900s, Spearman proposed the *g* Factor Theory for general intelligence, which laid the foundation for analyzing intelligence tests. Prior to his work, tests weren't highly correlated with the factors they attempted to measure.

In the 1900s, French psychologist **Alfred Binet**, along with medical student Theodore Simon, developed the first test to determine which children would succeed in school. His initial test, the Binet-Simon, focused on the concept of mental age and included memory, attention, and problem-solving skills. In 1916, Binet's work was brought to Stanford University and developed into the Stanford-Binet Intelligence Scale. It's since been revised multiple times and is still widely used.

In the 1940s, **Raymond Cattell** began developing theories on fluid and crystallized intelligence. His student, John Horn, continued this work. The Cattell-Horn Theory hypothesized that over one hundred abilities work together to create forms of intelligence. Fluid intelligence is defined as the ability to think and act quickly and to solve new problems, skills that are independent of education and enculturation. Crystallized intelligence encompasses acquired and learned skills, and is influenced by personality, motivation, education, and culture. In 1949, Catell and his wife, Alberta Karen Cattell, founded the Institute for Personality and Ability Testing at the University of Illinois. Cattell developed several assessments, including the 16 Personality Factor Questionnaire and the Culture Fair Intelligence Test.

In the 1950s, American psychologist **David Wechsler** developed intelligence tests for adults and children. His tests were adept at identifying learning disabilities in children. Wechsler began his career developing personality tests for the U.S. military. He disagreed with some aspects of the Stanford-Binet Intelligence Scale and believed intelligence had both verbal and performance components. He also believed factors other than pure intellect influenced intellectual behavior. Wechsler's tests are still used today for adults, as well as school-age and primary-age children. They include the Wechsler Adult

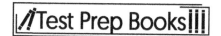

Intelligence Scale (WAIS-IV), the Wechsler Intelligence Scale for Children (WISC-IV), and the Wechsler Preschool and Primary Scale of Intelligence (WPPSI-III).

John Ertl, a professor working in Canada in the 1970s, invented a neural efficiency analyzer to more effectively measure intelligence. He believed traditional intelligence tests were limited to understanding an abstract degree of intelligence. Ertl's system measured the speed and efficiency of electrical activity in the brain using an electroencephalogram (EEG).

Arthur Jensen supported the *g* Factor Theory and believed intelligence consisted of two distinct sets of abilities. Level I accounted for simple associative learning and memory, while Level II involved more abstract and conceptual reasoning. Jensen also believed that genetic factors were the most influential indicator of intelligence. In 1998, he published the book *The g Factor: The Science of Mental Ability*.

Important Terms

Appraisal: Professionally administered assessment tools and tests used to evaluate, measure, and understand clients.

Behavioral Observation: Type of assessment used to document the behavior of clients or research subjects.

Bell Curve: Illustration of data distribution that resembles the shape of a bell.

Coefficient of Determination: Denoted by R^2, the proportion of the variance in the dependent variable that's predictable from the independent variable and the square of the coefficient of correlation.

Correlation Coefficient: Statistic that describes the relationship between two variables and their impact on one another. In positive correlation, both variables react in the same direction. In negative correlation, variables react in opposite directions.

Dichotomous Items: Opposing choices on a test, such as yes/no or true/false options.

Difficulty Index: Measure of the proportion of examinees who answer test items correctly.

External Validity: Describes how well results from a study can be generalized to the larger population.

Forced Choice Items: The use of two or more specific response options on a survey.

Free Choice Test: Also known as **liberal choice**; questions that allow for a subjective/open-ended response

Halo Effect: An overgeneralized positive view of a person from limited data. An example of this would be favoring a politician for their attractiveness and assuming that attractiveness extends to their ethical beliefs or personality.

Horizontal Test: A test covering material across various subjects.

Ipsative Measurement: A format that presents two or more equally attractive answer choices wherein the test taker chooses the one they favor most. This assessment is sometimes used in personality surveys and is also known as forced-choice measurement.

Likert Scale: Rating scale measuring attitudes to a degree of like or dislike.

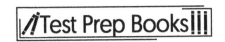

Mean: Provides the average of all scores and is calculated by adding all given test scores and dividing by the number of tests.

Median: Refers to the middle or center number in an ordered list of scores or data; also referred to as the midpoint. In an even data set, the two middle numbers are typically averaged to determine the median.

Measure: Score assigned to traits, behaviors, or actions.

Mode: The most common or frequent score that occurred in a group of tests. If a number/score doesn't occur twice, a test doesn't have a mode.

Normative Format: Means of testing to compare individuals to others.

Objective Test Items: Standardized questions with clear correct or incorrect answers that are not open to any interpretation.

Obtrusive Measurement: Assessment tools (such as observation) conducted without the knowledge of the individual.

Percentile: Determines how test scores rank on a scale of 100. Percentiles determine the number of individuals who are at or below a given rank. For example, a test taker who scores in the 65th percentile performed better than 65 percent of the other test takers.

Projective Test: Responses to ambiguous images that are intended to uncover unconscious desires, thoughts, or beliefs.

Psychological Assessment: An informal process of testing, interviews, or observations used to determine the psychological needs of an individual. Assessments can expose the need for more formal testing.

Psychological Test: Refers to any number of specific tests or measurements conducted to evaluate, diagnose, or develop treatment plans. It can include personality assessments, projective or subjective tests, intelligence tests, or diagnostic batteries.

Psychometrics: The process or study of psychological measurement.

Q-Sort: Self-assessment procedure requiring subjects to sort items relative to one another along a dimension, such as agree/disagree.

Range: Subtraction of the lowest score from the highest score.

Rapport: Development of trust, understanding, respect, and liking between two people; essential for an effective therapeutic relationship.

Rating Scale: Process of measuring degrees of experience and attitudes through questions.

Regression to the Mean: Statistical tendency of a data series to gravitate toward the center of a distribution.

Reliability: Four types of reliability are test-retest, parallel forms, inter-rater, and internal consistency. Each type measures whether a tool is producing consistent and stable results that must be quantified. Reliability doesn't indicate validity.

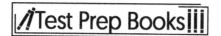

Scale: Used to categorize and/or quantify variables. The four scales of measurement are nominal, ordinal, interval, and ratio.

Score: Numerical value associated with a test or measure.

Skew: The measure a score deviates from the norm.

Standard Deviation: Measures dispersion of numbers and is calculated by taking the square root of the variance.

Standard Error of Measurement (SEM): Refers to test reliability and the difference between the true score versus the observed score. Since no test is without error, the SEM depicts the dispersion of scores of the same test to rule out errors, also referred to as the "standard error" of a score.

Subjective: Individual perceptions/interpretations based on feelings and opinions and not on fact.

Stanine (STAndard NINE): A nine-point scale used to convert a test score to a single digit. Stanines are always positive whole numbers from zero to nine.

T-Score: Specific to psychometrics, used to standardize test scores and convert scores to positive numbers. T-Scores represent the number of standard deviations the score is from the mean (which is always fifty).

Test: A measuring device or procedure.

Test Battery: A group or set of tests administered to the same group and scored against a standard.

Trait: Method of describing individuals through observable characteristics that are unique and distinguishable.

Validity: Indicates how well any given test or assessment measures what it's intended to measure. There are four major types of validity: content, construct, criterion, and consequential. Validity *does* indicate reliability.

Variance: How widely individuals in a group vary; how data is distributed from the mean and the square of the standard deviation.

Vertical Test: Same-subject tests given to different levels or ages.

Z-Score: Also referred to as a **standard score**, Z-Scores measure the number of standard deviations a raw score is from the mean. Z-scores use zero as the mean.

Precipitating Problems or Symptoms

The Process Used in Problem Formulation

The problem system refers to factors that are relevant to the client's presenting problem, which may include other people or environmental elements the client deems relevant to the situation. It is important that questions be asked to determine what the client's perception of the presenting problem is. Additionally, the practitioner should determine if there are other legal, medical, or physical issues related to the problem. For a comprehensive assessment, the client should also be asked how long the

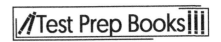

problem has been present and if there are any triggers they believe contribute to the problem. Identification of external supports and access to resources is also key when examining and discussing the problem system.

The presenting problem is generally revealed in the client's statement about why they have come in for treatment. If collateral sources are used, information can also be gathered from one or more of the collateral sources who have insight as to why the client is in need of assistance. Disclosure of the presenting problem allows the counselor to determine the prevailing concerns deemed important by the client. Counselors can gain a sense of how distressed the client is about the problem or situation and what client expectations are for treatment. The manner in which the client describes the presenting problem can also provide insight as to how emotionally tied the client is to the problem and whether or not the client came in under their own volition.

It is important to determine the true root causes of the presenting problem. Although a client may come in and voice a concern, it may not be the root cause of the issue. Rather, this concern may simply be an item the client feels comfortable discussing. For example, a client who is experiencing sexual issues may initially speak about anxiety before disclosing the actual problem. This may require an investment of time to allow the client to become comfortable trusting the practitioner. The history of the problem is important to address because it clarifies any factors contributing to the presenting problem, as well as any deeper underlying issues. Gathering background information on the problem history is also helpful for developing interventions. There are three key areas to address when reviewing the problem history: onset, progression, and severity.

Onset: Problem onset addresses when the problem started. It usually includes triggers or events that led up to the start of the problem; these events may also be contributing factors.

Progression: Assessment of the progression of the problem requires determining the frequency of the problem. The practitioner should ask questions to determine if the problem is intermittent (how often and for how long), if it is acute or chronic, and if there are multiple problems that may or may not appear in a pattern or recurring cluster.

Severity: Practitioners should determine how severe the client feels the problem is, what factors contribute to making the problem more severe, and how the situation impacts the client's adaptive functioning. This may be determined by addressing the following questions:

- Does the problem affect the client at work?

- Is there difficulty performing personal care because of the problem?

  - The practitioner should ascertain whether or not the client has access to resources that can provide adequate care (running water, shelter, and clothing).

  - The client's living situation should be explored if there are difficulties with personal care activities.

  - The practitioner should also ask if there are others for whom the client is responsible, like children or elderly parents/relatives.

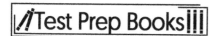

- Has the problem caused the client to withdraw from preferred activities?

- Has the client used alcohol or other controlled substances to alleviate or escape the problem? If so, for how long and to what degree?

Methods of Involving the Client System in Identifying the Problem

In addition to gathering information from the client through a verbal report, the client can participate by taking assessment tools to assist with identification and analysis of the presenting problem. The counselor may choose from a plethora of worksheets and exercises to engage clients in assessing the various systems in which they are involved. Some of them include the Social Support Network inventory, questionnaires, and perspective worksheets. The more common tools are noted, here:

Intake Assessment Form: Clients are asked to complete an assessment form prior to the first session. The counselor may review this form before or after meeting with the client to gain additional insight into the client's needs. The assessment form includes identifying information about the client's household, age, gender, and a brief description of the problem in the client's own words.

Genogram: The counselor can engage the client in creating a **genogram**, a diagram that depicts the client's family systems, in order to understand significant life events that may indicate familial patterns. Additionally, the genogram can provide insight on the perceived relationship between the client, family, and related support systems.

Ecomap: The ecomap also reviews the client systems, but this diagram extends beyond the family and examines all of the systems in which the client is involved. The client should construct a map of the social relationships in their life, such as work, friendships, church, organizations, and agencies. The social systems are placed in circles.

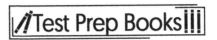

Next, the client should illustrate the connection between the self and relationships with lines. A solid line represents a strong relationship; a dotted or crossed line indicates a fractured relationship. Arrows and other items may be used to add more detail to the relationship status and to help the client and counselor understand the overall function of the relationships.

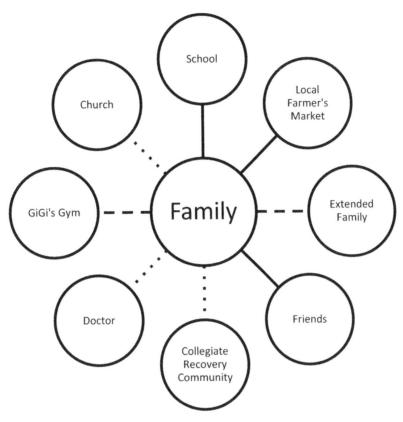

Process of Identifying the Client System Needs

While formulating the treatment plan, the practitioner should assess the level of care needed for a client with the whole person in mind and a desire for continuity of care. As the practitioner starts where the client is, the treatment plan process should reflect levels of care that are in line with the client's needs, adjusting the intensity up or down based on the level of need as reflected in ongoing assessments and review processes.

For example, geriatric care is similar to behavioral healthcare as the client may present with a need for the most basic level of care, conducted through routine visits with a practitioner, either at the practitioner's office or at the client's residence. The intensity may move up to increased sessions with the practitioner.

The highest level of intensity would be a multidisciplinary team approach in a residential or inpatient setting. For geriatric care, the highest level of need would be represented in a skilled nursing facility. For child welfare or special needs, an inpatient medical facility would also represent the highest level of need.

Indicators of Client's Strengths and Challenges

Noticing a client's different characteristics can indicate particular strengths. Strengths are biological, physical, mental, social, spiritual, or emotional abilities that help them to solve problems and keep the mind, body, and spirit in a stable state. The practitioner might also notice areas requiring intervention or treatment plans for the individual's overall growth. Focus is on the following indicators:

- Intelligence quotient (IQ) and cognitive ability
- Willingness to learn
- Willingness to understand oneself without judgment
- Ability to accept both positive feedback and constructive criticism
- Desire for personal growth
- Willingness to change
- Ability and desire to learn new concepts
- Temperament
- Optimistic or pessimistic thought patterns
- Reaction patterns to stressors (both initially and over time)
- Self-esteem
- Self-efficacy
- Self-worth
- Accountability for one's actions
- Emotional quotient (EQ), also called emotional intelligence (EI)
- Status and complexity of close relationships and friendships
- Ability to trust and depend on others
- Ability to be trustworthy and dependable
- Ability to empathize and sympathize
- Perspective on society at large
- Self-awareness
- Moods and what external events or internal thought processes affects them
- Involvement in social institutions (e.g., religious groups, social clubs)
- State of physical health
- State of finances
- Socioeconomic status

Indicators of Behavioral Dysfunction

Ideas about what is normal versus what is abnormal with regard to behavior are society-dependent. People tend to equate *normal* with "good" and *abnormal* with "bad," which means that any behavior labeled as abnormal can potentially be stigmatizing. Use of person-centered language is one way to reduce stigma attached to abnormal behavior or behavior health issues (e.g., saying "a person with schizophrenia," rather than "a schizophrenic.")

The "Four Ds" of Abnormality assist health practitioners when trying to identify a psychiatric condition in their clients. Deviance marks a withdrawal from society's concept of appropriate behavior. Deviant behavior is a departure from the "norm." The *DSM-5* contains some criteria for diagnosing deviance. The second "D" is dysfunction. Dysfunction is behavior that interferes with daily living. Dysfunction is a type of problem that may be serious enough to be considered a disorder. The third "D" is distress. Distress is related to a client's dysfunction. That is, to what degree does the dysfunction cause the client distress?

A client can experience minor dysfunction and major distress, or major dysfunction and minor distress. The fourth "D" is danger. Danger is characterized by danger to self or to others. There are different degrees of danger specific to various types of disorders. Duration is sometimes considered a fifth "D," as it may be important to note whether the symptoms of a disorder are fleeting or permanent.

Indicators, Dynamics, and Impact of Sexual Abuse Across the Lifespan

Sexual abuse is forced or coerced sexual contact or exposure, usually by someone older or in a position of authority over the victim. Sexual abuse can also include forcing someone to watch sexual acts or receive messages involving unwanted sexual content. The impact of sexual abuse is complex, and the emotional and psychological response to the trauma may evolve as the victim gets older and understands more fully what happened to them. Children who suffer sexual abuse may struggle from confusion about the abuse, especially if they are told by the perpetrator that it is right and good and if that person is someone with whom they have a relationship of trust. They may be blamed by the perpetrator for the abuse, which leads to further feelings of confusion and guilt. If they report the abuse to someone who does not believe it, the long-term effects of the abuse may be even greater, as well as the guilt, self-doubt, and shame. A history of sexual abuse will normally impact a person's relationships with others throughout life, and there may be issues of trust as well as confused feelings toward sex.

Indicators of Sexual Abuse (Child)
- The statement that one has been sexually assaulted
- Mistrust or fear of those who bear resemblance to the abuser, potentially due to gender or size (children may be mistrustful of all adults)
- Changes in behavior
- Depression
- Anxiety with presenting symptoms (hair loss, fluctuations in weight)
- Increased fearfulness (possible night terrors and enuresis/bed wetting from children)
- Withdrawal from preferred activities/social isolation
- Compulsive masturbation
- Substance abuse
- Overly-sexualized behavior

Parent, Spouse, or Caregiver
- Demonstrating inappropriate behaviors
- Role confusion, distortion of child's role in the family
- Jealousness or over-protection of the victim
- Excessive, abnormal alone time with the child
- Lack of appropriate social and emotional contacts outside the home
- Substance and/or alcohol abuse
- Parent or caregiver reports being sexually abused previously (possible normalization or continuation of the cyclic behavior)

Indicators, Dynamics, and Impact of Emotional Abuse and Neglect Across the Lifespan

Victims of abuse and neglect are most often children, the elderly, or someone suffering from a physical or mental disability. Because of their vulnerability, these populations are most at risk of mistreatment. One of the most challenging aspects of dealing with abuse or neglect is that victims are often hesitant to report abuse. This may be due to fear of the perpetrator or a conflicted sense of loyalty toward that person, who may be a close relative or friend. It is often communicated to victims that they are the cause of the abuse, and they mistakenly take on the responsibility for the bad things happening to them. The effects of abuse vary depending on many factors, including the severity level of the abuse, the response of other adults or caregivers when the abuse is reported, and the age of the victim at the time of abuse.

Physically, there may be injuries, wounds, or even sexually transmitted diseases in the case of sexual abuse. Oftentimes, these physical symptoms are what is observed by outsiders and can be the first sign of potential abuse. Evidence of neglect may also show up physically—e.g., if a person loses weight, is not wearing adequate clothes, or is not taken for necessary medical attention. A child inexplicably missing school for multiple days may also be an indication of a problem. Psychologically, abuse impacts a person in many ways. Their whole view of self may revolve around the abuse suffered, resulting in low self-esteem and feelings of worthlessness and loneliness. Additionally, mental illnesses, such as anxiety or depression, may arise, and victims may even engage in self-harm or attempt suicide. Behavioral changes may also occur, and a child may begin acting out at home or school. When a person endures sexual abuse, they may later begin acting out sexually or become either sexually promiscuous or sexually withdrawn. There is a higher level of drug and alcohol abuse among victims of abuse, as well as criminal activity. The wounds from abuse are varied and extensive, but with a strong social support and appropriate counseling, victims of abuse can be extremely resilient and even go on to help other survivors of abuse.

Indicators of Neglect (Child)
- Reports of no one around to provide care
- Appearance of being malnourished, always hungry
- Excessive sleepiness
- Untreated medical problems
- Parent or caregiver demonstrates lack of interest
- Parent or caregiver chronically ill (physically or mentally)
- Parent or caregiver history of neglect from their parent or caregiver
- Description of or visibly-unsafe home environment

Indicators of Psychological Abuse and Neglect
- Extreme fluctuations between aggression and passiveness
- Manifestation of emotional stress through nail biting, hair loss, rocking, bed-wetting
- Presence of low self-esteem with self-defeating statements. For example, *no one likes me, no one cares about me, I can't do anything right*
- Excessive desire to be a people pleaser
- Developmental delays or presentation being younger or slower (speech or movement) than age-appropriate
- Caregiver or parent belittles the child
- Client is treated lesser than other individuals in the family

Differentiating Substance Use, Intoxication, Withdrawal, and Other Addictions

Substance Use Disorders
The *Diagnostic and Statistical Manual,* generally referred to as the *DSM,* is a comprehensive handbook used by clinicians to determine which mental health diagnosis best fits with presenting symptoms. In

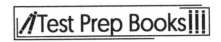

older editions of the manual, substance abuse disorders and substance dependence disorders were listed separately, the latter being seen as the more serious of the two. The latest edition, the *DSM-5*, has combined these two disorders into **substance use disorders**. The severity of these disorders is currently broken down by number of presenting symptoms. A client who displays two to three symptoms is considered in the mild range. One displaying four to six symptoms is scored as in the moderate range, and six or more symptoms indicate a severe level of addiction.

The primary distinction between milder and more severe substance use disorders involves the following variables, which are seen in the later stages of addiction:

- Tolerance: The need for increased quantities of the substance to achieve desired level of intoxication

- Withdrawal: Onset of undesirable symptoms when the drug or alcohol is not immediately available, which may include tremors, nausea, vomiting, confusion, abnormal heart rhythms, hallucinations, and seizures

- Cravings: Increasingly intense urges to consume one's drug or drink of preference

It should be noted that about 50 percent of persons who discontinue use of a substance may experience some form of withdrawal symptoms. Some are mild and do not require medical attention. A small percent experience stroke or seizures that can be life threatening. Clients wishing to attain sobriety by quitting "cold turkey" need careful evaluation and possible medical consultation before entering outpatient treatment for the addiction.

Substance Induced Disorders refer to psychiatric conditions that result from the use of one or more intoxicants. This can occur upon first time use of a substance, such as LSD or synthetic marijuana. More often, the condition is seen following a prolonged and intense use of substances, such as methamphetamines or hallucinogenic drugs. Long term uses of these drugs have, in some cases, caused permanent psychological damage that involves psychosis, depression, paranoia, and other symptoms. The following are the primary substances identified in the *Diagnostic and Statistical Manual*:

- Alcohol
- Inhalants
- Prescription medication
- Sedatives
- Opioids
- Cocaine
- Marijuana
- Hallucinogens

Effects of Substance Use
The following lists the effects of substance use. These include physical problems, mental health problems, social problems, and financial problems.

Physical Problems
Common physical problems include organ damage, gastrointestinal issues, birth defects in children exposed to drugs or alcohol during pregnancy, and increased exposure to HIV and hepatitis. In addition, there is a risk of death by overdose.

Mental Health Problems

Persons addicted to drugs or alcohol are prone to mental health disorders, such as depression, anxiety, memory loss, aggression, mood swings, paranoia, and psychosis. Some of these issues persist long after the person has stopped using the addictive substance.

Social Problems

As mentioned, the people closest to the addict suffer much emotional pain. Family and friends cannot rely on the person to follow through with important responsibilities. The addict may be involved in illegal activities leading to arrest, loss of income, and loss of custody of children. Others begin to distance themselves from the person for self-protection. Some families may disown or shun the addict and set up legal barriers to prevent contact. The addict may begin a series of revolving door stays at jails, hospitals, and halfway houses.

Financial Problems

Parents who struggle with addiction and alcoholics may experience dire financial consequences. They have trouble keeping steady employment. They may destroy their credit status, deplete savings accounts, or fail to do their share to meet financial needs of family and household. Medical and social problems, such as arrest, can impact financial stability. Prolonged unemployment causes loss of vehicles, homes, and other assets, and may eventually lead to homelessness.

Effects of Intoxication

Intoxication effects can vary considerably depending on what drug or combined drugs have been consumed. Depressants, such as alcohol, opioids, or some prescription drugs have some of the following components:

- Sense of euphoria
- Decreased coordination
- Staggering or unsteady gait
- Speech impairment
- Judgment impairment
- Memory impairment
- Disinhibited behavior
- Mental confusion

The following effects may be seen in those abusing cocaine or amphetamines:

- Increased energy/hyperactivity
- Sense of euphoria
- Increased heart rate
- Decreased need for sleep or rest
- Agitation
- Anxiety
- Paranoia
- Psychosis

Those persons abusing hallucinogens may experience the following:

- Sense of euphoria, wellbeing or relaxation

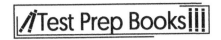

- Hallucinations
- Distorted perceptions of self, body, time, or space
- Increased heart rate and blood pressure
- Numbness
- Anxiety, sometimes leading to sense of panic

Effects of Withdrawal

Withdrawal symptoms vary from individual to individual, and the process is impacted by the type of drug consumed, the length of time the drug was used, and the current health status of the addict. Some withdrawal symptoms are psychological and do not involve physiological changes. There may still be a sense of anxiety, sadness, or irritability as one stops using the substance.

Withdrawal, in its more serious forms, can be life-threatening. There may be seizures, strokes, or heart attacks. Some withdrawal symptoms, such as those seen with methamphetamine parents who struggle with addiction, mimic mental illness. In areas where this drug is widely used, emergency rooms must use drug testing to determine if this is an onset of paranoid schizophrenia or the effect of amphetamine withdrawal. Those showing psychotic symptoms generally become asymptomatic after three or four days. Some people withdrawing from alcohol or other substances experience tactile hallucinations. They may see and feel insects on their skin or in their environment, causing them to aggressively scratch at their skin.

Withdrawal causes much physical discomfort that may include vomiting, diarrhea, stomach pain, profuse sweating, tremors, headaches, and spikes in heart rate or blood pressure. Persons with severe withdrawal symptoms or those with frail health should be monitored by a physician or placed in a hospital for observation. Withdrawal symptoms or the fear of experiencing them often propel the addict to seek more of the drug of preference in order to avoid these unpleasant and life-threatening experiences.

Indicators of Addictions to Gambling, Sex, Food, and Media

Addictions and compulsive behaviors can damage health, finances, social status, and relationships. Even some behaviors—such as exercise and work—are recognized as positive behaviors, but when taken to extremes, unpleasant consequences develop. For example, exercise addiction, in its least damaging form, may create anxiety when physical or weather conditions prevent participation. In more extreme cases, certain athletes will continue to train in spite of illness or injury, exacerbating the physical problem and sometimes causing permanent disabilities.

Those addicted to pornography find that having close and intimate contact with their long-term partner is less exciting than viewing stimulating films or pictures. This creates intimacy problems and difficulty in one's primary relationship. The Internet has made it easier for people to access these materials, sometimes at no cost, creating a greater number of persons who view it addictively.

Spending parents who struggle with addiction—sometimes called "shopaholics"—may become hoarders or financially destroy themselves and their family. They may make foolish purchases when more basic needs of the family are not being fulfilled. For example, many spending parents who struggle with addiction have closets full of clothes never worn or may own fifteen pairs of sunglasses.

Like exercise parents who struggle with addiction, overworking—sometimes referred to as "workaholism"—may also be viewed as positive by some standards. In the end, however, those working many hours of overtime may result in a life out of balance. They may also be using work as a means to avoid other responsibilities, such as family life. It can create stress and low energy, and it can lead to physical and emotional problems.

Overeating, based upon the number of obese and overweight persons in our culture, is on the rise. Some people use food much in the same way that others use alcohol or drugs—to feel a sense of pleasure or to numb feelings of depression or anxiety. The consequences of obesity are numerous from a social and physical standpoint, with the most severe of these being at higher risk for heart disease or stroke.

Some individuals are addicted to self-harm in the form of cutting, scratching, or mutilating themselves. This is often described as a means to bring relief from emotional pain as one focuses on the physical sensation of pain to distract from the emotional sensation. It may also be a type of self-punishment. Some people have horrendous scars from this compulsion. Others may contract infections. It is theorized that persons who self-mutilate are at higher risk of suicide than those who do not, making it a possible precursor to suicidal ideations.

The Co-Occurrence of Addiction and Other Disorders

Co-occurring disorders may also be known as **dual disorders** or **dual diagnoses**. Co-occurring disorders are more prevalent in clients who have substance use history (or presently use substances). Substance use is diagnosed when the use of the substance interferes with normal functioning at work, school, home, in relationships, or exacerbates a medical condition. A substance use diagnosis is often made in conjunction with a mood or anxiety related disorder, resulting in a dual diagnosis.

Co-occurring disorders or dual diagnoses may be difficult to diagnose due to the nature of symptom presentation. Some symptoms of addiction or substance abuse may appear to be related to another mental health disorder; conversely, some symptoms of mental health disorder may appear to be related to substance use. On the contrary, there are some signs that a co-occurring disorder is present:

- Mental health symptoms worsening while undergoing treatment: For example, a client suffering from depression may be prescribed anti-depressants to address depressive symptoms. However, if the client is using substances, they may mix other medications with anti-depressants. This can be dangerous in itself but may also create a prolonged false sense of wellbeing while under the influence. Once this feeling fades, it can be confusing for the client to realize whether the prescribed medications are working. Even worse, the client may increase recreational substance use, leading to worse overall mental health symptoms over time.

- Persistent substance use problems with treatment: There are some substance use treatment centers that titrate clients off of one medication and place them on another, such as methadone. This may result in transference of dependence and ongoing substance use while the client is receiving treatment for mental health disorders.

Another scenario is that a client may seek treatment from a substance use treatment center with clinicians that are not equipped to provide adequate mental health treatment for the client. As the mental health problems persist or worsen while undergoing withdrawal, the client may continue to engage in substance use as a coping skill, therefore making the substance use problem appear resistant to treatment.

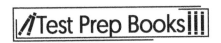

It is important for co-occurring disorders or dual diagnoses to be treated together because they occur simultaneously. This may be done utilizing a multidisciplinary team approach in an outpatient or inpatient setting. Treatment of dual diagnoses or co-occurring disorders at the same time in the same setting by the same treatment team is also known as an **integrated treatment** approach.

Symptoms of Mental and Emotional Illness Across the Lifespan

Mental and emotional illness can present in a number of ways and vary depending on the illness, the person, and the circumstances.

Some symptoms of mental and emotional illness include:

- Chronic feelings of sadness
- Inability to focus
- Extreme mood variation
- Loss of interest in activities one used to enjoy
- Lack of sexual interest or desire
- Intense, and sometimes unexplainable, feelings of guilt, shame, regret, fear, or worry
- Chronic fatigue
- Sleep problems, such as insomnia or sleeping too much
- Feeling overwhelmed by daily routines or tasks
- Substance abuse
- Compulsive or obsessive thoughts or behaviors
- Hallucination
- Thoughts of suicide
- Thoughts of harming oneself or others
- Excessive weight gain or weight loss
- Unexplained anger or irritability
- Detachment from loved ones
- Medically unexplained physical symptoms (psychosomatic) such as headaches, jaw pain, stomach pain, or joint stiffness.

Indicators of Biopsychosocial Stress

Stress can manifest itself in different forms and may result from a threat to the client's functioning, both real and imagined. Some common factors contributing to biopsychosocial stress are natural disasters and disruption of relationships (divorce, death, break-ups, or moving). Other events, such as childhood abuse, bullying, sexual abuse, problems at work, and worries about physical health, may compound or contribute to biopsychosocial stress and manifest in the following symptoms:

- Cognitive
  - Difficulty concentrating
  - Poor memory
  - Anxiousness and worrying
- Emotional
  - Excessive tearfulness
  - Agitation
  - Irritability
  - Feelings of loneliness

- o Depression
- o Unstable moods
- o Feelings of detachment
- Physical
  - o Abnormal weight loss or gain
  - o Swelling and aches from stiff muscles
  - o Digestive problems (nausea, diarrhea, constipation)
  - o Insomnia
  - o Heart palpitations
  - o Chest pain
  - o Feelings of being short of breath
  - o Breakouts (hives, acne, eczema)
  - o Frequent minor illness (colds, headaches)
  - o Fatigue
- Behaviors
  - o Decreased appetite
  - o Withdrawal from preferred activities
  - o Nail biting, pacing, pulling of hair, other nervous "tics"
  - o Hyperactivity to avoid problems, such as too much exercise
  - o Increased aggression

Indicators, Dynamics, and Impact of Physical Abuse and Neglect Across the Lifespan

Physical abuse is the intentional act of physical force that may result in pain, injury, or impairment to a child or other dependent. Physical abuse is typically thought of as violent acts such as hitting, kicking, burning, etc., but it may also include extreme physical discipline, force-feeding, and some uses of drugs or restraints. Physical indicators of physical abuse are multiple physical injuries in various stages of healing; physical injuries that are inconsistent with an individual's account of how the injuries occurred; multiple injuries, accidents, or unexplained illnesses occurring over a period of time; and injuries reflecting the object used to inflict the injury (e.g., cigarette burns, tooth marks, bruising in the shape of finger/hand marks). Behavioral indicators of physical abuse are flinching; offering inconsistent explanations of injuries or being unable to remember how injuries occurred; exhibiting wariness around adults or authority figures; aggression or abusive behavior toward others; and withdrawn, sad, depressed, or even suicidal behavior.

Indicators of Physical Abuse (Child)

- Presence of bruises or marks
- Mistrust of others, evidenced by cringing or shying away
- Fear of going home
- Increased aggressive behavior, bullying of others
- History of acting-out, suicidal behaviors, and/or school problems
- Frequent vomiting
- Parent or caregiver appears unconcerned about the child's physical condition, no explanations offered for injuries

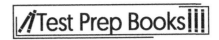

Indicators, Dynamics, and Impact of Intimate Partner Violence

Partner violence takes place in an intimate relationship where one of the partners is physically, verbally, or sexually aggressive towards the other. There is also typically a high level of social and financial control, as well as psychological manipulation or belittling. The most obvious indicators of partner violence are physical injuries such as bruises, broken bones, or black eyes. Emotional symptoms—such as excessive crying or fear—may also be observed, in addition to controlling or obsessive behavior on the part of the abusive partner. However, indicators of partner violence may also take the form of more subtle symptoms, such as depression, anxiety, or distrust of people. Drug or alcohol abuse is often associated with partner violence, and there is a higher risk of violence when drugs or alcohol are involved.

Intimate partner violence occurs when one of the partners seeks to exercise control over the other. While the majority of perpetrators of violence are men, this is not always the case, and domestic violence can be perpetrated by both men and women in either heterosexual or homosexual relationships. Overt physical acts of aggression are often intermittent and may be precipitated by an increase in anger on the part of the abusive partner. Other forms of control, manipulation, and psychological or verbal abuse are more continual, creating an atmosphere of fear and helplessness. In spite of the aggression and control of the abusive partner, the victimized partner of violence often hesitates to reveal the abuse to anyone and will choose to stay with the abusive partner. This dynamic results from the conflicted sense of loyalty the partner feels, especially in cases where they may have had children together.

In situations of intimate partner violence, the abusive partner often alternates abusive behavior with kindness and affection and may apologize and promise to change. This causes the victim to justify or minimize the periods of violence and emphasize the more positive aspects of the relationship. An abusive partner may use the acts of kindness as a constant form of guilt and manipulation, causing the other partner to feel ungrateful if they reveal the abuse to anyone. Additionally, fear of the abuser or a misplaced sense of shame may prevent the victim from telling anyone of the abuse. Only when the costs of leaving the relationship are outweighed by the benefits, will the victimized partner take steps to get out of the abusive situation. In such cases, counselors must provide a safe relationship of trust for the abused individual.

The impact of intimate partner violence is pervasive and profound. The abused partner not only bears physical scars, but also emotional and psychological wounds such as distorted self-image, insecurity, shame, and guilt. These can lead to depression, anxiety, self-harm behaviors, or suicide. In addition to the partner, children who are exposed to domestic violence are also deeply impacted and may struggle in school, at home, and in present and future relationships. There is also a high correlation between intimate partner violence and the perpetration of child abuse.

Indicators, Dynamics, and Impact of Other Forms of Exploitation Across the Lifespan

Exploitation is taking advantage of someone in a vulnerable position for personal gain

Financial exploitation of older adults:

- Indicators
  - Missing identification, money, credit cards, documents, or valuable possessions

- o Large or frequent checks made out to cash
- o Frequent or expensive gifts for caregiver
- o Older adult's unawareness of income or bills
- o Blank checks, cash withdrawals, or money wires/transfers

Sexual exploitation of children (includes both sexual acts and child pornography):

- Indicators
  - o Spending time with older individuals or an older "boyfriend" or "girlfriend"
  - o Spending time in inappropriate locations such as hotels or bars
  - o May show aforementioned signs of abuse
  - o Uncertain of where they are (as they have been moved around to various geographic locations)
  - o Missing from their home or not attending school
  - o Fearful or anxious around others
  - o Signs of grooming (someone building a connection with the child, either online or in-person, in order to gain trust and ultimately abuse and/or exploit the child):
    - Secretive about behavior
    - Possesses unexplained money or items
    - Has access to alcohol and/or drugs

Girls are disproportionately affected by sexual exploitation and trafficking. The majority of children and adolescents are exploited by someone they know.

Individual and/or Relationship Functioning

Typical and Atypical Physical Growth and Development

It is important to understand normal developmental milestones. While not all children progress at the same rate, one must have some guidelines in order to determine if the child has any developmental delays that prevent them from reaching goals by a certain age.

Infancy Through Age Five

During the first year of life, abundant changes occur. The child learns basic, but important, skills. The child is learning to manipulate objects, hold their head without support, crawl, and pull up into a standing position. The toddler should be able to walk without assistance by eighteen months. By age two, the child should be running and able to climb steps one stair at a time. By age three, the child should be curious and full of questions about how the world works or why people behave in certain ways. The child should have the balance and coordination to climb stairs using only one foot per stair. By age four, the child is increasingly independent, demonstrating skills like attending to toilet needs and dressing with some adult assistance.

School Age to Adolescence

By age five, speech is becoming more fluent, and the ability to draw simple figures improves. Dressing without help is achieved. By age six, speech should be fluent, and motor skills are strengthened. The youth is now able to navigate playground equipment and kick or throw a ball. Social skills, such as teamwork or friendship development, are evolving. The child must learn to deal with failure or frustration and find ways to be accepted by peers. They become more proficient in reading, math, and

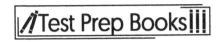

writing skills. Towards the end of this phase, around age twelve, secondary sexual characteristics, such as darker body hair or breast development, may occur.

Adolescence

This is a period of extraordinary change. The process of **individuation** is occurring. The teen views themselves as someone who will someday live independently of parents. More time is spent with peers and less with family. Identity formation arises, and the teen experiments with different kinds of clothing, music, and hairstyles to see what feels comfortable and what supports their view of the world. Sexuality is explored, and determinations are being made about sexual preferences and orientation. Sexual experimentation is common, and some teens actually form long-term intimate relationships, although others are satisfied to make shorter-term intimate connections. There is often a period of experimentation with drugs or alcohol. As the thinking process matures, there may be a questioning of rules and expectations of those in authority. Moodiness is common, and troubled teens are likely to "act out" their emotions, sometimes in harmful ways.

Typical and Atypical Cognitive Growth and Development

Cognitive development refers to development of a child's capacity for perception, thought, learning, information processing, and other mental processes. The **nature vs. nurture** debate questions whether cognitive development is primarily influenced by genetics or upbringing. Evidence indicates that the interaction between nature and nurture determines the path of development.

Some recognized milestones in early cognitive development:

- One to three months: focuses on faces and moving objects, differentiates between different types of tastes, sees all colors in the spectrum

- Three to six months: recognizes familiar faces and sounds, imitates expressions

- Six to twelve months: begins to determine how far away something is, understands that things still exist when they are not seen (object permanence)

- One to two years: recognizes similar objects, understands and responds to some words

- Two to three years: sorts objects into appropriate categories, responds to directions, names objects

- Three to four years: Demonstrates increased attention span of five to fifteen minutes, shows curiosity and seeks answers to questions, organizes objects by characteristics

- Four to five years: Draws human shapes, counts to five or higher, uses rhyming words

The **Zone of proximal development** is the range of tasks that a child can carry out with assistance, but not independently. Parents and educators can advance a child's learning by providing opportunities within the zone of proximal development, allowing the child to develop the ability to accomplish those actions gradually without assistance.

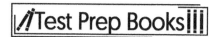

Piaget's Theory of Cognitive Development

Piaget was the first to study cognitive development systematically. He believed children have a basic cognitive structure and continually restructure cognitive frameworks over time through maturation and experiences.

Key Terms:

- Schema: Introduced by Piaget, a concept or a mental framework that allows a person to understand and organize new information

- Assimilation: The way in which an individual understands and incorporates new information into their pre-existing cognitive framework (schema)

- Accommodation: In contrast to assimilation, involves altering one's pre-existing cognitive framework in order to adjust to new information

- Equilibrium: Occurs when a child can successfully assimilate new information

- Disequilibrium: Occurs when a child cannot successfully assimilate new information

- Equilibration: The mechanism that ensures equilibrium takes place

Stages of Cognitive Development

The stages of cognitive development are sensorimotor, pre-operational, concrete operational, and formal operational. **Sensorimotor** occurs from birth to around approximately age two. The key accomplishment here is developing object permanence—the understanding that objects still exist even when the child cannot see them. **Pre-operational** is from two to seven years. Children become capable of symbolic play and using logic. **Concrete operational** is from seven to eleven years of age. Children are able to make generalizations by drawing conclusions from what they observe (inductive reasoning), yet they are generally unable to come to a conclusion or predict an outcome by using logic pertaining to an abstract idea (deductive reasoning). **Formal operational** occurs from adolescence through early

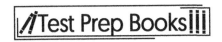

adulthood. People develop abstract thought, metacognition (thinking about thinking), and problem-solving ability.

Typical and Atypical Social Growth, Development, and the Socialization Process

Social development refers to the development of the skills that allow individuals to have effective interpersonal relationships and to contribute in a positive manner to the world around them.

Social learning is taught directly by caregivers and educators, but it is also learned indirectly by the experience of various social relationships.

Social development is commonly influenced by extended family, communities, religious institutions, schools, and sports teams or social groups. Positive social development is supported when caregivers engage in these behaviors:

- Attune to a child's needs and feelings
- Demonstrate respect for others
- Teach children how to handle conflict and solve problems encountered during social experiences
- Help children learn to take the perspective of another person and develop empathy
- Encourage discussion of morals and values and listen to the child's opinions on those topics
- Explain rules and encourage fair treatment of others
- Encourage cooperation, rather than competition

Social development begins from birth as a child learns to attach to their mother and other caregivers. During adolescence, social development focuses on peer relationships and self-identity. In adulthood, social relationships are also important, but the goal is to establish secure and long-term relationships with family and friends.

Another important contributor to social development are social institutions, such as family, church, and school, which assist people in realizing their full potential. Lev Vygotsky was a pioneer in this field with his concept of cultural mediation. This theory emphasizes that one's feelings, thoughts, and behaviors are significantly influenced by others in their environment.

Typical and Atypical Emotional Growth and Development

Emotional development encompasses the development of the following abilities:

- Identifying and understanding the feelings that one experiences
- Identifying and understanding the feelings of others
- Emotional and behavioral regulation
- Empathy
- Establishing relationships with others

Caregivers who are nurturing and responsive enable children to learn to regulate emotions and feel safe in the environment around them.

- By age two to three months, infants express delight and distress, begin smiling, and may be able to be soothed by rocking.

- By three to four months, infants communicate via crying and begin to express interest and surprise.

- Between four to nine months, infants respond differently to strangers in comparison to known individuals, solicit attention, show a particular attachment for a primary caregiver, and have an expanded range of expressed emotions that include anger, fear, and shyness.

- At ten to twelve months, babies show an increase in exploration and curiosity, demonstrate affection, and display a sense of humor.

- Children at age twelve to twenty-four months often demonstrate anger via aggression, laugh in social situations, recognize themselves in a mirror, engage in symbolic play, and have a complete range of emotional expression.

- Around age two, children begin using different facial expressions to show their emotions, begin to play cooperatively, and may transition from being calm and affectionate to temperamental and easily frustrated.

- At age three, children engage in more social and imaginative play, show interest in the feelings of others, begin to learn to manage frustration, and are often inconsistent and stubborn.

- Children at age four show improved cooperation, express sympathy, and may exhibit lying and/or guilty behavior.

- At age five, children can play rule-based games, often want to do what is expected of them, express emotion easily, and choose friends for themselves.

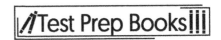

- Children at age six typically describe themselves in terms of their external attributes, have a difficult time coping with challenges and criticism, prefer routines, and show inconsistent self-control.

- Around age seven, children can typically describe causes and outcomes of emotions and show better regulation of emotions in most situations.

- From ages eight to ten, children have an increased need for independence, want to be viewed as intelligent, experience and better understand emotional subtleties, and may be defiant.

- During adolescence, children begin to master emotional skills to manage stress, increase self-awareness, develop identity, show increased ability for empathy, and learn to manage conflict.

Normal versus abnormal behavior is difficult to distinguish because each person is unique, so creating a standard of normal can be challenging. Though labeling behaviors as normal or abnormal can be problematic, it is important to have some standard by which it is possible to identify those behaviors that are indicative of an underlying psychological condition. Notwithstanding the challenges, it is possible and helpful to have general definitions of normal and abnormal behavior.

Normal behaviors are those that are common to the majority of the population, as related to emotional functioning, social interactions, and mental capacity. **Abnormal behavior** is considered that which is maladaptive, dysfunctional, and disruptive to life. These behaviors may be an exaggeration of a normal behavior or even an absence of a typical response. They do not conform to the accepted patterns or common behaviors of society. Sadness over the death of a loved one is considered normal but disabling depression that interferes with school and work responsibilities is not. The *DSM-5* is the current standard for determining the diagnostic criteria that distinguishes abnormal behavior from normal.

Typical and Atypical Sexual Growth and Development

While not everyone develops sexually on exactly the same timeline, there are certain expectations that define healthy and unhealthy sexual development. These expectations differ based on age. During the early stage of life, from birth until age two, the child is focused on developing a relationship of trust with caregivers. Eventually, children become aware of their genitals and explore these through self-touch. By ages two to five, they begin to develop the ability to name and describe genitalia. They understand that male and female bodies are different. They have little inhibition about nudity.

As children enter middle childhood (ages six to eight or nine), they begin to understand the concept of puberty and what to expect about future body changes. They have a more sophisticated knowledge of reproduction and may become more inhibited about nudity.

By the age of nine or ten, some children show signs of puberty, although the typical age of onset is eleven for girls and thirteen for boys. During puberty, there is a dramatic development in both primary and secondary sex characteristics. Children at this age show an increased interest in sex and may have questions about sexual orientation, sexual practices, or how the opposite sex behaves. By age twelve or thirteen, they begin to understand the consequences of sexual behavior, such as pregnancy or STDs. As they enter later adolescence, they may form longer relationships with their love interests, but many prefer casual dating. They are beginning to form an identity in terms of sexual orientation, preferences, and values.

It is important to understand red flags that may be signs of unhealthy sexual development. These may be brought on by abuse or by exposure to sexually explicit scenes. Children who are preoccupied with sexuality at an early age and whose behaviors differ from peers their own age may be at risk. Other indicators include attempting adult-like sexual interactions. These behaviors may include oral to genital contact or some form of penetration of another person's body.

These issues should raise concerns:

- A child overly pre-occupied with sexual thoughts, language, or behaviors, rather than in more age-appropriate play
- Child engaging in sex play with children who are much older or much younger
- Child using sexual behavior to harm others
- Child involved in sexual play with animals
- Child uses explicit sexual language that is not age appropriate

A sexually-reactive child refers to one who is exposed to sexual stimuli prior to being sexually mature enough to understand the implications. The child becomes overly preoccupied with sexual matters and often acts out what they witnessed or experienced.

Spiritual Growth and Development

Spiritual development encompasses a broad search for finding meaning in life. Children learn spiritual concepts from family, church, and sometimes school. Observing and copying others is part of the groundwork for spiritual development. As children move toward adolescence, they may begin to question the beliefs once held. As adulthood approaches, they become more interested in a broader worldview.

Child Behavior and Development

The term **child development** refers to the process of human growth from birth until the end of adolescence. It encompasses physical, emotional, and psychological changes that take place during those years. Child development examines the process of growth and life transitions during the first eighteen years of life as the infant moves from complete dependency to increasing autonomy. It is recognized that there are certain sequential milestones, but each individual is unique in terms of developmental advancement. Child development is influenced by social, economic, and cultural factors. Because the way in which children develop today impacts how society will function in the future, it is essential that parents, educators, child care providers, and those in the medical field have a clear grasp of what elements are crucial in terms of successfully transitioning a child into the role of an independent adult.

Adolescent Behavior and Development

Adolescence is the sometimes-rocky path from the end of childhood to the onset of adulthood. It is a time of tremendous change, experimentation, and learning lessons. The changes are far-reaching, with the most apparent being changes in physical appearance and the emergence of sexuality. At the same time, adolescents are changing cognitively and emotionally and learning to view the world through new eyes. Adolescent development is usually categorized into three stages. These are early adolescence (ages ten to fourteen), middle adolescence (ages fifteen to sixteen), and late adolescence (ages seventeen to twenty-one).

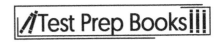

During **early adolescence**, the child's sense of identity is beginning to emerge. They are less interested in time spent with parents and more interested in being with peers. Close friendships may be forged during this time. In this stage, the child may be moody, sometimes rude, and occasionally oppositional. Limit testing is common, as is experimentation with drugs, alcohol, or cigarettes. Girls are more likely to exhibit early signs of sexual maturity than boys at this point. It is a period of exploration of the body and becoming more aware of new sensations. This leads to concerns about being physically attractive.

In **middle adolescence**, the child continues to move toward eventual independence. The peer group becomes more central, and parents are viewed as less likable than before, due to a new awareness of parental flaws. There is a greater preoccupation with body image, personal style, and intellectual interests. The child can now experience insight and may spend time analyzing inner experiences or relationships. Sexual orientation and identity is becoming more clearly defined, but is still in a formative stage.

In **late adolescence**, there is greater movement towards independence as demonstrated by a stronger ability to feel compassion, expressing ideas through words, expanding interests in career paths, self-reliance, and a concern for the future. Sexuality is expressed in more mature and more stable relationships. The child can now set goals and follow through with them successfully. Some sadness may be present due to the inevitable separation from parents and their changing social relationships.

Knowledge of adolescent development is a standard for the practice of counseling with adolescents.

Physical Development

Puberty encompasses the physical changes of adolescence, indicated by a substantial growth spurt and sexual maturation. **Sexual maturation** means becoming capable of sexual reproduction.

For girls, the growth spurt typically begins between ages ten and twelve and ends between ages seventeen and nineteen. For boys, the growth spurt typically begins between ages twelve and fourteen and ends around age twenty. Accompanying changes for girls are breast budding (age ten or earlier) and onset of menstruation (typically around age twelve or thirteen). Accompanying changes for boys are testicular enlargement (around age eleven or twelve) and first ejaculation (around ages twelve to fourteen).

Development of body hair for both sexes and voice changes (boys) often occur later in puberty, rather than at the onset. Adolescents who mature early may also be at increased risk for early sexual activity, teenage pregnancy, and STDs. For boys, late maturation appears to be more problematic than early maturation; late maturing boys are at increased risk for bullying, parental conflict, academic problems, and depression.

Identity Development

Identity includes **self-concept** and **self-esteem**. Self-concept is the beliefs one holds about one's self. Self-esteem is how one feels about one's self-concept.

The physical changes of adolescence can have a strong influence on an adolescent's self-esteem. Adolescents also incorporate comments from others, particularly parents and friends, into their identity. Counselors can help with adolescent identity development simply by asking questions and being available to listen, while suspending judgment.

Adolescents also undergo important emotional development and begin to hone the skills that are necessary for stress management and effective relationships with others. Some of the skills necessary for stress management are recognizing and managing one's own emotions, developing empathy for others, learning appropriate and constructive methods of managing conflict, and learning to work cooperatively rather than competitively.

A normal part of adolescence is a yearning for independence. Counselors can help parents understand that the desire for independence is healthy and age-appropriate. They can educate both parents and adolescents about the importance of positive peer relationships during this time. Peer groups help adolescents learn about the world outside of their families and identify how they differ from their parents. Adolescents who are accepted by their peers and who have positive peer relationships may have better psychosocial outcomes in both adolescence and adulthood.

An increase in conflict with parents is normal during adolescence and seems to be most prevalent between girls and mothers. Parents may need reassurance that this conflict does not represent rejection, but rather a normal striving for independence.

Some theories seek to explain the prevalence of risk-taking behaviors among adolescents. One theory of risk-taking behavior explains that the need for excitement and sensation seeking outweighs any potential dangers that may come from sensation seeking. Another theory says that risk-taking often occurs within groups as a way to gain status and acceptance among peers. Additionally, adolescents who engage in risk-taking behavior may be modeling adult behavior that has been romanticized.

There are many ways in which counselors and parents can provide guidance to young people with regard to their risk-taking behavior. They should become comfortable discussing uncomfortable topics, so that adolescents can safely talk about their decision-making and peer pressure. Additionally, it is wise to steer adolescents toward healthy outlets that channel their talents or get them involved in positive activities.

Adolescent resilience and positive outcomes are associated with these factors:

- Having a stable and positive relationship with at least one involved and caring adult (e.g., parent, coach, teacher, family member, community member)
- Developing a sense of self-meaning, often through a church or spiritual outlet
- Attending a school that has high, but realistic, expectations and supports its students
- Living in a warm and nurturing home
- Having adequate ability to manage stress

Young Adult Behavior and Development

Adult development includes any of the physical, psychological, or social changes that occur from the end of adolescence through the remainder of an individual's life. It is important to understand that the term **adulthood** has different meanings and expectations across cultures. A person is legally considered an adult when they reach the **age of majority**, the age at which their society considers individuals legally responsible for themselves and their behaviors. In the U.S., the age of majority is eighteen. In other cultures, it may be as low as sixteen or as high as twenty-one.

Seasons of Life Theory (Levinson)
This theory of adult development is classified by development stages, with each stage defined by different—yet meaningful and developmentally necessary—tasks. There are transition periods where stages overlap.

Pre-Adulthood Stage
- Ends at age twenty-two

- Beginning at birth, this is the stage when a person develops and prepares for adulthood. It is a time of major growth and transition.

- The individual develops a state of independence.

Early Adulthood Transition
- Roughly age seventeen to twenty-two

- Pre-adulthood is ending, and early adulthood is beginning, but the time of transition is actually part of both periods.

- Physical development is completed, but this time of transition can be compared to the infancy of a new period of development.

- Adolescence ends, and the individual begins to make decisions about adult life. They further develop independence and separate from the family of origin.

Early Adulthood Stage
- Roughly age seventeen to forty-five

- This stage begins with the early adult transition.

- From a biological perspective, an individual's twenties and thirties are at the peak of the life cycle.

- This stage can be the time at which individuals have their greatest energy but are also experiencing the greatest amount of stress as they try to establish families and careers simultaneously.

Midlife Transition
- Roughly age forty to forty-five

- Another time of transition that bridges the end of early adulthood and the beginning of middle adulthood.

- At this time of life, people tend to become more reflective and compassionate and less concerned with external demands.

- Values may change, and it is possibly a time where crisis is experienced due to limited time to reach goals.

- Individuals become aware of death and leaving a legacy.

Middle Adulthood Stage
- Roughly age forty to sixty-five

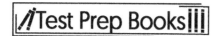

- There is a diminishment of biological capacities, but only minimally. Most individuals are able to continue to lead fulfilling and energetic lives.

- Many take on a mentoring role and responsibility for the further development of young adults.

- Choices must be made about livelihood and retirement.

Late Adulthood
- Roughly age sixty

- A transition period occurs from around sixty to sixty-five.

- Late adulthood is a time of reflection on other stages and on accomplishments.

- During this stage, retirement takes place, and the individual gives up their role in the workplace. Crisis occurs at this stage due to declining power and less accolades of work performed.

Middle Adult Behavior and Development

Adult development refers to the psychological, physical, cognitive, and social changes that occur from age eighteen until the end of life. Broadly speaking, adulthood can be divided into three phases:

Early Adulthood
Early adulthood includes the ages of eighteen to forty. It is a transitional time as the young adult leaves home, begins a higher level of education, or ventures onto a career path. During this period, a spouse or partner may be chosen, and children may be born.

Middle Adulthood
Middle adulthood occurs from ages forty to sixty-five. These are the years in which skills attained earlier become more polished, and one may climb the ladder of vocational success. The family changes as older children leave the nest to establish their own places in life, and elderly parents become less independent and more infirm.

Late Adulthood
Late adulthood occurs from the age of sixty-five until the end of life. This is a time for reflection on the quality of life, the goals achieved, and the need to adapt to changes such as retirement, a decreased income, health issues, and the loss of people dear to them.

Older Adult Behavior and Development

In gerontology, **aging** is viewed as occurring in four separate processes:

Chronological aging: based on actual years lived

Biological aging: based on physical changes that have an impact on the performance of the body's organs and systems

Psychological aging: based on changes in personality, cognitive ability, adaptive ability, and perception

- Basic personality traits appear to be relatively stable through the lifespan, as does an individual's self-image.

42

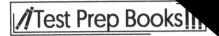

- One aspect that does tend to change, however, is the tendency to become more inwardly focused, which may also result in reduced impulsivity and increased caution.

- Studies have shown that a pattern of age-related changes in intelligence can typically be observed after age sixty, although changes vary widely across individuals. Furthermore, the somewhat poorer testing results are reflected in **fluid intelligence** (i.e., reasoning, problem-solving, and abstract thinking unrelated to experience or learned information), but not in **crystallized intelligence** (i.e., knowledge based on skills, learning, and experience).

- Normal age-related changes in memory typically involve acquisition of new information and retrieval of information from memory storage.

- **Sensory decline** is also a common experience for aging individuals.

Social aging: based on changes in one's relationships with family, friends, acquaintances, systems, and organizations

- Most older persons experience a narrowing of their social networks. However, they are more likely to have more positive interactions within those networks, and they are more likely to experience more positive feelings about family members than younger persons do.

- **Disengagement theory** states that it is natural and inevitable for older adults to withdraw from their social systems and to reduce interactions with others. This theory has been highly criticized and is incompatible with other well-known psychosocial aging theories.

- **Activity theory** proposes that social activity serves as a buffer to aging; successful aging occurs among those who maintain their social connections and activity levels.

- **Continuity theory** proposes that with age, individuals attempt to maintain activities and relationships that were typical for them as younger adults.

Social Clock Theory (Bernice Neugarten)

Neugarten proposed that every society has a **social clock**: an understood expectation for when certain life events should happen (e.g., getting married, buying a home, having children). When individuals do not adhere to this timeframe, they often experience stress, the sense of disappointing others, or the experience of an internal "clock ticking" and reminding them that time is running out.

Basic Human Needs

Abraham Maslow is the most notable researcher in the area of basic human needs. Maslow theorized that human needs could be described in the form of a pyramid, with the base of the pyramid representing the most basic needs and the higher layers representing loftier goals and needs. Unless the basic needs are met, a person cannot move on to higher needs. For example, a homeless woman living under a bridge will need food, shelter, and safety before she can consider dealing with her alcoholism.

Prep Books

...ational layer in Maslow's hierarchy is physiological needs, and the final layer at the pinnacle of ...id is self-transcendence.

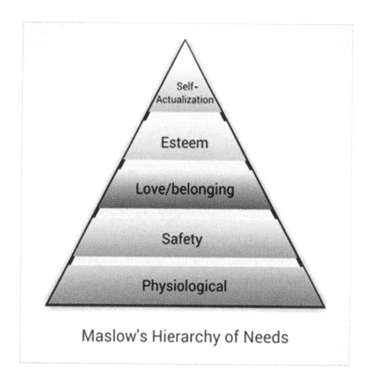

Maslow's Hierarchy of Needs

Maslow's Hierarchy of Needs

Physiological Needs: These needs must be met first and pertain to what humans need to survive. This includes basics, such as food, water, clothing, and housing.

Safety Needs: Once primary needs are met, the person may now focus on safety issues. This would include safety from abuse and neglect, natural disaster, or war.

Love and Belonging: Once the first levels of need have been satisfied, people are next driven to find a sense of acceptance and belonging within social groups, such as family, community, or religious organizations. Maslow suggests that humans have a basic need for love, affection, and sexual intimacy. Failure to achieve this level can lead to difficulty in forming and maintaining close relationships with others.

Esteem: The need for esteem is driven by a desire for recognition, respect, and acceptance within a social context.

Self-Actualization: The U.S. Army slogan, "Be All You Can Be," expresses this layer of need. Reaching one's highest potential is the focus. According to Maslow, this cannot be achieved until all the others are mastered.

Self-Transcendence: Devised by Maslow in his later years, he felt self-actualization did not completely satisfy his image of a person reaching their highest potential. To achieve self-transcendence, one must commit to a goal that is outside of one's self, such as practicing altruism or finding a deeper level of spirituality.

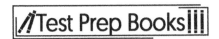

Attachment and Bonding

Understanding attachment and bonding has become more important than ever, especially in relation to changes within the U.S. culture's attitudes about child welfare over the last fifty years. Child Protective Service Teams have become more active in every city. The medical profession, the educational system, and the mental health profession are more informed about children at risk. As a result, more children are being taken from parents, sometimes as early as the day of birth. An older child victim may travel from relative to relative, back to the mother, then into foster or group homes. These children do not have an opportunity to form attachments with their caregivers, nor do caregivers have the opportunity to bond with the children.

Bonding refers to a mother's initial connection to her baby. This occurs within the first hours or days of the birth. Mothers who are able and willing to hold their child close to them shortly after birth generally have more positive relationships with the child. When a mother fails to bond, the child is at greater risk for having behavioral problems.

Attachment, on the other hand, refers to a more gradual development of the baby's relationship with their caretaker. A secure attachment naturally grows out of a positive, loving relationship in which there is soothing physical contact, emotional and physical safety, and responsiveness to the child's needs. The baby who has a secure attachment will venture out from their safe base, but immediately seek their mother when fearful or anxious, having learned that mommy will be there to protect them. This type of secure relationship becomes impossible if the child is moved from home to home or has experienced abuse or neglect.

A child whose needs have not been met or who has learned through mistreatment that the world is unfriendly and hostile may develop an avoidant attachment or ambivalent attachment. An **avoidant attachment** is characterized by a detached relationship in which the child does not seek out the caregiver when distressed but acts independently. A child with **ambivalent attachment** shows inconsistency toward the caregiver; sometimes the child clings to them, and at other times, resists their comfort. Establishing a secure, positive attachment with a caregiver is crucial to a child's life-long emotional and social success. The development of attachment disorder is often present in foster children or those adopted later in life and can create much frustration and heartache as the more stable parents step in and attempt to bond with them.

Impact of Physical, Mental, and Cognitive Impairment on Human Development

Approximately 7 percent of U.S. children have some type of disability. The most common physical disabilities that impact development are cerebral palsy, hearing issues, and visual issues. Learning disabilities are also common—these could be Down's syndrome or other developmental delays. Common psychiatric disabilities are ADHD and autism spectrum disorders. Others include mood disorders, oppositional disorders, anxiety disorders, and, in rare cases, schizophrenia. The impact upon the child and family corresponds to the family's ability to adapt to the condition, and their ability to connect to community resources.

How the individual develops and copes with the disability depends upon the social context and the child's own personal attributes. Raising a disabled child puts tremendous stress on parents and siblings. There are issues of stigma, financial burden, missed days of work for parents, and the time and energy needed to seek useful resources. Siblings may be called upon to take roles of parenting to help out. These siblings may be bullied by peers who make fun of their disabled family member. They may feel neglected by parents. Additionally, there may be a need for special housing and special schools. Low-income families may face barriers to accessing services such as transportation, medical specialists, or assistance with childcare.

Components of a Sexual History

Sexual history can be a difficult topic to discuss. It helps to gently emphasize that discussing the topic may assist with providing a holistic assessment of the individual's case and, consequently, providing an optimal treatment plan. When assessing an individual's sexual history, the data that is typically collected include:

- Sexual orientation
- Cultural and personal views on sexual behavior
- Number of partners
- Gender of partners
- Length of relationships
- Satisfaction with partners
- Sexual desires
- Ability to become aroused and orgasm
- Types of sexual behaviors
- History of sexually transmitted diseases or infections
- Contraception use and type
- Reproductive or pregnancy history
- Role of substance use or abuse in relation to sexual desires, sexual behaviors, or arousal

Assessing the Client System's Communication Skills

One of the most common means of assessing client's communication skills is through use of verbal dialogue. It is important to note the dialect the client chooses to use, the syncopation of speech, and the length of responses to questions (Are the answers short? Does the client go off on tangents often?) The client's responses are indicators of the presenting problem and an extension of the mental status examination process. There are numerous areas of communication that can be assessed and addressed, the most common of which are listed here:

Alertness
A common primary indicator of the client's level of consciousness is discernible alertness, commonly assessed with the client's orientation and indicated by a value from one to three.

- If a client is alert and oriented x1, they are only aware of a person.
- If a client is alert and oriented x2, then they know the person and place.
- If a client is alert and oriented x3, then they can state a person, the place, and provide a time period.

The client's level of alertness can also be described with adjectives such as lethargic, apathetic, or confused. The practitioner can ask questions to determine these elements:

- "What's your name?"
- "How old are you?"
- "Do you know what you're here for?"

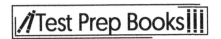

- "What is today's date?"
- "Who am I?"

Speech Patterns

The rhythm, syncopation, and other behaviors of a client's speech are important in assessing communication. The practitioner should document how articulate the client is and note qualities, such as the formation of complete sentences, presence of stuttering, mumbling, curt responses, immature colloquialisms, cursing, and sentence syntax.

Additionally, the quality of the client's voice should be assessed for communication patterns. The counselor should observe whether or not the client's tone is appropriate, if the fluctuations are in response to the mood presented, and any persistence of a mechanical tone or rapidity of speech. Moreover, the client's response to the practitioner should be noted, gauging the client's degree of cooperation during sessions.

Nonverbal Cues

Not all communication is verbal; nonverbal communication is just as important in client communication. One important nonverbal cue includes the client's facial expressions. Just as it is important to note whether the speech patterns and tone match the flow of conversation, it is equally important to assess whether or not the client's facial expressions are congruent with the present mood and conversation. The counselor should make note of any cues/facial expressions that are in opposition to the words spoken or stated mood (for example, the client stating she is happy, but grimacing or crying).

The client's mannerisms should also be observed for communicative deficits or distinctions like fidgeting, flapping, excessive blinking, avoidance of eye contact, rocking, a tense or relaxed posture, and balance. The rate and consciousness of these movements should also be noted.

In addition to facial expressions and mannerisms, the manner in which a client dresses and the degree of hygiene presented can provide insight to the client's overall functioning.

Assessing the Client System's Strengths, Resources, and Challenges

Once the client has identified the existing problem and systems, the client's **internal support systems** should be assessed, which includes examining the client's strengths and coping abilities. As with other facets of the assessment process, the client can provide a verbal report answering an open-ended question about what they view as current strengths and weaknesses.

Additionally, the counselor can ask the client to provide a narrative related to a recent experience (it does not necessarily have to be linked to the presenting problem), in order to showcase strengths and weaknesses. Using finding questions can guide the client to describe their reaction to events comprehensively, to identify what favorable actions were taken, and to research what alternative actions could be taken. The counselor may then summarize back to the client the strengths they heard in the narrative. This ensures that the client feels heard and understood.

The counselor may also use scales to assess the client's strengths and weaknesses. A **dual perspective worksheet** may be utilized to identify the supports and obstacles perceived by the client in current social interactions. The worksheet helps create a visual map of the areas of strength the client can rely on as a means of improving areas of functioning, while simultaneously allowing the client to see areas

47

that could use additional improvement. The counselor can create a treatment plan with the client to develop or enhance coping skills, focusing on strengthening weaker areas and utilizing stronger ones.

Assessing the Client System's Ability and Motivation to Engage in the Intervention Process

Counselors must be able to identify indicators of motivation and resistance in order to determine how to engage the client and progress through treatment effectively. If a client is motivated, then they are likely to be more participative in treatment and positively respond to interventions.

Indicators of motivation are transparent and include a client voluntarily coming in for treatment and expressing a willingness to be actively involved in treatment. As time progresses, the client's level of engagement with the practitioner is an indicator of motivation, as well. It is important for practitioners to determine whether the client feels empowered with the interventions to remedy the problem or if the client is dependent upon the practitioner to provide the solution.

Resistance is likely to be more present in clients who are involuntarily seeking treatment, like through a court order. Resistance may take the form of clients minimizing the effects of their behaviors, rationalizing their behaviors, or believing there is no problem to address. A client may also appear disengaged during sessions or directly state that they will not take the recommended steps toward resolution. Resistant clients may frequently arrive late, cancel, or fail to show up for sessions.

Assessing the Client System's Coping Abilities

Ego strength is the ability of the individual to be resilient in the face of stressors. Generally, individuals with high ego strength will be able to return to a normal emotional state after experiencing crisis. They will be able to appropriately process it and cope with the demand of doing so. Positive or high ego strength is marked by:

- The ability to acknowledge mood shifts without getting overwhelmed
- The ability to cope positively with loss and setbacks
- Realizing painful or sad feelings will decrease in intensity over time
- Taking personal responsibility for actions and reactions
- Self-discipline in the face of temptation or addictive urges
- Setting and respecting firm limits and boundaries
- Avoiding people who are negative influences
- Learning from mistakes rather than blaming oneself or someone else

Consequently, the absence of these indicators may reveal areas around which to tailor intervention or treatment. These indicators may be determined through verbal discussion or standardized assessments.

Assessing Community Functioning

Community often has a strong impact on the development of the individual. To pinpoint the strengths and challenges of a community, the practitioner can examine indicators such as:

- What is the socioeconomic status of the community?
- What are the demographics of the community?
- How many people are employed?

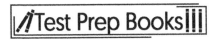

- How many people are living under the poverty level?
- What is the instance of violence, misdemeanors, and/or gang activity in the community?
- How safe do community members feel on a daily basis?
- What is the median household income level?
- What are the community centers (faith-based organizations, social agencies, recreation and development facilities, schools) that serve the population? How well are they funded, what types of programs are offered, and how much of the community is engaged?
- How does the community interact with public agencies such as law enforcement or the labor department? What are the community's feelings toward these agencies?
- Who are the leaders of the community? How did they come to their positions of leadership, and how are they perceived by the community?
- What does the community feel it needs?
- These points of information can be obtained from U.S. Census reports, surveys, and interviews. It's important to collect this data from reliable, varied, and quality sources.

Effects of Addiction on the Client

The effects of drugs and alcohol can be far reaching, and when abuse occurs, it can cause changes in body, mind, and spirit. The organ that is most impacted is the brain. The brain regulates bodily functions and provides responses and interpretation to everything experienced through the senses. Substances of abuse tap into the brain's communication center and interfere with the processing of information. When drugs and alcohol are introduced, the brain's pleasure circuits are stimulated. While this brings a sense of euphoria initially, other responses soon follow if the substance is consumed in large quantities.

One consequence is **tolerance**—the need to use larger quantities to achieve desired effects. When drugs enter circulation, the brain adjusts by producing fewer neurotransmitters that produce a sense of well-being. As a result, the ability to experience pleasure naturally is reduced, leaving one feeling depressed and lifeless. The addict continues to take substances to feel better and creates a vicious cycle, requiring more and more of the substance to derive a sense of euphoria.

As mentioned in earlier sections, drugs can diminish inhibitions. This means the processes usually in place to manage unacceptable urges become disabled. As a result, engagement in foolish or risky behaviors increases. Some examples are as follows:

- Deciding to operate a motor vehicle while impaired
- Believing one is physically capable of certain feats when they are not (e.g., during annual spring breaks when young adults risk their lives by attempting to dive from hotel balconies into swimming pools)
- Engaging in sexual activities in unsafe places with unsafe people
- Failure to consider risks of pregnancy or STDs
- Getting into physical altercations
- Committing criminal acts
- Failing to censor one's words that could damage relationships with others
- Spending money foolishly

Other effects involve physical consequences, such as the following:

- Contraction of life-threatening medical disorders, such as HIV
- Respiratory and heart issues

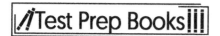

- Kidney and liver damage
- Birth defects in children if using substances when pregnant
- Loss of bladder or bowel control
- Seizures, stroke, and brain damage
- Death

Interplay of Biological, Psychological, Social, and Spiritual Factors

The **biopsychosocial model** (developed by George Engle) posits that health and illness result from the interplay between biological, psychological, and social factors. This model incorporates more factors than the traditional biomedical model of illness, which attributed causation only to biological factors, disregarding any other influences.

Biological Factors: Genetics and other biological factors play a substantial role in human development. Examples of these factors are physical features, such as height, weight, or degree of attractiveness. Is the person healthy or disabled? Can he or she walk, talk, see, and hear? While most believe that others should not be judged by physical appearance, studies show that healthy, attractive, fit persons have certain advantages in life. More people will be attracted to these individuals, which creates an expanded circle of friends and eligible partners. In general, being disabled restricts social, educational, and vocational opportunities.

Psychological Factors: Psychological factors encompass a wide range of symptoms and conditions. These can range from a diagnosis of schizophrenia to mild social anxiety. Many psychological factors can directly impact biological ones and vice versa. Depression may cause insomnia. Anxiety can cause gastrointestinal distress. Anorexia causes restricted food intake to the point of starvation. Chronic pain can cause irritability, anger, depression, and social withdrawal.

Social Factors: Social factors are intimately intertwined with both biological and psychological factors. These are developed in response to the social institutions and influences that one is exposed to. These can include family, school, religious organizations, government, and neighborhoods. The media contributes to people's social context, telling them what is desirable, what is undesirable, and what they need in their lives to be happy. Media influences attitudes about sexuality, violence, consumption of goods, the government, and the way people treat one another. Experiences are based on interpretation, and interpretation is influenced by social context.

In Western culture, particularly in medicine, psychology, and counseling, it is commonly accepted that the interaction of the aforementioned factors determines health outcomes. An individual's health status, their perceptions of and beliefs about health, and their barriers to accessing healthcare exert a combined influence on the likelihood of that individual engaging in healthy behaviors, such as exercising, getting physical exams, or eating well-balanced meals.

For counselors, the biopsychosocial model is helpful in understanding why some individuals are more likely to develop mental health problems. This perspective is also helpful in fighting the stigmatization of mental illness because it promotes the understanding that anyone can develop mental health problems, if there is a disruption to the balance of biological, psychological, or social influences. In counseling, this perspective is often expanded and referred to as the **biopsychosocial-spiritual perspective**—the idea that one must also consider the ways in which individuals find meaning in their lives.

Relevant Family Issues

Components of a Family History

Family history can provide insight into an individual's influences. The family unit is the most immediate system to which an individual belongs, so understanding it can provide invaluable perspective.

Counselors often use a genogram to understand the individual's family dynamic. A genogram is a visual chart that depicts an individual's familial relationships over a specified period of time by collecting relationship dynamics, attachments, interactions, and behavioral patterns. It can also aid clients with self-understanding and help the counselor choose appropriate assessments.

Inquiries about family history may explore:

- Ethnic and cultural background
- Immigration status and experiences
- Family composition (i.e. nuclear, blended, fostered or adopted children, divorced parents, co-parenting status)
- Socioeconomic status
- Educational levels of family members
- Employment status of family members
- Personal and occupational goals and ambitions of family members
- Achievements of family members
- Traumas or loss experienced by any family members
- Medical, financial, or domestic problems
- Values held by each family member, and the priority of each value
- Any perceived favoritism experienced to certain children or adults
- Roles held within the family

Some of these topics may be sensitive to discuss and should be approached empathetically.

Effects of Addiction on the Family System and Other Relationships

The repercussions of addiction can affect many significant aspects of life. The impact of addiction is felt not only by the person using, but everyone in that person's family and circle of social support. Those most powerfully affected are the immediate family members—particularly those who live under the same roof as the person experiencing addiction issues. Friends, extended family, co-workers, and employers also experience fallout.

The spouses or partners often feel depressed, anxious, and angry. Persons in the throes of addiction often lie and steal to maintain their habit. It is not uncommon for people struggling with addiction to steal from friends, family, or employers. Families must deal with the anxiety of not knowing when their loved one will come home or what mood or condition the person may demonstrate upon arriving home. Some families must deal with the shame of seeing their loved one arrested or knowing that this person harmed others while under the influence. Others simply become embarrassed by behaviors loved ones exhibit in public or their failure to show up for an important event, such as a graduation.

Children of addictive parents experience embarrassment, fear, anxiety, and sadness. They are more likely to be abused or neglected, especially in single parent homes. Children may suffer when money intended for basic needs is spent on drugs or alcohol instead. When abuse and/or neglect are reported to CPS, these children may be taken from parents and placed in a series of group or foster homes. In some cases, custody is completely severed. Such experiences may lead to deep psychological scars for those closest to the person who battles addiction.

Family Theories and Dynamics

Family systems theory is an iteration of the basic systems theory. When seeking to explain the behavior of an individual, one must look also at the interrelationships of the individual's family.

Assumptions:

- A family is a unique unit and is unlike any other family.
- A family is interactional, and its parts vary in their resistance to change.
- Healthy family development depends upon the family's ability to meet the needs of the family and the individuals comprising the family.
- The family undergoes changes that cause differing amounts of stress to each family member.

External Boundaries

External boundaries define the family and distinguish it from individuals and systems outside of the family. Boundaries in systems theory are not physical or tangible, but can be observed, in a sense, via a family's attitudes, rules, and use of space. Some families have **closed** boundaries. Families that use closed boundaries are characterized by having many rules about associating with non-family, physical barriers used to limit access to the family, rigid rules and values, few connections with others, and are traditional and wary of change. Families that have open boundaries are characterized by having many connections to individuals outside the family, fluid rules and spontaneous decision-making skills, minimal privacy, uniqueness is valued more than tradition, and there is no fear of change. Open boundaries may lead to the family experiencing more chaos.

Internal Boundaries

Internal boundaries are rules that develop and define the relationships between the subsystems of the family. A **subsystem** might include the parents, the males of the household, or members of the family who share the same hobby. **Role organization** within a family is influenced by the size of the family, its culture and history, lifestyle, and values. In a healthy, well-functioning family, roles should be both clear and flexible.

As a family grows, rules develop that define how family members relate both to each other and to the world around them. Rules may be explicitly stated or implicitly understood. Families vary greatly in the type of rules that they have, as well as regarding whether rules can be easily discussed or modified.

Distribution of power in a reliable manner is important to the functioning of a family, though this distribution may change over time in response to changing needs of family members. Effective communication is also necessary for the family system. Roles, behaviors, and rules are all established through some type of communication. Communication can be open (clear and easy to understand) or closed (confusing and unclear).

Family life cycle theories assume that, as members of a family unit, individuals pass through different stages of life. Although various theories will break down the stages somewhat differently, the following is a common conceptualization of the stages:

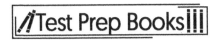

Unattached Young Adult

The primary tasks for this stage are selecting a life style and a life partner. Focus is on establishing independence as an adult and independence from one's family of origin.

Newly-Married Couple

The focus in this stage is on establishing the marital system. Two families are joined together, and relationships must be realigned.

Family with Young Children

The focus in this stage is on accepting new family members and transitioning from a marital system to a family system. The couple takes on a parenting role. Relationships must again be realigned with the extended family (e.g., grandparents).

Family with Adolescents

The focus here is on accommodating the emerging independence of the adolescents in the family. The parent-child relationship experiences change, and the parents may also begin to take on caregiving roles with regard to their own parents.

Launching Family

The focus in this stage is on accepting the new independent role of an adult child and transitioning through the separation. Parents also must face their own transition into middle or older age.

Family in Later Years

In this stage, spousal roles must be re-examined and re-defined. One focus may be the development of interests and activities outside of work and family. Another focus is on navigation of the aging process and losses that may occur.

The basic family life cycle can vary significantly as a result of cultural influences, expectations, and particular family circumstances (e.g., single-parent family, blended family, multi-generational family).

Family dynamics are the interactions between family members in a family system. As discussed previously, under "Family Theories," each family is a unique system. However, there are some common patterns of family dynamics.

Common influences on family dynamics:

- The type and quality of relationship that the parents have
- An absent parent
- A parent who is either extremely strict or extremely lenient
- The mix of personalities in the family
- A sick or disabled family member
- External events, particularly traumatic ones that have affected family members
- Family dynamics in previous generations or the current extended family

Common roles in the family that may result from particular family dynamics:

- The problem child: child with problematic behavior, which may serve as a distraction from other problems that the family, particularly the parents, do not want to face

- Scapegoat: the family member to whom others unjustly attribute problems, often viewed as "bad," while other family members are viewed as "good"

- Peacekeeper: a family member who serves to mediate relationships and reduce family stress

The Effects of Family Dynamics on Individuals

There are many ways in which the family influences the individual socially, emotionally, and psychologically. All family systems have their own unique characteristics, with both good and bad functional tendencies. The family interactions are among the earliest and most formative relationships that a person has, so they define the relational patterns that the individual develops and utilizes with all subsequent relationships. Parenting styles, conflict resolution methods, beliefs and values, and coping mechanisms are just a few things that a person learns from their family of origin. It is also within the family that a person first develops an image of self and identity, often having to do with the role that they are given within the family system and the messages communicated by parents. If a child has a secure and healthy relationship with the family members, this will likely lead to overall wellbeing and emotional stability as an adult.

When it comes to physical or mental illness, the role that the family plays is critical in lowering risk factors and minimizing symptoms. A strongly supportive family will help a person function at the highest level possible. Oftentimes, family members can serve as caregivers or play less formal—but still critical—roles in supporting a person's health.

Family Practice Approaches

One of the main goals of family therapy is to allow each family member to function at their best while maintaining the functionality of the family unit. When working with families, the counselor must:

- Examine and consider all systems affecting a family and each individual member to determine problems, solutions, and strengths, and must also consider the functionality of the family subsystems.

- Respect cultural, socio-economic, and non-traditional family systems and not automatically define those systems as dysfunctional if they are not the norm. The overall and individual family functioning should be accounted for.

- Work to engage the family in the treatment, while considering the specific traits of the family (i.e., culture, history, family structure, race, dynamics, etc.).

- Assist in identifying and changing dysfunctional patterns, boundaries, and family problems.

Important Concepts

Boundaries: Healthy boundaries around and within the family must exist for families to function effectively. The boundaries must be clear and appropriate.

Emotional Proximity and Distance: These are the type of boundaries that exist within a family system.

Enmeshed: Boundaries are unclear and pliable. Families that have very open boundaries within the family unit may have very fixed boundaries between outside forces and the family.

Disengaged: Boundaries are rigid with little interaction and emotional engagement. Families that are disengaged within the family system tend to have very open boundaries around the family unit.

Family Hierarchy: The power structure within the family. For families to function effectively, there must be a clear delineation of authority. There must be an individual or individuals who hold the power and authority in a family system. In a traditional family, this should ideally be located within the parental system.

Homeostasis: Family systems should maintain homeostasis or remain regular and stable. When life events become too stressful and the family can no longer function as it normally would, the state of homeostasis is threatened. This is usually when many families seek help.

Alliances: Partnerships or collaborations between certain members of a family. When alliances exist between some members of a family, it can lead to dysfunction (i.e., parent and child have an alliance that undermines the parental subsystem).

Couples Intervention/Treatment Approaches

Many couples enter treatment after experiencing long-standing problems and may seek help because all other options have failed. One of the goals of couples' therapy is to help clients develop effective communication and problem-solving skills so they can solve problems throughout and after treatment. Other goals include helping the couple form a more objective view of their relationship, modifying dysfunctional behavior/patterns, increasing emotional expression, and recognizing strengths. Workers should create an environment to help the couple understand treatment goals, feel safe in expressing their feelings, and reconnect by developing trust in each other. Interventions for couples are often centered on goals geared toward preventing conflicting verbal communication and improving empathy, respect, and intimacy in a relationship. Therapeutic interventions, along with exercises, are designed to help couples learn to treat each other as partners and not rivals. Cognitive Behavioral Therapy is also used in working with couples. It uses cognitive restructuring techniques to help change distorted thinking and modify behavior.

Counseling and Psychotherapy

Ethical Standards and Practice

Professional relationships with clients develop in six stages. In the first stage, counselors focus their efforts on building rapport and trust with clients. This involves the development of a comfortable and trusting working relationship using listening skills, empathic understanding, cultural sensitivity, and good social skills. In the second stage, the practitioner identifies the problem(s) that led the client to seek the assistance of a counselor. Together, the practitioner and client identify the initial problems that will be addressed, check the understanding of each issue through a conversation, and make appropriate changes as necessary. The third stage involves the counselor using skills that allow him or her to understand the client in deeper ways. The practitioner begins to make inferences based on his or her theoretical orientation about the underlying themes in the client's history. Once these inferences are made, then goals can be established based on these overarching themes.

The fourth stage of professional relationship development involves working on the issues that were identified and agreed upon between the practitioner and client. The client takes responsibility for and actively works on the identified issues and themes during and between sessions. As the client successfully works through issues, it becomes increasingly clear that there is little reason for the meetings to continue. Therefore, in stage five, the end of sessions is discussed, and both the client and the counselor work through feelings of loss. The sixth stage occurs after the relationship has ended if clients return with new issues, if they want to revisit old ones, or if they want to delve deeper into their self-understanding. This stage is the post-interview stage and occurs with many—but not all—clients.

Principles and Processes of Informed Consent

When providing services, it is important to ensure that clients understand all aspects of the treatment they will receive. In addition to the plan of treatment, it is also necessary to ensure that clients understand the possible risks involved, the costs associated, the length of treatment, and any limitations that might exist due to both mandated reporting laws and third-party payers. Alternatives to the therapeutic plan may also be discussed with clients before beginning treatment. Clients need to be given the opportunity to ask questions and receive answers to ensure they completely comprehend what their therapies will entail. Informed consent should require that the client sign legal documentation stating that they fully understand what will be involved—including all the risks, limitations, and alternatives— prior to beginning treatment. This documentation should become a part of the client's chart.

In certain instances, a client may have difficulty in fully understanding the information being presented. This could be true especially if there is a language barrier or if the person receiving services either is not fully alert or is disoriented. Appropriate measures should be taken to ensure that the person receiving services fully understands the information provided to satisfy that informed consent has been achieved. This may require utilizing a translator or a third party, such as a durable power of attorney or family member, if the person is not able to make their own decisions. In the event that a client has a conservator or power of attorney acting on his or her behalf, it is also the role of the counselor to ensure that this person is making decisions that coincide with the wishes of the client.

There will be circumstances in which a person may be receiving treatment on an involuntary basis. In these situations, the counselor should fully explain the terms of the treatment as it pertains to the individual's situation, as well as any rights the person does have in regard to refusal. An example of this type of situation would be someone who is court mandated to receive treatment, such as drug and alcohol counseling, anger management, or other therapies.

Sometimes client information needs to be shared with other individuals such as the client's family or other professionals for referrals. In these situations, the client must agree to these disclosures, and consent for disclosure of information must be obtained.

In this day and age, it is common for professionals to use electronic means of communication, such as email or text. It is important that the risks associated with using these avenues are fully disclosed. Depending on the nature of the professional relationship and the needs of the individual, a treatment may necessitate audio taping, videotaping, or observation by a third party. The informed consent of the client should be obtained before any recording takes place. Some practitioners will have audio and videotaping as a part of the informed consent documentation when clients begin therapy, and others will have a separate form to be used if and when the need should arise. As long as the client has signed that they understand and give consent, either way will suffice.

Identification and Resolution of Ethical Dilemmas

Ethical dilemmas occur when three different conditions are met in a situation. The first is that the practitioner must make a decision. If the situation does not require that a decision be made, then there isn't an ethical dilemma. The second is that there are different decisions that could be made or different actions one could take. The third condition is that an ethical ideal will be conceded no matter what decision is made.

One type of ethical dilemma occurs when you have a situation in which two ethical principles are conflicting. This is a pure ethical dilemma because either choice of action involves conceding one of these principles, and there is no way to keep both principles intact. Another type of ethical dilemma occurs when ethical principles conflict with values and/or laws. In these types of situations, a counselor's values may conflict with an ethical principle, and a decision must be made.

Legal and Ethical Issues Regarding Confidentiality, Including Electronic Information

Counselors have a duty to protect confidential information of clients. Ethically, client information should not be discussed with anyone other than the client. Legally, a client has a right to keep their medical and therapeutic information confidential. The Health Insurance Portability and Accountability Act of 1996 (HIPAA) requires that medical information (including therapeutic and mental health information) be protected and kept confidential. However, there are certain limitations to confidentiality. These generally involve risk of harm to the individual being served, as well as others.

Counselors are not as protected as some other professionals when it comes to confidentiality and often find themselves being called to testify in court cases related to their clients. There are also certain situations in which counselors may have to release confidential information to protect the client or satisfy the duty to warn.

Providing services to minors can be challenging when it comes to confidentiality issues, especially since the legal rules and regulations vary from state to state. At times, there can be a conflict between the counselor's feeling of ethical responsibility to maintain the privacy of the minor and the legal right of parents to be informed of issues discussed. Adolescents in particular may discuss concerns with a counselor that they do not want their parents to be aware of, and it can be a violation of trust if these issues are subsequently revealed to parents. It is imperative that at the start of treatment, the expectations of the counselor's relationship with each person are discussed with the parents and minors, as well as the benefits and limits of confidentiality. Minors should never be promised confidentiality when the counselor cannot keep that promise, but the privacy and individuality of the minor should be maintained as much as possible. In cases where private information about the minor is going to be revealed, counselors should always inform the minor. This holds true regardless as to whether it is with the client's consent, mandated reporting, or due to the parent utilizing their right to information.

When disclosing information due to legal requirements, it is always important to discuss the situation with the client. It should be noted that the counselor should evaluate their own safety when discussing disclosure of confidential information with the client. If the counselor believes the situation to be unsafe if/when the client learns of the disclosure, then it is not necessary to alert the client prior to disclosing the confidential information. This is something that should be discussed in detail with clients during the informed consent process and throughout the relationship.

One of the difficulties associated with breaking confidentiality to protect a third party is that the threat isn't always clearly established. If a client discloses during treatment that he is going to go home and stab his neighbor, this is clearly a plan of intended harm. However, what about an HIV-positive client who fails to warn sexual partners of her HIV status? What if the client fully understands the risk to her partners and has no intention of disclosing her status? This is a situation which would require thorough documentation, thoughtful debate, and possibly conferencing with colleagues to decide upon the best course of action.

Confidentiality also becomes more complicated when a counselor is working with two or more people, either in a family or group session. All participants must agree that any information shared within the context of treatment will be kept confidential and not shared with others. However, the counselor should stress with clients that they cannot force other members to abide by the confidentiality agreement and that breach of confidentiality is a risk.

With technology being utilized extensively by helping professionals, confidentiality of electronic information is another important issue. Counseling sessions are now being provided by telephone, video chat, and online simulation, and these media open up new possibilities for information abuse. If a practitioner provides a video therapy session, they should be aware that it is possible for the client to have someone else in the room, off-camera, without informing the clinician or other participants. The same could be true with electronic communication such as texting or email. There is no way to know if a client is forwarding electronic information to third parties without the clinician's knowledge.

Other issues relating to confidentiality include the storage and maintenance of records and charts. All confidential material should be kept in a secure location and locked at all times. For example, if a counselor takes a clipboard into client rooms to make notes for later documentation, that clipboard should be locked in a drawer when not in use so that no one can turn it over and see confidential information when the counselor is away from their desk. With the use of electronics and computers, there should be policies in place to lock computers when away to avoid anyone seeing notes or other confidential information. Collaboration between colleagues in which clients may be discussed should be done behind closed doors to avoid anyone else hearing the conversation.

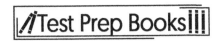

Counselors are to provide clients with reasonable access to records. Counselors are permitted, however, by the Code of Ethics to withhold all or part of the client record from the client if the counselor determines there is a great risk of harm in releasing the information. In these cases, it is important to fully document the request, whether or not the records were released, and the rationale for either releasing or not releasing them.

There may be instances in which a counselor is sued for malpractice. In these cases, the Code of Ethics states that it is permissible for the counselor to share confidential client information to aid in self-defense, but only so far as is necessary to adequately defend oneself.

Ethical and Legal Issues Regarding Mandatory Reporting of Abuse

Some clients may disclose intent to harm themselves. It is necessary in these situations to fully assess suicidal intent and determine if the client is serious about carrying out a plan for self-harm. It might be sufficient, in cases where a client has considered self-harm but has no clear plan, to complete a safety plan with the client. The safety plan will outline what the client agrees to do should they begin to experience the desire to engage in self-harm. However, if the client has a clear plan of action and access to items necessary to carry out the plan, then confidentiality should be broken to protect the client. This would involve notifying police and having the client committed for observation for their own protection.

In addition to protecting clients from themselves, counselors also have a duty to warn third-party individuals if there is threat of harm. Duty to warn was established by the 1976 case Tarasoff vs. Regents of the University of California. In this case, a graduate student at the University of California-Berkley had become obsessed with Tatiana Tarasoff. After significant distress, he sought psychological treatment and disclosed to his therapist that he had a plan to kill Tarasoff. Although the psychologist did have the student temporarily committed, he was ultimately released. He eventually stopped seeking treatment and attacked and killed Tarasoff. Tarasoff's family sued the psychologist and various other individuals involved with the university. This case evolved into the duty to warn third parties of potential risk of harm. Satisfying the duty to warn can be done by notifying police or the individual who is the intended victim.

Because ethical dilemmas can involve legal situations, they may also have legal consequences for a counselor or necessitate involving the legal system. For example, a client may disclose that he frequently drinks large amounts of alcohol and then drives his children to school. Ethically, there is an obligation to keep what the client has said in confidence. However, the client's children are being placed in a situation in which they are in great danger of being injured or harmed. Due to laws protecting the welfare of children, the counselor would need to make a report to Child Protective Services. In some states, if someone has a good faith reason to believe that a child is being neglected or abused, and does not report the situation, that person may face a civil lawsuit and even criminal charges.

Ethical and Legal Issues Regarding Mandatory Reporting of Abuse

Mandatory reporting laws require counselors, and other professionals, to report any suspected abuse or neglect. This means that any professional who has a suspicion of abuse or neglect of a child or a vulnerable adult must legally make a report to either Child Protective Services or Adult Protective Services. Note that some states, such as Tennessee, have laws that require all citizens to report suspected abuse or neglect, making everyone a mandated reporter.

Often when abuse or neglect is suspected, the concern about breaking confidentiality is at the forefront of the mind of the counselor. During informed consent, this requirement to report any signs of abuse or neglect should have been disclosed to the client. When such breaks in confidentiality occur, they can damage the relationship. In some cases, it may be necessary or appropriate to disclose to the client that a report is being made. For example, if a new mother has tested positive for cocaine and the infant has tested positive for cocaine while in the hospital, the infant will remain in the Neonatal Intensive Care Unit due to withdrawal. Disclosing to the mother that a report is being made, and why it's being made, could prepare her and create an opportunity to speak further with her about treatment options and other important considerations. It's important to note that counselors who fail to report suspected abuse or neglect can be subject to civil penalties and/or prosecution.

Current and Continuing Trends

Legal counseling licensing standards have influenced current and continuing trends in the profession. However, not all states recognize licensing obtained in other states. This is something that may yet face reform. Additionally, the types of services that are considered counseling have expanded. Counselors can be found in vocational, medical, organizational, school, sports, and life coaching settings. In particular, licensed mental health counselors are largely influencing the field of psychiatry. It's expected that they'll handle more of the behavioral and therapeutic cases in the country, while psychiatrists will focus primarily on cases where the client must utilize psycho-pharmaceuticals to manage their diagnosis. Psychologists have opposed counselor licensure in the past, claiming that counselors do not have qualification to practice. However, more and more states have agreed to pass state licensure laws, granting counselors their right to practice in the field. Finally, technology has impacted all aspects of living. Online counseling and the leveraging of social media as a counseling tool have greatly influenced the field. However, research does not currently exist on whether technology is helpful or harmful to the profession and its clients.

ICD, PL94-142, and the 1958 National Defense Education Act

The International Classification of Diseases (ICD) is a resource published by the World Health Organization (WHO). It provides a snapshot of health statuses, disease concerns, and other epidemiological data by country and population. It is used for research purposes and to manage available, global health resources. The latest edition (ICD-10) was published in 1994, but revisions are currently underway for the next edition (ICD-11) to be published in 2022.

Public Law 94-142 (PL94-142) is known as the Education for All Handicapped Children Act and, more recently, as the Individuals with Disabilities Education Act (IDEA). Enacted by the United States Department of Education in 1975, it declared that tailored public education is guaranteed for all disabled children.

The 1958 National Defense Education Act was a key initiative for the field of counseling and provided funding in the form of federal grants and loans to individuals who wanted to pursue a formal counseling education. This act was responsible for expanding school guidance services as well as improving guidance for gifted children.

Principle of Ethical Decision-Making and the Purpose of the ACA Code of Ethics

In general, counselors follow basic ethical guidelines to do no physical or psychological harm to their clients or to society, and to provide fair, honest, and compassionate service to their client and society when making professional decisions. The ACA Code of Ethics exists as a resource to provide clear guidelines for counselors to practice by, and as a resource for counselors to consult when facing an

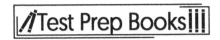

ethical decision that they're unsure of making. This Code supports the mission of the counseling profession as established by the ACA.

Ethical Issues

Ethical issues can present themselves in any field. In counseling, ethical issues often center on the confidentiality and anonymity of clients, client cases, and data collected about the client (especially in group or family settings). However, counselors are obligated to report any instances of abuse, self-harm that could lead to a fatality, or harm to others that could lead to fatalities. Counselors also need to ensure that clear personal and professional boundaries are maintained between themselves and their client. In all instances of counseling, practitioners must exhibit respect and tolerance for individuals of all backgrounds, attitudes, opinions, and beliefs.

ACA Code of Ethics

The foundation of the ACA Code of Ethics is defined by the following six core values:

- Autonomy: Freedom to govern one's own choices for the future
- Nonmaleficence: Causing the least amount of harm as possible
- Beneficence: Promoting health and wellbeing for the good of the individual and society
- Justice: Treating each individual with fairness and equality
- Fidelity: Displaying trust in professional relationships and maintaining promises
- Veracity: Making sure to provide the truth in all situations and contacts

The Code of Ethics is comprised of nine sections that cover ethical guidelines to uphold these core values. These nine sections focus on the following:

Practitioner-Counselor Relationship

The counselor-client relationship is one that is built primarily on trust. Counselors have the obligation to make sure the confidentiality and privacy rights of their clients are protected, and therefore should protect and maintain any documentation recorded during services. Additionally, clients have rights regarding informed consent. Open communication between the client and counselor is essential; in the beginning of the relationship, the counselor must provide the client with information on all services provided, with sensitivity to cultural and developmental diversity. Counselors should also pay special attention to clients who are incapacitated in their abilities to give consent and should seek a balance between the client's own capacities and their capacity to give consent to a more capable individual. Finally, with mandated clients, counselors should seek transparency in areas regarding information they share with other professionals.

Confidentiality and Privacy

With trust as the cornerstone of the counselor-client relationship, counselors must ensure the confidentiality and privacy of their clients in regards to respecting client rights through multicultural considerations, disclosure of documentation to appropriate professionals, and speaking to their clients about limitations of privacy. Some exceptions to confidentiality include the potential for serious harm to other individuals, end-of-life decisions, information regarding life-threatening diseases, and court-ordered disclosure. Counselors are encouraged to notify clients when disclosing information when possible, with only the minimal amount of information shared.

Professional Responsibility

Counselors have the obligation to facilitate clear communication when dealing with the public or other professionals. They should practice only within their knowledge of expertise and be careful not to apply or participate in work they are not qualified for. Continuing education is part of the counselor's development as a professional, and the counselor should always be aware of evolving information. It's important for counselors to also monitor their own health and wellness, making sure to refer clients to other competent professionals if they find themselves unable to practice due to health or retirement.

Relationships with Other Professionals

Developing relationships with other professionals is important for counselors in order to provide their clients with the best possible resources. Being part of interdisciplinary teams is one way for counselors to provide the best, well-rounded services to clients. Counselors should always be respectful to other professionals with different approaches, as long as those approaches are grounded in scientific research. It is important for counselors to develop and maintain relationships with other professionals.

Evaluation, Assessment, and Interpretation

In order to effectively plan for a client's treatment, general assessments should be made at the beginning of the counselor-client relationship regarding education, mental health, psychology, and career. Clients have a right to know their results and should be informed of the testing and usage of results prior to assessment. Counselors must take into account the cultural background of clients when diagnosing mental disorders, as culture affects the way clients define their problems. Counselors should take care not to evaluate clients they are counseling and vice versa.

Supervision, Training, and Teaching

It is important for counselors to foster appropriate relationships with their supervisees and students. A client's wellbeing is encouraged not only by counselors but everyone the counselor works with. For counselors who are involved in supervising others, continuing education is important in providing the students or trainees with correct information. Any sexual relationship with current supervisees or students is prohibited, as well as any personal relationship that affects the counselor's ability to be objective. Finally, counselors should be proactive in maintaining a diverse faculty and/or a diverse student body.

Research and Publication

When conducting research, counselors must take care to make sure they adhere to federal, state, agency, and institutional policies in dealing with confidentiality. Counselors should keep in mind the rights of their participants and facilitate safe practices during research that do not harm the client's wellbeing. As any objective research, counselors should take care not to exaggerate or manipulate their findings in any way, even if the outcome is unfavorable. Counselors should take care where the identity of participants is concerned. All parties involved in the research of case examples must be notified prior to publication and give consent after reviewing the publication themselves. It's important for researchers to give credit to all contributors in publication.

Distance Counseling, Technology, and Social Media

The field of counseling is evolving to include electronic means of helping clients. Counselors should take into consideration the implications of privacy and confidentiality when treating clients online and take precaution in securing these, notifying the clients of any limitations to privacy. It's important to verify the client's identity when using electronic sources throughout the duration of treatment. In distance counseling, counselors must also be aware of the laws in their own state as well as the client's state.

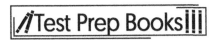

<u>Resolving Ethical Issues</u>

This section ensures that all counselors act in an ethical and legal manner when dealing with clients and other professionals. It's important for counselors to make known their allegiance to the ACA Code of Ethics and try to resolve ethical issues following this manner. If the conflict cannot be resolved this way, counselors may be obligated to solve the conflict through the appropriate legal and/or government authority.

The ACA keeps an updated copy of their Code of Ethics, as well as other media and interactive resources relating to ethical practices, on their website at www.counseling.org.

Ethical Issues Regarding Termination

Termination of the relationship occurs when the client and the counselor have reached treatment goals. Even though the relationship is terminated, the client may feel warmly toward the counselor, and congruence and empathy may still be part of the relationship. Some clients may require maintenance sessions to continue stability, but when termination is the next clear stage in the relationship, psychotherapy sessions should end.

In the case of a client choosing to prematurely terminate services, the counselor should clearly explain the risks to the client and also carefully document all meetings and interactions to protect against legal ramifications. Abandonment, which refers to the counselor terminating services prematurely without adequate reason or in an improper manner, is considered malpractice and can lead to lawsuits. When the counselor decides to end the working relationship, they must ensure that the client is adequately prepared and warned about the end of services, and that the client is emotionally equipped to deal with the termination. Counselors can refer clients to other types of providers, who can continue working with the client after their own services have ceased. If a counselor needs to terminate services early, such as in the case of leaving a job, they should connect the client to a new counselor who can continue to provide the same level of services.

Responsibility to Seek Supervision

Sometimes it may be necessary to seek supervision if the counselor experiences burnout, secondary trauma, compassion fatigue, countertransference or the inability to develop a trusting relationship with the client. Although the focus is often on the supervisor's role of ensuring that clients are provided with ethical services by training and evaluating the supervisee, the supervisee's role in supervision is not passive. The counselor should fully engage in the process of supervision and use this relationship to grow and improve. In order to do that, the supervisee must be willing to discuss areas of ethical or legal concern that have arisen in their interactions with clients. They must also be ready to honestly address their own struggles and identify their learning needs, and seek the help and advice of the supervisor. This can only happen effectively through genuine self-assessment, which flows from a desire to become a better counselor. The process of self-assessment in supervision can help them see any biases or weaknesses that may be holding them back from fully meeting their clients' needs. If the counselor is defensive or resistant to the supervisory relationship, then they will make little progress.

Factors to consider when receiving feedback during supervision/consultation:

- Counselors can benefit from feedback during supervision or consultation, especially with difficult clients/cases or at significant times in treatment, such as termination.

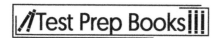

- When discussing cases, client confidentiality should be protected as much as possible, and client consent to release information should be acquired.

Impairment is a professional issue that should be addressed swiftly. Impairment occurs when a counselor's personal problems (e.g., mental health conditions, difficult life circumstances, or alcohol/drug use) have an impact upon their practice. The Code of Ethics states that counselors should seek to rectify their impairment by consulting with colleagues or supervisors, seeking their own treatment, limiting work, and/or terminating client relationships until the impairment has been fully addressed. In the event that a colleague is suffering from some sort of impairment, a counselor should address the concern with the colleague and encourage the colleague to rectify the issue. If the issue continues without proper attention, the counselor should go through appropriate channels to seek additional help for the colleague and to prevent consequences to clients. The same is true if the counselor feels there has been unethical behavior by a colleague. The counselor should discuss the behavior with the colleague and possibly with a supervisor. If a colleague is unfairly accused of unethical behavior, assisting the colleague in rectifying the situation is the best course of action.

Counselor/Client Roles

Building Counselor and Client Relationships

Creating rapport with clients requires counselors to engage in specific approaches using appropriate therapeutic techniques. In addition to the use of theory, they must convey a genuine attitude of empathy and respect for their clients. Using positive regard, as well as a nonjudgmental style, is essential to creating a sense of comfort and willingness for clients to open up to their counselor. Counselors should carefully evaluate each client and develop a plan for services that will best meet his or her needs. The plan should be communicated and agreed upon with the clients, ensuring that they feel the counselor is trustworthy and competent.

Person-Centered Approach

Carl Rogers developed the person-centered, or humanistic, approach to counseling, which stressed the importance of the counseling relationship, as well as the need to evaluate therapy for effectiveness. Rogers believed that three core conditions must exist for therapy to facilitate change: empathy, positive regard, and congruence. Rogers's work was continued by Robert Carkhuff, who created a five-point scale to measure the core conditions and effectiveness of a counselor. This scale attempts to measure the degree to which the counselor is providing effective levels of empathy, genuineness, concreteness, and respect.

- Level 1. Therapist is contradictory in statements and nonverbal cues and exhibits defensiveness.
- Level 2. Therapist is superficially professional but lacks genuineness.
- Level 3. Therapist does not express defensiveness; there is implied but not overt professionalism.
- Level 4. Therapist is genuine and nondefensive.
- Level 5. Therapist is open and honest and accurately and genuinely reflects ideas and reactions to client.

In his 1967 book, *Toward Effective Counseling and Psychotherapy*, Carkhuff found that therapeutic interventions did not always have a long-term positive impact, and in some cases, clients worsened after counseling. Carkhuff's findings were summarized in a famous quote that "therapy may be for better or for worse." This led him to conduct further research on specific attributes of the counselor that contributed to successful outcomes.

Additional Counseling Skills

The following are additional counseling skills:

- Restatement: Clarification through repeating back the client's words, as understood by the counselor

- Reflection: Restatement of what the counselor heard from the client, emphasizing any underlying emotional content (can be termed **reflection of feeling**)

- Paraphrasing: Repeating back a client's story while providing an empathic response

- Summarizing: Reiteration of the major points of the counseling discussion

- Silence: Moments during which neither the client nor the counselor speak; can be used for reflection but may indicate resistance from the client

- Confrontation: Technique in which the counselor identifies discrepancies from the client in a supportive manner (counselor may also ask for clarification to determine if content was misheard prior to exposing possible inconsistencies)

- Structuring: Used to set goals and agree upon plan for counseling; also used within sessions to make effective use of time and respect boundaries

Motives for Helping Others Through Counseling

Just as clients are motivated to seek counseling to resolve issues and/or improve their lives, counselors exhibit motivation to help others. Counseling, as a profession, allows an opportunity to positively impact the lives of individuals and help improve society. It is important as part of professional development for counselors to explore their motivation to join the profession. Some graduate programs may require individuals to receive counseling as part of their education to ensure they have adequately addressed their own issues and prevent using the clients to get their own needs met. In some specific areas of counseling, such as addictions, it is more common for counselors to have experienced addiction and recovered, thus motivating them to assist others.

Coping Skills

Teaching coping skills is an important role of the counselor in the therapeutic relationship. Coping skills enable individuals to manage stressful situations, solve problems, handle uncertainty, and develop resilience. Coping skills can include solution-focused problem solving, removing negative self-talk, learning mindfulness or other stress management techniques, and gaining support through friends, family, and community. Individuals may learn how to identify specific patterns to their feelings and behaviors, and thus, learn new and healthier responses. As there are many ways for individuals to develop and practice coping skills, counselors can provide options and unique plans for clients to best meet their needs.

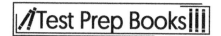

Empathy

Empathy is considered an essential counseling skill. It is used not only to initially build trust but also throughout the counseling process. The process of empathy is used to help the counselor understand the client's viewpoint. It is more complex than sympathy, which is somewhat passive and a sense of feeling bad for another person. Empathy focuses on gaining insight into the client's experience to offer effective means to deal with any issues or concerns. Although psychologist Edward Titchener was the first to use the term, it is strongly associated with the client-centered approach of Carl Rogers. Rogers believed empathy extended beyond understanding a person's situation; it involved the counselor imagining him or herself in that situation. This level of empathy requires genuineness, acceptance, and a small measure of vulnerability on the part of the counselor.

Cultural Awareness

Counselors must be adept at working with diverse populations. Diversity includes race, culture, gender, ethnicity, sexual orientation, socioeconomic status, religion, and age. As part of the profession, counselors will provide services to individuals and families with whom they have no cultural similarity. Thus, it is essential for counselors to develop and maintain a level of cultural competence. The first step is for them to engage in self-awareness and gain an understanding of their own identity, including their belief systems and biases. As part of the counseling process, counselors should be able to acknowledge differences and communicate to clients with trust and credibility while demonstrating mutual respect. They should engage in ongoing professional development, both to gain skills and awareness of differing cultural needs, as well as from an ethical standpoint to ensure they are providing competent services. To maintain credibility and trust, counselors must clearly define issues and goals for counseling, taking into consideration cultural variations.

Initial Phase of Relationship Building

At the onset of the process, the counselor and client will progress through the relationship phase, which has four specific phases. These phases may be completed at a varying pace, depending on both parties. Some phases can be completed quickly, while others may take several sessions.

- Phase 1. Initiation, or entry phase: This is the introduction to the counseling process, which sets the stage for the development of the client/counselor relationship.

- Phase 2. Clarification phase: This phase defines the problem and need for the therapeutic relationship.

- Phase 3. Structure phase: The counselor defines the specifics of the relationship, its intended outcomes, and responsibilities of both parties.

- Phase 4. Relationship phase: The client and counselor have developed a relationship and will work toward mutually agreed-upon goals.

Stages of Positive Interaction

Once a working relationship is established, the client and counselor will need to develop and maintain positive interactions to ensure the effectiveness of counseling. Positive interactions ensure the

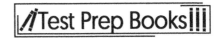

therapeutic relationship advances and supports clients in meeting their goals. The counseling relationship has four stages.

- Stage 1. Exploration of feelings and definition of problem: Counselors will use rapport-building skills, define the structure of the counseling process and relationship, and work with their clients on goal setting.

- Stage 2. Consolidation: This is the process of the clients integrating the information and guidance from the counselor, allowing them to gain additional coping skills and identify alternate ways to solve problems.

- Stage 3. Planning: During this phase, clients can begin employing techniques learned in counseling and prepare to manage on their own.

- Stage 4. Termination: This is the ending of the therapeutic relationship, when clients feel equipped to manage problems independently and have fully integrated techniques learned in counseling.

Silence

Silence can be an effective skill in therapy but must be used carefully, especially in the early stages of the process. Initially, clients may be silent due to many factors, such as fear, resistance, discomfort with opening up, or uncertainty about the process. Counselors who use silence in initial sessions must ensure clients do not perceive the counselor as bored, hostile, or indifferent. As counseling progresses, clients may gain additional comfort with silence and use it as a way to reflect on content, process information, consider options, and gain self-awareness. Newer counselors may have more difficulty with silence, as they may believe they are not being helpful if they are not talking. Silence is also viewed differently by culture, so cultural awareness is important in understanding and using it as a therapeutic tool.

Transference

Transference is a concept from psychoanalysis that refers to the process of the clients transferring any feelings toward others onto the counselor. These feelings are likely unconscious, as they arrive from childhood experiences and relationships. For example, the counselor may remind clients of their distant parent, and the clients will project feelings about that parent onto the counselor. Transference can be very powerful, although both positive and negative forms exist. Positive or good transference allows clients to work through issues with the counselor, who is safe and nonreactive. Clients can project negative feelings or emotions onto the counselor, thus being able to resolve them in the absence of the parent or individual. Negative or bad transference exists when clients project negative emotions and become angry or hostile toward the counselor. This type of transference can create a blockage and diminish the effectiveness of therapy. It is the role of the counselor to understand and manage transference as it arises in the relationship. Transference can also occur for the counselor with clients. Supervision and consultation are both helpful and necessary should this occur.

Attending

Attending is the act of the counselor giving clients his or her full attention. Attending to the client shows respect for their needs, can encourage openness, and can create a sense of comfort and support in the counseling process. There are several ways for counselors to attend actively to clients, including maintaining appropriate eye contact, using reassuring body language and gestures, and monitoring their tone and expressions. Counselors can communicate support and a nonjudgmental attitude through an open posture and eye gaze that shows interest but not intimidation. They should use a caring verbal tone and facial expressions, which indicate attention to what their clients are saying, and can be used in addition to silence to create a positive environment for counseling.

Client Resistance

Resistance to counseling, at some point, may be unavoidable. The process of change is difficult, and clients may become overtly or unconsciously oppositional when faced with the need to adjust thoughts or behaviors. In psychoanalytic terms, clients are resistant in an attempt to avoid anxiety brought up through the counseling process. Resistance can be very obvious, such as canceling or delaying appointments, not following through, or not fully engaging in the process. Resistance can also be subtler; clients can display resistance through disinterest or noncompliance. The counselor can contribute to client resistance through inadequate therapeutic interventions, such as having an agenda that does not meet clients' needs. Although resistance can interfere with the process, it can also be very powerful when dealt with effectively. Counselors need to pay close attention to resistance, understand its origins, and work to help clients recognize and work through blockages.

Questions

As part of any counseling session, counselors will ask both open and closed questions. Open questions are more likely to provide helpful information, as they require the client to express feelings, beliefs, and ideas. Open questions often begin with "why," "how," "when," or "tell me …". Closed questions may be less helpful, as they may elicit brief responses of one or few words.

Counselors do need to be aware of the limitations of asking questions. Any questions asked should have purpose and provide information that will be meaningful to the counselor and the relationship. Curiosity questions should be avoided, as well as asking too many questions, which may feel interrogating to the client. A counselor can ask follow-up questions for clarification as needed. The counselor should provide the client adequate time to answer questions and elaborate but also allow time for the client to talk freely.

Reflecting

Reflecting is a basic counseling skill designed to build rapport and help clients become aware of underlying emotions. Counselors "reflect back" what a client says, both to indicate they are attending and also to analyze and interpret meanings. Reflecting is more than simply paraphrasing a client's words, as it involves more in-depth understanding and an attempt to elicit further information. An example would be a client stating, "I'm not sure what to do about my current relationship. I can't decide if I should stay or leave." The counselor would reflect by stating, "It sounds like you are conflicted about what to do; this is a difficult decision to make," and follow up with a probing question or time for the client to process and react.

Errors

Reflecting is one of several active listening and rapport-building skills but should not be overused. It is essential that the counselor be able to offer back meaningful restatements and not simply repeat back what is heard. It is also important that the counselor accurately reflects any feeling and does not project or misinterpret. In some cases, misinterpretation can help the client further clarify and is not detrimental to the relationship. By using reflection and clarification, any errors can be corrected. Even when errors occur, when the counselor clarifies what the client means, it communicates that the counselor is invested in understanding the client. From a cultural awareness standpoint, the counselor should be sensitive to any differences and ensure there is a level of trust prior to engaging in more in-depth reflection.

Guidelines for Giving Advice

There are two main types of advice: substantive and process. Substantive advice can be considered directive and may involve the counselor imposing his or her opinions onto clients. Process advice is more empowering and helps clients navigate options for solving their own issues. An example would be a client who is struggling with anxiety. Substantive advice would be the counselor telling the client he or she should practice deep breathing. Process advice, in the same example, would be teaching the client how relaxation techniques can lessen anxiety and providing examples. Counselors can offer process advice to help clients better understand their problems and possible solutions. Clients may ask for advice, and in some situations, it may be appropriate for the counselor to offer process advice; it is less likely that substantive advice should be given. Providing counseling is more complex than simply giving advice; thus, counselors should explore when, why, and how to give advice, if needed. As the goal of counseling is to help individuals gain a better self-awareness and competence, giving advice may undermine the process by not allowing clients an opportunity to learn ways to solve their own issues both within and after counseling.

Summarizing

Summarizing is another active listening and rapport-building technique. The counselor listens to the content provided by the clients and summarizes the essential points of the conversation. This process can help isolate and clarify the essential aspects of issues and ensure that both the client and the counselor can focus on the most critical tasks. Additionally, summarization can be helpful in goal setting or at the end of a session.

Phases of a Crisis Period

In 1964, psychiatry professor Gerald Caplan defined the recognizable phases of a crisis:

- Phase 1. This first phase consists of the initial threat or event, which triggers a response. The individual may be able to employ coping skills or defense mechanisms to avoid a crisis.

- Phase 2. This second phase is the escalation, during which initial attempts to manage the crisis are ineffective and the individual begins to experience increased distress.

- Phase 3. The third phase is the acute crisis phase, during which anxiety continues and may intensify to panic or a fight-or-flight response. There are still attempts to problem-solve during this phase, and new tactics may be used.

- Phase 4. The fourth phase is the climax of the crisis when solutions have failed; the individual may experience personality disorganization and become severely depressed, violent, and possibly suicidal.

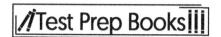

Crisis Intervention

A crisis situation requires swift action and specially trained mental health personnel and can occur at any time in any setting. Albert Roberts proposed a seven-stage model to deal with a crisis and provide effective intervention and support. Roberts's stages are as follows:

- Stage 1. Conduct thorough biopsychosocial assessments of client functioning and identify any imminent danger to self or others.

- Stage 2. Make contact, and quickly establish rapport; it is important that the counselor is accepting, nonjudgmental, flexible, and supportive.

- Stage 3. Identify specific problems and the possible cause of crisis; begin to prioritize the specific aspect of the problem most in need of a solution.

- Stage 4. Provide counseling in an attempt to understand the emotional content of the situation.

- Stage 5. Work on coping strategies and alternative solutions, which can be very challenging for an individual in crisis.

- Stage 6. Implement an action plan for treatment, which could include therapy, the 12-step program, hospitalization, or social services support.

- Stage 7. Follow up and continue to evaluate status; ensure that the treatment plan is effective and make adjustments as needed.

Critical Incident Stress Debriefing

Designed to support individuals after a traumatic event, Critical Incident Stress Debriefing (CISD) is a structured form of crisis management. Specifically, it is short-term work done in small groups but is not considered psychotherapy. Techniques used include processing, defusing, ventilating, and validating thoughts, experiences, feeling, and emotions. CISD is best for secondary trauma victims, not primary trauma victims. For example, in cases of workplace violence, any employees who witnessed an event or who were indirectly impacted could benefit from CISD. Employees who were first-degree victims would need more individualized, specialized care and therapeutic intervention. It is important that CISD is offered as quickly as possible after an event; research has indicated it is most effective within a 24- to 72-hour time frame and becomes less effective the more time lapses after the event. CISD can be managed by specially trained personnel and could include mental health workers, medical staff, human resources, or other professionals. Trained Crisis Response Teams can be ready or quickly available to provide support directly following a traumatic situation.

Support

Support is a broad term for the way in which a counselor provides assistance and care to clients. Nonjudgmental support helps clients to open up, identify issues and the need for counseling, and set personal goals. A counselor can support a client by providing reassurance, acting as a sounding board, and simply listening without reaction. For the client, support from the counselor can allow a sense of being temporarily unburdened, which can facilitate healing. Support groups allow for peers or individuals experiencing similar issues (such as single parents and those struggling with addiction or eating disorders) to provide companionship and comfort through shared experiences.

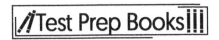

Grief

Grief is the emotional reaction to any type of loss. Emotions can range from sadness to despair, anger, or guilt. A loss could include a person, pet, job, or relationship. Bereavement is grief specific to the loss of a loved one. Although individuals can experience a range of emotions, there are two types of grieving. Instrumental grieving is considered more cognitive and focuses on managing emotional reactions and problem solving. It is more *thinking* than *feeling* and is considered a masculine way of dealing with grief. Intuitive grieving is more *feeling* than *thinking*. It is thought to be a more feminine way of grieving and focuses on expressing feelings, sharing, and processing emotions. Elisabeth Kubler-Ross developed the most well-known model for grief in 1969. The five-phase model suggests that individuals pass through at least two of five linear stages: denial, anger, bargaining, depression, and finally, acceptance. Individuals can also cycle back through certain stages.

Counselors can assist clients in dealing with grief by providing support and helping them process emotions and develop skills to adjust to life after a loss. It is important for counselors to understand that individuals experience grief in unique ways and to recognize when grief becomes unmanageable and can lead to more serious concerns, such as depression.

Reassurance

Reassurance is an affirming therapeutic technique used to encourage and support clients. Reassurance can help alleviate doubts and increase confidence. Counselors use reassurance when a client experiences setbacks or an inability to recognize progress. Clients can be reminded of past successes to help bolster their ability to solve current problems. It is important that reassurance is genuine and not overused by counselors to pacify clients, but rather as a tool to validate and inspire continued growth.

Promoting Relaxation

As part of the counseling process, clients may need to learn basic relaxation techniques, which can be simple to learn and practice. Stress can cause increased anxiety and tension; thus, relaxation techniques help reduce both mental and physical stress. Clients may present with racing thoughts, fatigue, or headaches; techniques such as awareness, breath work, and progressive relaxation can be of great benefit. Clients who have a reduction in their stress level may be more engaged in the counseling process and better able to manage difficulties outside of sessions. Meditation is a powerful relaxation tool to help build awareness and the ability to calm oneself. Relaxation can help diminish the activity of stress hormones in the body, reduce feelings of anger and frustration, lower heart rate, and improve confidence.

Goals

Setting goals is an important aspect of the therapeutic process. Talk therapy may seem unstructured or capable of lasting for long periods of time; however, both the client and the counselor are responsible for setting and working toward measurable change. Goals of counseling can include the desire for physical change, such as getting into shape or losing weight, and career aspirations and/or social goals, such as gaining increased support or modifying relationships. Other types of goals can include emotional, spiritual, and intellectual. Goals can be immediate, short term, or long term, and clients may want to achieve several goals at different paces. Goals can take the form of SMART goals, which are specific, measurable, achievable, relevant, and time-bound. Specific means detailing why you want to accomplish the goal, what specifically there is to accomplish, who is involved, the setting for the goal, and what kind of resources are involved. Measurable means designating a system of tracking your goals in order to stay motivated. Achievable is making sure that the goal is realistic, like looking at financial factors or other limitations. Relevant means making sure it's the right time for the goal, if it matches your needs, or if the goal seems worthwhile to pursue. Finally, time-bound is developing a target date so that there is a clear deadline to focus on.

Flaws in Goal Setting

Goal setting must be specific to each client and should be mutually agreed upon. Setting clear time frames, supported by the counselor, is essential to success. Goal setting may cause issues if goals are too ambitious or vague or have no identifiable benefit. It is also important to explore what motivation exists for a client to work toward a goal. If adequate motivation is present, the counselor also needs to consider what will happen if the goal is not met. In some cases, failure to meet goals can cause a client to become highly discouraged and unwilling to stick with the process of reformulating goals. During the process of working toward goals, a client may realize another goal is better suited. It's important to reevaluate goals during the process to help the client grow and embrace personal change.

Rational Problem-Solving Process

Rational problem solving is based on facts and clear consequences. It is an analytical approach that relies on predictability and understood outcomes. The rational decision-making process has distinct steps to define a problem and then weigh and rank the decision-making criteria. Next, the client must develop, evaluate, and select the best alternative. It is also important to explore consequences as well as what might happen if no decision is made and no action is taken.

Intuitive Problem Solving

Intuitive problem solving is based on feelings and instinct. It is an approach based on emotions and a "gut feeling" about what might be the right decision. Although in some cases it may be the right way and result in the correct decision, it is important for the counselor and client to work together on understanding any problem and possible solutions. It is also important to know when to utilize rational decision making versus intuitive or when to employ both strategies.

Modeling

Modeling is a technique used in therapy to allow clients to learn healthy and appropriate behaviors. Counselors "model" certain actions and attitudes, which can teach a client to behave in a similar fashion in his or her own life. Modeling is somewhat indirect. It is not suggested to the client to act in specific ways; rather, the counselor demonstrates desired behaviors, and the client begins imitating them.

Reinforcement When Analyzing Behavior

Reinforcement is a tool of behavior modification, used to either encourage or discourage specific thoughts or behaviors. Positive reinforcement rewards desired behaviors, thus encouraging the client to continue them. Counselors can provide positive verbal reinforcements, for example, to a client sharing difficult feelings, which in turn will encourage the client to continue sharing. The term **positive** in this case does not refer to a "good" outcome but to the act of applying a reward, such as a positive reaction from the counselor. Negative reinforcement works to discourage unwanted thoughts or behaviors by

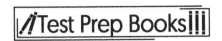

removing a stimulus after a specific action. The negative does not make it "bad"—rather, it is the act of removing a negative stimulus to eliminate a specific thought or behavior.

Extinguishing

Extinguishing is the process of ending, or making extinct, a specific maladaptive thought pattern or behavior. Previously occurring behaviors were reinforced, and when reinforcement (either positive or negative) ceases, the behavior will eventually be extinguished. It may be a goal in counseling to extinguish unwanted thoughts or behaviors that are harmful or a hindrance to the client.

Contract

As part of the intake process, counselors may wish to develop and agree upon a contract with the client. Contracts outline goals and responsibilities of both parties and may help to alleviate potential miscommunication. Important components of a contract include an outline of the service being provided, a description of the counselor's qualifications, and any explanation of the scope of practice. A clause outlining client rights and confidentiality should be included. Lastly, the counselor may wish to include specifics about session time, fees, and consequences of a client being late, missing, or canceling sessions. Contracts can serve to empower clients by clarifying service and allowing clients to take an active role in their therapeutic care. They may also be flexible, allowing either party to modify the contract as needed.

In-Life Desensitization

Desensitization is a behavior modification technique designed to replace an anxiety-producing stimulus with a relaxation response. Also known as systematic desensitization, it is a process to help the client manage fear or phobias. The client is taught relaxation techniques, which can include breathing, mindfulness, and muscle relaxation. Next, a "fear hierarchy" is created to rank stimulus from least to most fearful. The client is gradually exposed to the object or action that causes anxiety and then moves up the fear hierarchy and practices relaxation techniques. The goal is for the client to reach the most feared object or action and be able to react with calmness and control.

Symptoms of Burnout

At times, counselors may experience a sense of disinterest or disengagement from their work, which may signal burnout. Symptoms of burnout can include physical symptoms, such as fatigue, headaches, insomnia, and decreased resistance to illness. Emotional symptoms can include depression, anxiety, boredom, lack of empathy, cynicism, and anger. Burnout may be a result of overworking and/or providing service to clients who are not progressing in therapy, thus causing counselors to feel incompetent and ineffective. It is important to know the warning signs of burnout and engage in self-care, which may involve taking a vacation; getting increased supervision or therapy; making changes to one's hours, fees, or practice; or seeking continuing education options.

Warning Signs to Consider Before Expressing Personal Feelings

In rare cases, it may be appropriate for counselors to self-disclose to clients. It is important to remember that the therapeutic process is to help clients, not indirectly benefit counselors. First and foremost, counselors should consider the intent and who will benefit from their self-disclosure. It is not appropriate for clients to be burdened with counselors' emotions, as it could shift the atmosphere and

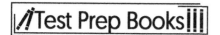

power dynamic of therapy. Counselors can disclose an emotional reaction to content from clients, provided it is for the benefit of the clients. Counselors should be cognizant of their clients' level of functioning and issues prior to any purposeful self-disclosure to ensure professional boundaries are maintained.

Support System

As part of the intake process and initial sessions, counselors need to explore and understand clients' existing support systems. All individuals have varying degrees of social support, which can include friends, family, and community. Counselors can help clients evaluate their level of support and determine how the support system can help during counseling and after it has ended. It may be necessary to help clients find ways to develop additional support, such as through groups or organizations. A support system is necessary to provide help, encouragement, and care.

Characteristics of Willingness to Change

Entering into counseling can provoke anxiety, fear, and resistance to change. Clients may have both internal and external reasons to want or need to change but exhibit some unwillingness to do so. Clients with internal or intrinsic motivation understand that they need to change to move forward, grow, and achieve personal goals. External factors, such as mandated counseling, can be motivating, but may create additional resistance. Clients will be more motivated and willing to change when they have a vested interest in the process and believe they will achieve a successful outcome. Commitment to the process is essential, especially considering that counseling may not seem enjoyable or even interesting but may be necessary.

Group Work

Individuals seeking counseling may benefit from group work in addition to, or in place of, individual counseling. Groups focus on nonpathological issues, such as personal, physical/medical, social, or vocational, and act to support and encourage growth. Groups are popular for addictions, eating disorders or weight loss, grief, anxiety, and parenting. They can be homogenous and share demographic information and goals or can be heterogeneous and diverse with multifaceted goals. Group members benefit from the process through sharing and the ability to learn new ways to react and cope with difficulties. It is essential that groups have a trained leader to help create structure, boundaries, and rules and keep the group on track.

Spirituality

Spirituality is a component of overall wellness and can be incorporated into the counseling process. It must be noted that spirituality is different from religion, although individuals may define the concepts in different ways. A client's spiritual views may encompass his or her higher sense of purpose, meaning, the reason for existence, worldview, and sense of place in the universe. Counselors need to be aware of their own spirituality and be able to appropriately support a client without imposing or rejecting their spiritual views. Spiritual practices that can be helpful in counseling include meditation, prayer, mindfulness, and reflection.

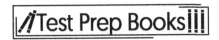

Maslow's Hierarchy of Needs

Abraham Maslow believed that all humans have basic needs, that, once filled, allow movement onto higher-level functioning. The hierarchy is depicted as a pyramid with biological and psychological needs at the base. The base level includes the need for food, shelter, warmth, air, and sleep. The next level, safety, is the need for personal security, stability, laws, and social order. The third level reflects the need for love and a sense of belonging, which can include both personal and professional relationships. The fourth level is esteem needs and was updated to include cognitive and aesthetic needs. These include the need for self-esteem, status, prestige, knowledge, and an appreciation for beauty and balance. The top level of the pyramid is self-actualization when an individual has reached his or her potential, is fulfilled, and finds meaning in life. It can also include the process of helping others achieve self-actualization. It's important to realize that if clients are not having their very basic needs met (food, shelter, etc.), they will have great difficulty working on higher goals that contribute to their mental and emotional wellbeing.

Wellness

The concept of wellness is multidimensional and includes six aspects of health: occupational, physical, emotional, spiritual, intellectual, and social. Wellness is holistic and stresses the need for individuals to find balance and maximize their potential. It can be considered to be more of a luxury than an essential need. Wellness is a higher level of functioning for those who have their basic needs met and are seeking a more successful existence.

Finding Happiness

Happiness can be defined in many ways, and individuals may have challenges in arriving at a state where they feel entirely happy. Research on happiness shows that it is small things, like activities, and not hypothetical future events or material possessions that create the most happiness. Counseling can assist in helping individuals explore times when they felt happy and work on ways to increase and maintain their happiness. By asking clients about past happy times and what about those times made them feel happy, the counselor will be able to help clients explore how to feel happier in the present. It is important to recognize that future achievements may not produce desired happiness, such as "I will be happy when …". Rather, counselors should focus on helping clients appreciate what makes them happy in the present moment and how to use that happiness to feel more fulfilled each day.

Structured and Unstructured Helping Relationships

Individuals can get help and support from many types of relationships, both structured and unstructured. Structured relationships include those with professional helpers, such as counselors, therapists, medical professionals, and counselors. These relationships have clear goals and are time-limited both in session and overall duration. Unstructured relationships also provide support but are more ambiguous and ongoing. These can include community support, groups, friends, family, and activities such as workshops or retreats.

Models of a Helper

Gerard Egan developed a model for helping outlined in his book, *The Skilled Helper*. Egan drew from several theorists, including Rogers, Carkhuff, and Albert Bandura, to create a three-stage model for helping. The phases of the model are identifying the present situation or scenario, defining the desired scenario, and developing a strategy to achieve it. The model provides a framework and map that clients can internalize for use when faced with a problem. It was designed to empower individuals to develop skills and confidence to solve problems outside of a helping relationship.

Congruence

The term **congruence** is associated with the person-centered work of Carl Rogers. Congruence can be defined as genuineness on the part of counselors, in that there is agreement on their words and actions. Counselors display congruence when their body language, affect, and words correspond to demonstrate genuine concern for the client. Lack of congruence is revealed when counselors express concern but at the same time seem bored, disinterested, or use language that does not indicate a true understanding of the client. Counselors who are nonreactive or act as a blank screen for clients are not expressing congruence. Rogers considered congruence to be essential for effective counseling.

Touch

There is some controversy over the use of touch in counseling. Studies have found that touch, such as a pat on the shoulder or a hug, can be very beneficial to some clients. Touch can provide comfort, reassurance, grounding, and support. However, there is an argument that touch violates personal boundaries and can be considered unethical. Touch is also interpreted in widely different ways across cultures; the United States is considered a "low touch" culture. For counselors, it is important to understand ethical and intercultural issues surrounding the use of touch and to use it only if and when it is needed and can be therapeutically beneficial.

Imagery

Guided imagery can be a powerful tool in the counseling process. Guided imagery, which draws upon the mind-body connection, can be used to help the client alleviate anxiety, relax, and control or change negative thoughts or feelings. A counselor, who helps the client envision a place of relaxation and calm, guides the process. The counselor encourages the client to visualize and relax into the details of the image. Clients can also envision the successful outcome of a situation or imagine themselves handling a stressful situation. Once learned, clients can practice imagery on their own to help reduce stress and anxiety.

External Stress, Internal Distress, and Transitional Stress

Crisis situations and stress have a variety of causes. External stress exists outside of a person's control and can include natural disasters, loss, illness of self or a family member, crime, poverty, or job change. Internal distress is the reaction to external stress but may be chronic and exist at all times due to an individual's coping skills and personal choices. Positive events, such as marriage, childbirth, a new job, or relocation, can cause eustress, which is considered positive stress. Major life changes can cause transitional stress, which may be short term but still requires strategies for managing. Stress management techniques include maintaining one's physical health, adequate sleep, relaxation techniques, and engaging in enjoyable activities or hobbies.

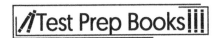

Professional Boundary Issues

Difficulties in Setting and Maintaining Professional Boundaries

Professional boundaries in counseling are clearly defined limits on the practitioner-client relationship that provide a space for the creation of safe connections. Some helpful things to keep in mind include: the line between being friendly and being friends; being with the client versus becoming the client; and understanding the limits and responsibilities of the counselor role.

Conflicting values occur when the counselor's values and knowledge about best practices are at odds with the client's values, history, relationships, or lifestyle. **Vicarious trauma** may happen when a counselor experiences symptoms of trauma after listening to a client's experience. These symptoms may arise due to the practitioner sharing a similar history of trauma. Boundaries may be difficult to maintain if the counselor feels that they need to rescue the client due to an unhealthy attachment to positive results in practice. This is termed the **rescuer role**. Professional boundaries may also be difficult to set and maintain if there is poor teamwork between colleagues in the counseling organization. This is evident when counselors assume the roles of other team members because they believe they are not fulfilling their responsibilities to the client.

Professional Boundary Issues

Professional boundary issues occur when counselors have multiple types of relationships with a client. This may include a professional, business, or personal relationship. For example, it is permissible to see a client out in public at a restaurant, but not to invite a client to dinner for business or personal reasons. When encountering a client in public, the relationship with the client must be kept confidential. However, if the client chooses to say hello, saying hello in return and quickly ending the encounter would be acceptable.

There are several boundary issues that come with working with clients. These issues are:

- Intimate contact: This refers to things such as hugging a client at the end of a working relationship or patting a client on the hand during a crying session. Sexual contact also falls into this category.

- Personal gain: This refers to instances in which a counselor engages in activity with a client that results in a monetary (or otherwise valuable) benefit to the counselor. This could involve situations such as referring a client to a business owned by the counselor or a friend/family member of the counselor, selling something to a client, or even asking a client for professional suggestions.

- Emotional and dependency issues: This refers to instances in which a counselor's own personal issues cause the counselor to have impaired judgment, possibly resulting in other boundary issues, such as a dual relationship with the client.

- Altruistic instincts: In some instances, a counselor's own good intentions and concerns for a client can result in boundary violations and confusion about the relationship between the counselor and the client. An example of this would be going to a client's bridal shower or retirement party.

Strategies for Setting and Maintaining Professional Boundaries

Despite these difficulties, counselors must set and maintain boundaries with their clients and colleagues to ensure an effective practice. Practitioners should consistently monitor how their professional boundaries enhance or harm relationships with clients, colleagues, supervisors, and administrators. They must also gauge the impact of their boundaries on the amount of time they devote to work, their ability to cope with stress at work, and the amount of time and energy that they spend on extraneous activities and relationships.

There are several strategies for building and maintaining appropriate professional boundaries and relationships. First, practitioners should examine their motivations for giving extra time and attention to a client. If a counselor treats one client differently, this indicates that the boundary may be overextended. Counselors can manage this situation by determining whether the services provided are in line with the client's care plan, the organization's mission, the job description, and scope of practice.

Counselors should also avoid encouraging clients to contact them through personal channels. Clients should use the channels of communication set in place by the organization, such as work email, voicemail, cell phones, pagers, receptionists, on-call staff, and procedures for after-hours referrals to 911, emergency rooms, or mental health crisis centers. Extending the professional boundaries of the counselor role puts colleagues and the organization at risk for failure. It also sets an unfair expectation that other colleagues will extend their professional boundaries. If boundaries are inconsistent between colleagues and within the organization, then clients may become confused and distrust the entire organization.

A third strategy for building appropriate professional boundaries is establishing clear agreements with clients during the initial sessions about the role of a counselor and the dynamics of a client-practitioner relationship. When warning signs indicate that healthy boundaries may be in jeopardy, counselors must address the issues with the client clearly, quickly, and sensitively. This involves clarifying the roles and boundaries with the client and asking the client to restate these boundaries to ensure understanding.

A fourth strategy is limiting self-disclosure about the counselor's personal life to information directly related to the client's goals. If there is a dual relationship between the counselor and client, the practitioner must preserve the client's confidentiality, physical security, and emotional well-being in social situations.

A fifth strategy is avoiding social media within professional practice. Practitioners should not connect with clients on social media. This includes adding clients as friends on Facebook or following clients on Twitter. Counselors should use discretion and limit the amount of online information that is made available to the public or social network connections to prevent conflicts of interest. Counselors also shouldn't attempt to access online information about clients without prior informed consent. Finally, practitioners shouldn't post negative information about colleagues or the organization online.

A sixth strategy is for counselors to foster strong work relationships with their colleagues at the organization. These connections will help practitioners cope with stresses, think through questions of ethics and professional relationships, and help maintain a sense of humor. Practitioners should be sensitive to signs of bullying in the workplace, as each practitioner deserves respect and dignity to ensure social justice for others. It's important that counselors use appropriate channels of supervision and consultation to determine appropriate boundaries in difficult situations. Supervision can also be useful when trying to remedy concerns with existing organization procedures that address or inhibit needs.

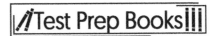

A final strategy for maintaining professional boundaries is ensuring appropriate self-care. This includes taking time for nurturing oneself throughout the workday, maintaining a regular work schedule, and taking time away from the office each day to refocus. Practitioners should limit communication when they are away from work to ensure time for rejuvenation, especially during vacations or personal time. They must also be aware of how they handle work stress and monitor how often they take work home. This includes physical work, emotional strain, or hyper-vigilance about work situations. If a practitioner consistently struggles to maintain professional relationships and work boundaries, they should seek supervision or outside mental health counseling.

Dual Relationships

Dual relationships are clearly outlined in the NBCC Code of Ethics. The Code of Ethics states that counselors should not engage in dual relationships with clients or former clients in which exploitation of the client may occur. The Code of Ethics does recognize that there might be situations where dual relationships are unavoidable. For example, a counselor might have two jobs, one of which involves providing group therapy to survivors of sexual abuse. It is possible that a member of the aforementioned therapy group could become an employee or client at the counselor's second place of work. In these types of situations, the Code of Ethics suggests that the counselor establish clear boundaries that are sensitive to the client/former client.

Under no circumstances should a counselor ever become involved in a sexual relationship with a client. In addition, the Code of Ethics establishes that counselors must avoid sexual relationships with anyone who is related to or has a close personal relationship with a client or former client. The Code of Ethics also states that counselors should not become involved in sexual relationships with former clients because of the high risk of harm that may occur with such relationships. If, however, a counselor does become involved in a sexual relationship with a former client, the counselor is responsible for demonstrating that the former client entered into the relationship without manipulation or exploitation. The Code of Ethics also specifies that, due to the obvious risk of harm, a counselor should not provide professional services to anyone with whom the counselor has had a previous sexual relationship.

Situations called "boundary crossings" are when a counselor does not intend to create a dual relationship but inadvertently does so, as would be the case were a clinician to self-disclose personal information during a therapy session. This is distinguished from a boundary *violation*, which occurs when a dual relationship is established that is inherently coercive or manipulative and therefore harmful to the client. What are some clues about whether a boundary crossing is unethical?

- It hinders the counselor's care
- It prevents the counselor from being impartial
- It exploits or manipulates the client or another person
- It harms clients or colleagues

Dual relationships are sometimes unavoidable in practice, particularly in small communities. However, it is possible to avoid dual relationships that involve boundary violations and ethical violations.

Counseling in Relation to a Plan of Treatment

Building and Maintaining a Helping Relationship

As the principal conduit for client change and acceptance, the counselor/client relationship is primary to the problem solving and therapy process. If the counselor cannot develop a positive relationship with the client, the change process is hindered. The worker/client relationship should be based on trust, empathy, and acceptance by both parties in order to facilitate growth. Some clients may have difficulty building trust with the counselor, and the counselor may need to be patient with the client in order to make treatment goal progress. If the counselor cannot develop an appropriate trusting, empathetic, and accepting relationship with the client, the counselor should seek supervision. In some cases, the counselor will need to transfer the client because it will be very challenging for the client to make progress if trust does not exist. Counselors should be alert for countertransference issues in the relationship with the client and address these issues promptly if they occur.

Principles of Relationship Building

Rapport building begins during the initial contact the counselor has with the client, a crucial time for establishing trust and harmony. After building rapport, the client and the counselor can begin working on client issues and continue developing the relationship on deeper levels. The relationship that the client has with the counselor is representative of the relationships the client has in other areas of life; the counselor needs to engage with the client within this framework to effect the greatest change.

Developing, Evaluating and Establishing a Measurable Intervention Plan

To develop an intervention plan, the practitioner and individual may collaborate. If that isn't possible, the practitioner may want to involve the individual in order to have an informed, engaged, and receptive participant. The methodology may include:

- Clear discussion and a written definition of the presenting issue, including supporting anecdotal evidence, observations, and (possibly) statistical data

- Discussion of what may contribute to or cause the problem, and how it affects other aspects of the individual's daily life

- Discussion of possible resolutions to the presenting issue

- Discussion of components of the individual's life that support resolution—and what may be obstacles

- Development of objectives for success that are specific, measurable, achievable, relevant, and time-specific (known as SMART)

- Establishment of a method to evaluate progress

Techniques to Establish Measurable Intervention or Service Plans

Creating SMART objectives allows for data-driven and measurable intervention plans. When creating objectives, practitioners should be able to measure the following:

- The desired behavior that is exhibited

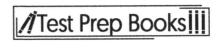

- The number of times the desired behavior is exhibited over a period of time
- The conditions in which the desired behavior must be exhibited
- Progress from the undesired behavior to the desired behavior through baseline evaluation and evaluation at pre-determined intervals

Techniques Used to Engage and Motivate Client Systems

When determining a client's motivation, the engagement and assessment stage is crucial. When clients voluntarily seek services and/or are facing a crisis, the commitment and motivation will likely be high. Non-voluntary clients are identified as those who are seeking assistance based on pressure outside of the legal system (i.e., a woman gives her spouse an ultimatum to get help or she will leave). When working with non-voluntary or involuntary clients who are mandated legally to seek treatment, the counselor must help determine client-identified problems. This should be in addition or complementary to the presenting problem. The worker and client collaboratively should create a treatment plan that addresses both types of issues.

Additionally, the worker must help the client overcome any negative feelings of anger or mistrust about treatment. With all clients, appropriate relationship building between the worker and client is a necessary part of engagement and motivation. Clients must feel they are in a safe, empathetic environment. They also should experience a sufficient level of trust for the counselor in order for treatment to be effective. To create an effective treatment relationship, the counselor must project an attitude free of judgment, recognize the client's individual attributes, strengths, and abilities, and encourage the client's right to be an active participant in their own treatment.

Working with Involuntary Client Systems

Clients who are involuntary/mandated may need extra encouragement from the counselor to adhere to treatment, and so the counselor may need to contract with the client for additional motivation. Counselors may show extra empathy to involuntary/mandated clients and offer clear communication of therapy parameters. Counselors may need to verbally explain the therapy process to the mandated client and explain the benefits of the therapeutic alliance, because often mandated clients have never before been involved in the therapeutic process. Counselors often need to report to the client's legal agency concerning the therapeutic progress of the client, and the client needs to be made aware of the parameter of this report so that there is clarity of client responsibilities for the therapy and change process. Clients who are involuntary/mandated are often required to attend therapeutic sessions with the counselor, and their attendance is monitored. Mandated clients need to be made aware of this reporting, so that perhaps they are motivated to attend therapy on a regular basis.

Contracting with Client Systems

Goal setting is a necessary factor in both the treatment and evaluation of direct practice. Counselors should work collaboratively with clients to determine goals. To be effective, goals need to be specific, measurable, achievable, realistic, and timely. They also should be directly related to the target problem. During the assessment process, begin identifying possible goals for treatment. Depending on the identified issues, goals may focus on desired behavioral, cognitive, or emotional changes.

Reciprocal goals: Complimentary goals agreed upon by members of a system related to the same target problem (i.e., a father's goal is to offer more compliments to his son, while son agrees to increase verbal acknowledgement to father's positive feedback).

Shared goals: When members of a system choose the same goal that addresses an identified problem (i.e., spouses each agree to communicate needs more frequently).

Contracts

Once goals are determined, a contract is the next step to engage the client in services. Contracts can be formal or informal, and written or verbal depending on the policies of the agency and the nature of treatment. A contract between client and worker provides a set of expectations and guidelines for treatment. Clients should be made aware the contract is a commitment by both parties, but not a legal document. Components of the contract include goals, assignments of tasks, timeframes, frequency of sessions, methods for determining progress, and how updates or revisions of the contract can occur. Other items that can be included are lengths of sessions, financial arrangements, procedures for cancelling appointments, etc.

Clarifying the Roles and Responsibilities of the Client System

The client system can include not only the client, but those who are in the client's immediate environment, or who have an influential role in the client's life and treatment. A client system may also consist of an organization or community, which may involve many people. It is important to clarify and define the roles of each person involved in the client system, including the counselor, individual client, or the different members of the organization.

Client systems and counselors may initially have differing expectations of their roles in the helping relationship, so it is important that the roles and responsibilities of each are clarified as soon as possible. Although the client may have the expectation that the counselor will have the most active role in treatment, it is important for the client to also be fully engaged and proactive. While the counselor plays a supportive, helpful role, there should be a collaborative effort in which everyone in the client system is working together toward goals that have been set cooperatively. Clients must be actively involved in identifying areas of strengths and weaknesses, setting goals for treatment, choosing providers, and working towards the changes that are needed. In situations where the client system consists of many people, the counselor's role will be to maintain unity and cohesiveness so that goals can be achieved.

Termination and Follow-Up

An important part of treatment planning is discharge planning. There are numerous reasons that services for a client may end. Clients may feel that they no longer need the services, that they are not compatible with the counselor providing the services, that an increased level of care is needed that is beyond the scope of the practitioner, or they may have successfully met goals for treatment.

Discharge planning should begin with the onset of the initial assessment for the client. The practitioner should not delay discharge planning, as discharge may occur at any time. Making the client aware of the choices for discharge and the discharge planning process empowers the client during treatment. It also provides continuity of care for the client.

The main purpose of discharge planning is to develop a plan of care that goes beyond the current treatment sessions to promote success once services have concluded. In the event the client is going to a higher level of care or to a different professional, effective discharge planning is useful in disseminating pertinent information about the client to assist in continuity of care and effective treatment. In this sense, the current practitioner should prepare to become a collateral resource linked to the client's level of care for the next professional.

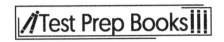

In addition to benefitting the other practitioners the client may meet with, effective discharge planning is a benefit to the client as well. If services have been completed successfully and the client has met the stated goals, then discharge planning ensures the client has a plan to sustain a stable level of function and maintain the successes achieved. This is particularly useful with clients who suffer from substance use or other addictive behaviors, as effective discharge planning can prevent relapse.

Upon the conclusion of the client discharging from services, a discharge summary should be created and placed in the client's file. The **discharge summary** should include the following information:

- Reason for discharge
- Description of treatment goals and the degree to which they were met
- Client's response to the interventions
- Description of the client's levels of functioning
- Baseline
- Progress during treatment
- Functioning at discharge
- Recommendations for follow-up care
- Links to community resources
- Appointment dates for other providers (if available)
- Provision of additional contacts, client supports
- Description of potential risks post-discharge
- Contact information for post-discharge support and crisis intervention

Follow-Up Techniques

At the final session, the counselor and client can schedule a follow-up session at a predetermined time to evaluate the client's continued progress after termination. Another option is to propose a time to meet and alert the client that the worker will contact the client to schedule a follow up. The follow-up session enables the counselor the opportunity to determine how well the client has progressed and to determine the effectiveness of the intervention(s) used during sessions.

Effect of Caseload Management on Client Systems

A caseload refers to the number of clients that are assigned to a particular counselor. Managing heavy caseloads can be a challenge for counselors, as it means balancing the needs of many clients with limited time and resources. This may result in poorer quality of services, which directly impacts the client system, and can lead to exhaustion and burnout for the counselor. When possible, a counselor's caseload should be minimized so that more comprehensive services are provided for each client. Unfortunately, there are various and complicated reasons that often contribute to higher caseloads in counselor organizations, such as financial restrictions, understaffing, and high numbers of clients. When large caseloads are unavoidable, then counselors must use other strategies to minimize stress and optimize services, including effective time management and more frequent referrals to other providers who can help meet the various needs of the clients. Additionally, it is important for counselors to prioritize client systems according to the complexity of their needs. Balanced and well-managed workloads, although difficult to achieve, can make a significant difference in the level of services provided to client systems and will result in better overall outcomes.

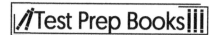

Crisis Intervention Approach

Crisis intervention is typically a short-term treatment usually lasting four to six weeks and is implemented when a client enters treatment following some type of traumatic event that causes significant distress. This event causes a state of disequilibrium when a client is out of balance and can no longer function effectively.

Gerald Caplan's Stages of Crises: Caplan theorized that individuals need to maintain homeostasis or remain in balance with their environment. A crisis is caused by an individual's reaction to a situation, not by an actual incident. Following a crisis event, an individual experiences the following stages.

- Stage 1: Increase in feelings of stress immediately following the event. Client may experience denial and typically tries to resolve the stressful reactions using past problem-solving and coping skills.

- Stage 2: Client experiences higher levels of stress as the usual coping mechanisms fail. Client may employ higher-level coping skills to alleviate the increasing stress levels.

- Stage 3: As stressful feelings continue to escalate, client experiences major emotional turmoil, possible feelings of hopelessness, depression, and anxiety.

- Stage 4: Final stage is marked by complete psychological and emotional collapse, or the individual finds a method to resolve the situation. However, there may be remaining emotional and psychological dysfunction or impairment if the coping mechanisms used were maladaptive.

Counselors can either use generic crisis intervention models for varied types of crises or can create an individualized plan for assisting the client. The main goal of crisis intervention should be to help clients develop and use adaptive coping skills to return to the level of functioning prior to the crisis.

Crisis Intervention Process

Engage and Assess
Counselors participate in client engagement by helping to de-escalate volatile emotional states through establishing rapport, using empathy, employing emotional management techniques, and accessing outside systems (family, friends, and support groups). Additionally, the counselor assesses the crisis situation to determine the level of care required (general triage may include intensities ranging from one to three) and how the client has been impacted.

Set Goals and Implement Treatment
Goal setting should occur in collaboration with a client's treatment plan. Intervention strategies, tasks, and timeframes should correspond with the desired goal and objectives. The primary goal should be to assist clients in returning to pre-crisis functioning. However, there will likely be additional and related goals and tasks as the plan of action is implemented.

Evaluate and Terminate
Worker concludes treatment and evaluates completion of goals. It is important to discuss with the client what coping skills have been developed and how they might be able to use those skills for future crises and challenges.

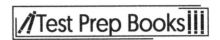

Cognitive and/or Behavioral Interventions

Cognitive Approaches

Cognitive approaches to the counseling process involve changing the way the client thinks in order to facilitate progress and problem-solving skills. Cognitive approaches tend to be evidence based and favored by insurance carriers, as they are efficacious for a variety of client issues, including substance use and personality disorders. Cognitive approaches focus on changing maladaptive thinking and cognitive distortions, and thus may help clients engage in behavior change. Cognitive distortions involve fallacious thinking patterns engaged in by the client, such as black-and-white thinking. Types of cognitive approaches may include cognitive behavior therapy, rational emotive behavior therapy, and solution focused brief therapy. There are many modalities of cognitive therapies and counselors should implement them when necessary.

Behavioral Approaches

Behavioral approaches, which originated with Skinner and Pavlov, include methods of changing and motivating client behaviors toward reaching constructive goals. The underlying concept is that if clients can change behavior, they may also alter the way they think. Skinner and Pavlov believed that all behavior is learned, and they believed in conditioning. Tokens may be awarded for positive behavioral changes in the client; this occurs in what is called a token economy. Cognitive behavioral therapies, which focus on both the cognition and the behavior of the client, are considered evidence based and are favored by managed care insurers.

Strengths-Based and Empowerment Practice

Empowerment is a strengths-based modality, and the goal is that all clients should feel empowered based on their personal identities. Clients need to feel in control of most of their lives and circumstances, and this is what empowerment permits. Working from a strengths-based perspective empowers clients to facilitate change in their own lives. Counselors may seek to empower clients by focusing on strengths and bolstering clients' social constructs. Clients may need to be empowered from a racial, ethnic, religious, gender, or age perspective because they have suffered discrimination in these areas. Counselors may act as political advocates in these realms to combat social oppression affecting clients. The counselor should take into account the differences each client possesses due to their race, religion, or circumstance, and use these differences as strengths.

Problem-Solving Approaches

The problem-solving therapeutic model serves to teach clients how to manage stressors that come in life. Often clients do not possess skills that allow them to effectively navigate negative events or emotions without increasing personal harm. The goal of the problem-solving model is to teach clients the skills necessary to deal with negative life events, negative emotions, and stressful situations. In particular, goals of this model should be to assist clients in identifying which particular situations may trigger unpleasant emotions, understanding the range of emotions one might feel, planning how to effectively deal with situations when they arise, and even recognizing and accepting that some situations are not able to be solved.

The counselor, however, may be an instructional guide to facilitate problem solving for the client. Because problem-solving skills are one of the primary methods of resolving issues, and often are skills that clients lack, the counselor may need to model them for the client so that the client can then develop their own skills. Counselors need to maintain empathy and congruence with the client during

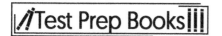

the problem-solving process, and even though they may have verbally instructed or modeled problem-solving methods, they need to maintain rapport in the relationship.

Components of the Problem-Solving Process

When working with clients to develop problem-solving skills, counselors must first engage and prepare clients by discussing the benefits of improving such skills and encouraging clients to commit to the problem-solving process during the goal setting/contracting phase.

Steps in the problem-solving process:

- Step 1: Assess, define, and clarify the problem. As with goal setting, counselors should assist clients in clearly determining and defining the specific problem. Workers should focus on the current problem and ensure clients do not become distracted by other past or current difficulties. Examine specific aspects of the problem, including behaviors and the needs of those involved.

- Step 2: Determine possible solutions. Counselors should lead discussion among participants to determine possible solutions and encourage client(s) to refrain from limiting options at this point. The purpose is for clients to gain practice in solution development. In the case of family work, all capable members should be allowed to offer solutions and should feel safe to do so without fear or criticism from other members.

- Step 3: Examine options and select/implement a solution. Workers should assist clients in examining the benefits and drawbacks of each possible solution and choose an option that best meets the needs of those involved.

- Step 4: Evaluate and adjust. Counselors should help clients to determine the success of the solution. Client(s) can use a practical form of tracking solution effectiveness (charts, logs, etc.). If it is determined the solution is not working, the client can return to the solution-generating stage.

Techniques Used to Teach Skills to Client Systems

Clients frequently need to develop better coping strategies or improved social, communication, or life skills. Examples of skills that counselors may help clients develop include anger management, parenting, and substance abuse management. Skill training can take place in individual, family, group, or classroom formats. Steps in skill development include:

- Step 1: Skill identification. Identify and describe the skill(s) to be developed and how the client will benefit by acquiring the new skill(s). Engage clients and garner motivation to build skill development.

- Step 2: Demonstrate use of the skill. Give the client a visual example of what the skill looks like by modeling and performing role-play of the desired skill. This can be completed by a counselor and the client or in a family or group situation with another client.

- Step 3: Use of the skill outside of session and evaluation. The client should use the skill in everyday situations. The counselor can use sessions to discuss and evaluate a client's mastery of the skill and whether further skill development is needed.

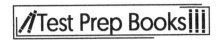

Client Self-Monitoring

Client self-monitoring can be a useful technique for turning subjective qualitative information into more quantifiable data. Clients may engage in self-assessment techniques and practices that include journaling, questionnaires, and evaluations. Clients collect data about goals, objectives, and the targeted behavior. This technique collects important information about client progress, but it also adds to clients' feelings of empowerment and self-determination as they become collaborators in treatment. Clients can either track information related to thoughts or behaviors or can use more formal charting techniques. Counselors should assist clients with defining and identifying which type of information to track and then demonstrate how to use the selected tracking technique. Self-monitoring methods serve several purposes. As clients become more invested in treatment, their awareness of strengths and areas in need of improvement may also increase. This will enable the client to monitor behaviors as they occur, allowing for the development of insight related to behavioral change.

Role-Play

Role-play is a type of modeling, also called behavior reversal. This technique enables clients to view the different ways a person may handle a challenging situation. It also allows a client to view a non-tangible behavior in a more tangible way. When clients practice skills and develop new and more productive methods of coping, they are able to take an active role in treatment, increasing their sense of empowerment and self-determination.

Assertiveness Training

Assertiveness training is an intervention that can be used in multiple settings with an assortment of interpersonal difficulties. This type of training helps individuals learn to express their emotions, thoughts, and desires, even when difficult, while not infringing on the rights of others. There are ways in which individuals can assert themselves, including saying no to a request, having a difference of opinion with another person, asking others to change their behavior, and starting conversations. Counselors must respect cultural differences when working with clients to develop assertiveness skills. For example, some cultures feel it is inappropriate for women or children to assert themselves. Role-play is an effective technique to help clients develop assertiveness skills.

Role Modeling

Role modeling, which offers the client a real-life view of desired target behaviors, can be an important tool to learn new skills. The counselor can request that clients demonstrate the behavior before modeling it, thereby allowing the worker to assess a client's current skills and abilities. Counselors can demonstrate a coping model showing the skill or desired behaviors, including difficulties, anxieties, or challenges. The worker can also demonstrate a mastery model, which shows confidence and competence with the desired behaviors. Each method has benefits and drawbacks. In coping mode, the client and worker can process the interaction and identify improvements or changes that can be made to the desired behaviors or actions. There are several types of modeling:

- Symbolic Modeling: Client watches a visual representation of the modeled behavior (i.e., video, TV, images)

- Live Modeling: Client watches while a person performs the behavior

- Participant Modeling or Guided Participation: Client observes model performing behavior and then performs the behavior and/or interacts with the model

- Covert Modeling: Client visualizes the desired behavior

Use of Cognitive Behavioral Techniques

Cognitive Behavioral Therapy (CBT) is typically a short-term treatment that focuses on transforming behavior by modifying thoughts, perceptions, and beliefs. Conscious thoughts affect behavior. Consequently, to promote consciousness of behavioral patterns in the client, the counselor (in the therapist role) will often assign homework in the form of exercises or journaling. The premise is that by identifying and reframing negative or distorted thoughts, the desired behavioral change can occur. CBT combines techniques and traits of both behavioral (positive and negative reinforcement) and cognitive therapies (cognitive distortion and schemas).

Cognitive restructuring is a concept used in CBT. The goal of cognitive restructuring is to help clients change irrational or unrealistic thoughts so that, ideally, change will lead to development of desired behaviors.

Cognitive Restructuring Steps:

- Accept that negative thoughts, inner dialogue, and beliefs affect one's feelings and emotional reactions.
- Identify which thoughts and belief patterns or self-statements lead to the target problems. Clients use self-monitoring techniques, including a log to track situations as they occur and the accompanying thoughts or feelings.
- Identify situations that evoke reoccurring themes in dysfunctional thoughts and beliefs.
- Replace distorted thoughts with functional, rational, and realistic statements.
- Reward oneself for using functional coping skills.

Providing Education and Information to Client Systems

Counselors often don multiple roles in their profession, one of which includes providing information and assisting with access to educational services. When providing educational services, the counselor must determine what skills, information, or knowledge needs to be acquired, as well as the capabilities of the client and the amount of time available for the development of new skills. The provision of education may be done in individual, family, or small group classes, or large group forums. Workers may also recommend resources such as books, articles, or websites that may help clients acquire new information.

Teaching Coping Strategies to Client Systems

Counselors may act in the role of teacher to instruct clients about coping and other skills. Coping skills may include relaxation techniques, deep breathing, time out, and improved communication skills. Common diagnoses that often require the instruction of coping skills include stress reduction, anxiety, and major depression. Clients may be able to utilize coping and acceptance skills for these diagnoses because they are frequently chronic, and clients will need to cope with them on an almost daily basis. Clients often need to learn a plethora of new skills to manage their issues and complex problems, and they and the counselor should collaborate on coping and other skills to manage these circumstances. Counselors can partialize and brainstorm with clients concerning coping and other treatment skills. Clients sometimes need detailed instructions in order to succeed with treatment goals. Clients need to be engaged in therapy outside of sessions and learn how to cope when the counselor is not present, so assigning clients' homework between sessions is a method of skills building. While the counselor may

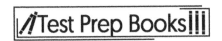

offer suggestions to the client for coping and other skills, the client is ultimately the most effective arbiter of their own treatment.

Group Work Approaches

Group work can be defined as a goal-directed intervention with small groups of people. The intention of this work is to improve the socioemotional and psychoeducation needs of the individual members of the group through the group process. There are two types of groups in social work: therapeutic and task groups. Task groups are created to perform a specific task or purpose. These groups differ in the amount and type of self-disclosure, confidentiality, and communication patterns. There are several types of treatment groups, including support, educational, and therapy groups. Groups can also be long-term or short-term, depending on the type and purpose.

Groups can be open or closed. Open groups are ongoing and allow for new members to enter at any time. Open groups are typically used for support and life transitions. There are challenges to this type of group, since the members are at different stages in the group process. The frequently changing membership can be disruptive to the group process because members may not feel as emotionally safe to share with others. Closed groups are time-limited, and new members can only join during the beginning stage. The advantages to this type of group is more engagement and better trust by the members, since the group process is more stable. A disadvantage is that if several members leave the group, the group process may not be as effective. There are several variations by theorists that describe the stages of group development. A general method of categorizing the group process is the beginning, middle, and end stages. Each stage is classified by different activities, processes, and tasks:

Beginning Stage
Counselors determine the group's purpose, members, objectives, and other logistical tasks (time, location, etc.). Group formation occurs at this stage as new members come together. The counselor fosters a safe and trusting environment by establishing acceptable group norms. As group members become more comfortable, conflicts arise as power and control behaviors emerge. Group roles and alliances begin to form. The worker's role is to help guide the group through these challenges and process any conflicts that arise within the group.

Middle Stage
This stage is where most group work is done. Members share information, openly address issues, and work through conflicts. Some groups do not make it to this stage for several reasons, including member dynamics and a lack of investment of the group members. Group cohesion or the connectedness of the members is extremely important at this stage. The role of the worker is to help members focus on methods and the meaning of communication, working through group differences and confronting members when necessary. Workers should also help develop more intensive levels of cohesiveness while building on member individuality.

End Stage
Group members come to resolutions on the issues addressed during the group process. Members may have strong reactions to termination, especially if there was a high level of cohesion developed during the group process. The counselor should lead the group in discussing feelings about termination and be aware of negative reactions that may surface. When these types of emotions occur, counselors should address any challenges that arise with members. The counselor should also help group members identify and reflect on the skills learned in the group process and how those skills can benefit the members with future challenges.

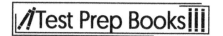

Working with Individuals in the Group Context

It is the role of the counselor to encourage all members to participate in the group process. The worker can solicit feedback from each member of the group throughout the group process. Clients typically take on various roles during group treatment. Roles can be defined as functions the individual members of the group are fulfilling or performing that facilitate the group process. Some roles include that of a clown, scapegoat, mediator, etc. The worker must be aware of the roles of each individual and how those roles are affecting the group, so interventions can be made when necessary.

Social Policy Development and Analysis

The social change process is one in which interested groups (i.e., community members, lawmakers, businesses, government agencies, community organizations) can work together to create change or solve an identified community or societal problem. Collaborative social planning increases the chances of positive change and allows community members to take ownership of the change and resulting policies. It also encourages the community to become more energized and more likely to make positive changes in the future. The role of the counselor as a leader in this process includes:

- Community engagement
- Problem identification
- Organization and engagement of community members
- Identification of resources, challenges, and solutions
- Creation and implementation of a plan
- Evaluation and follow-up

Techniques for Social Policy Analysis

Social policy analysis is a process of systematically and strategically examining policies to determine overall effectiveness. When analyzing policies, counselors must:

- Determine both the intentional and unintentional effects of the policy
- Examine whether the policy is cost-effective and feasible
- Identify potential problems with the policy
- Determine how the policy is viewed by those affected. Look at who benefits and who doesn't
- Identify possible policy alternatives

Techniques for Influencing Social Policy

Counselors may act in a macro capacity for the common public good and serve as policy advocates, or provide leadership in the policy change process. There are many types of societal influences that can affect social policy.

- Cultural: Societal perceptions or beliefs can shape policy. For instance, a general belief that children should have access to healthcare can aid in the development of child healthcare laws. Additionally, the media can bring problems/issues to the forefront and have a huge impact on public opinion, which can then influence policy development.

- Economic: Lack of or an availability of resources has a significant impact on policy development. Additionally, those who control the resources also impact how policy is shaped.

90

- Institutional: The capabilities, resources, and structure of government offices affect policy development. The institutions that create and implement policies have to be able to do so in an effective manner for those policies to be successful.

- Social: The social environment, including events or situations such as recessions, wars, or poverty, all affect how policies are developed.

- Legal: Existing laws and policies can influence future trends in policy development. New policies may or may not be adopted, depending on how they complement those already in existence and the current social climate. Legal events may also influence new policies.

- Political: The political climate directly influences social policy, since the parties in control of governing bodies directly affect which policies and laws are implemented and repealed.

Techniques for Working with Large Groups

Counselors might spend a significant amount of time in groups, including staff meetings, conferences, or community meetings. Group meetings must be run effectively and efficiently to be productive and to accomplish the intended purpose. Depending on the type of meeting and the level of structure required, parliamentary procedures may be used to help keep order and aid in decision-making. Generally, to conduct effective group meetings, counselors should:

- Determine the logistical needs. Choose the time and place, considering any costs or other resources that are needed. Secure any audiovisual needs.

- Establish and clarify the purpose, goals, and objectives of the meeting. The reason for the meeting should be clear to all participants.

- Make a plan/agenda. Create a plan for the meeting, including a written agenda, listing any speakers and anticipating the time needed for each item. Make sure presenters are aware of their time restrictions.

- Determine who will attend the meeting and ensure appropriate notice is given.

- Prepare meeting materials ahead of time, including handouts and other items.

- Start meetings on time, keep the group on target, and end at the expected time.

Classical Organizational Theories

Organizational theories provide explanations for organizational function and identify how certain concepts interrelate. Knowledge of these theories helps counselors gain an understanding of the agencies with which they work and can also be useful in leading change in those organizations. One important concept to remember is **organizational behavior**, or how individuals and groups behave in and interact within an organization. Another important concept is **management**, which is the use of planning and organizing tasks and skills to achieve organizational objectives.

Classical Organizational Theories emphasize a formalized and inflexible organization and employee structure. Here are some examples:

Scientific Management Theory

Emphasis on strong boundaries between the management who delegate tasks and the counselors who perform those tasks. Scientific methods were used to define jobs and tasks and select employees.

Administrative Theory

Hierarchical system that uses five basic functions to be administered by management that relate to planning, coordination, and control. Emphasis is placed on levels of authority and the separation of duties/tasks.

Bureaucracy Theory

Emphasis is placed on specialized areas with well-defined duties. Uses a hierarchical, impersonal structure with a heavy reliance on rules and procedures with the goal of maintaining control.

Neoclassical Organization Theories

Neoclassical Organization Theories focus on an individual's needs and inter-organizational/systemic interactions. They emphasize task coordination and cooperation between people or systems. Neoclassical theories reflected a change in focus to motivating employees with salaries and benefits as opposed to control.

It introduces two important terms:

- Inducements: Salary and benefits
- Contributions: What an employee offers (i.e., work, skills)

Human Relations Theory

Human Relations Theory has roots in psychology and theorizes that higher levels of employee job satisfaction and morale lead to better performance and more loyalty to an organization. If an organization provides better work conditions, it will experience increased productivity. Human Relations Theory introduced two types of management style: X and Y.

Theory X

Theory X is the classical style that emphasizes authoritarian management and the view of workers as unmotivated and uninterested in working.

Theory Y

Theory Y theorizes that workers are internally and intrinsically motivated and will seek responsibilities and ways to develop, given the opportunity.

Other Important Theories:

Feminist Theory: Emphasizes the protection of women from gender-based discrimination and encourages self-determination and empowerment

Economics Theory: Places emphasis on organizations and employees obtaining maximum profits

Chaos Theory: Describes organizations in terms of the complexity of all the forces affecting them and their ability to function

Contingency Theory: Centers on how systems within an organization are dependent on each other, and how all systems and factors must be considered collaboratively for organizations to function

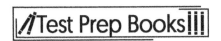

Culture Quality Theory: Focuses on organizational culture, common values, and quality improvement

Systems Theory: Emphasizes how all systems work together to create input and output, and the importance of assessments and modifications

Intervening with Organizations

One aspect of counseling is intervening with organizations. Social work organizations often begin with the admirable desire to help vulnerable populations. However, developing and sustaining such an organization can be an overwhelming challenge. Organizational policy development can improve the efficiency and effectiveness of the organization, by providing assessments and identifying the strengths and weaknesses. This type of policy development is also important to ensure that the goals and objectives of the organization are being met, and that they are in compliance with legal and ethical standards. Another aspect of organizational development has to do with the leadership hierarchy, or the formal power structure. This outlines the various positions of authority and leadership in relation to one another and is necessary for the smooth functioning and decision-making of the organization. However, in addition to the formal power structure, there is also informal power, which has more to do with the influence of relationships and skills than with structured influence. Organizational intervention in this area may address issues of team building, skills enhancement, and interpersonal skills. Intervention and development in both informal and formal power structures are necessary for a successful and sustainable organization.

Impact of Agency Policy and Function on Service Delivery

Counselors may be employed in a variety of agencies. Some organizations, such as hospitals or government entities, employ diverse professionals. Other types of organizations, such as direct service non-profits or private practice agencies, maintain predominantly social services staff. Agency policies directly and significantly impact the working environment, the services provided, and as a result, the effectiveness of the care clients receive. All agencies should have a mission statement that gives the agency purpose and serves as an umbrella for the agency's smaller goals and objectives. Agency policies must be in the best interest of the client and must support the ethical guidelines to which counselors adhere. They must also be clearly written and available to counselors and clients where appropriate. Counselors and all those providing care to clients should be able to help shape policy development to ensure consistency with client and worker needs and protection. Policies must address:

- Appropriate confidentiality, consent, and information protection.
- Case management and supervision.
- Cultural competency guidelines.
- Professional development and ongoing trainings.
- Anti-discriminatory/diversity practices

Referral Information

Making Referrals

In some cases, a client may require specialized service that is out of the scope of the counselor. At these times, a counselor may need to refer the client to another professional. It is important that the counselor is familiar with community resources and any specialized care a client may need. It is also essential to discuss with the client why a referral is recommended and ensure the client is comfortable with the decision and understands next steps. The counselor must be familiar with ethical guidelines surrounding referrals and not refer out simply due to discomfort with or dislike for a client. A counselor who refers out for such personal reasons risks clients feeling abandoned, and the ACA Code of Ethics states that the needs of the clients must be put before those of the counselor. In these situations, the counselor should seek supervision and consultation regarding his or her personal issues. If the counselor is unable to provide appropriate care, then the client should be referred out.

Process of Referring the Client for Additional Evaluations

Counselors frequently encounter clients who need assistance beyond the scope of the agency/counselor from whom they seek help. During assessment or throughout services, a counselor may need to refer a client to another agency for assistance. The NBCC Code of Ethics requires that counselors are knowledgeable about and able to identify community resources. Workers should also make referrals to those resources in alignment with the best interests of the client. Agencies may also have partnerships with other local organizations that their target population would frequently access. For example, a mental health agency may have an interagency agreement or partnership with a substance abuse provider. When making referrals and sharing information with other providers, counselors must always obtain client consent.

Additionally, the assessment phase is crucial to identifying needed referrals so that clients are referred to appropriate services early in the treatment process. Counselors should work to ensure clients are aware and have access to these services by helping clients make connections and overcome barriers. Workers should lead the process but still encourage self-determination and empowerment by allowing clients to play an active role in accessing and obtaining resources.

Activities related to referring clients for services may include:

- Contacting other providers: phone calls, meetings, letters, etc.
- Assisting clients with completion of paperwork.
- Ensuring clients qualify for the referred services.
- Monitoring clients' progress to ensure services are being provided and no barriers exist.
- Evaluating effects of referred services in meeting clients' goals and objectives.

Client Referral for Services

Clients may be referred to other entities or agencies for service outside the scope of the counselor's practice, such as legal, medical, and psychological testing agencies. Counselors must have the client sign a release of information to discuss the client case with outside service providers. Workers should be prepared to refer to services that fall outside their scope of practice, and they should inform the client about their framework of practice so that there is clarity of services provided. They may need to act as an advocate so clients receive continuity of care with other service providers, and they may need to be involved in arranging appointments and transportation for the client in order to effectively refer for services. Sometimes clients with complex needs require additional assistance from the counselor in order to most effectively receive outside referral services.

Coordination of Client Services

Counselors may consider the coordination of client services so that the client is not overwhelmed by service providers, and so that the services provided are appropriate for the client. They should request

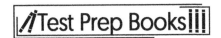

that the client coordinate among service providers so that there are smooth treatment transitions. Clients should focus on services that first address physical or psychological harm and then triage services for other aspects of their issues. Maslow's Hierarchy of Needs may be a map to use to coordinate client services according to most imperative needs first, and so on. Counselors should collaborate with clients to coordinate services and contract clients to follow through.

Methods of Networking

Networking provides counselors with additional resources for their clients and within their scope of practice. Counselors may network in person, telephonically, or by video teleconferencing. It is imperative that they network to provide additional resources to clients. Networking can occur in a variety of settings, including through the supervision process and conferences. Workers may network through continuing education opportunities where they may meet colleagues and presenters. Networking is important for counselors to stay informed of changes and progress in the counseling field.

Administration, Consultation, and Supervision

Case Notes, Records, and/or Files

The Use of Objective and Subjective Data in Written Assessments and Case Notes

Both objective and subjective data are used during the assessment and treatment processes. The client provides their perspective on what happened and the correlated feelings and experiences felt, which is the **subjective data**. Subsequently, the counselor uses the information and may ask finding questions to better understand where the client is emotionally, while teasing out facts related to the client's situation. These facts are **objective data**.

The information from both the subjective and objective data is combined to formulate a concise, yet comprehensive, assessment for the client. In some note-taking practices, the identification of the subjective and objective data, along with assessment formation, is required. This style of documentation is known as the *SOAP method*, an acronym that stands for Subjective, Objective, Assessment, and Plan. Another note-taking style that focuses on the subjective and objective data is the BIRP documentation method. *BIRP* stands for Behavior, Intervention, Response, and Plan. It is not as commonly used as SOAP.

Methods to Interpret and Communicate Policies and Procedures

Counselors have direct contact with clients and are in strategically critical positions to develop, implement, evaluate, and communicate policies and procedures. Policies and procedures are necessary to allow clients and employees to be aware of treatment and agency goals, objectives, resources, and limitations. Policies can sometimes be a barrier to client services, so counselors must be aware of this possibility and point out these barriers when necessary.

Factors in policy and procedure development:

- Front line health workers should be involved in policy and procedure development, since they are in the best position to determine and evaluate how clients are affected.

- Policies should be clearly written and communicated to clients/counselors with copies available for distribution. Workers should receive periodic training on current policies and procedures.

- Polices should be in the best interest of clients, but also protect the agency and staff.

Factors to consider when evaluating the effectiveness of policies and procedures:

- The origins of the policy and/or procedure, including values and the related ideology
- Client reactions, thoughts, and feelings about the policy
- Alignment with ethics and values
- Intentional and unintentional consequences and benefits
- Regular re-evaluation to ensure policies and procedures are still relevant and in the best interests of clients, counselors, and the agency

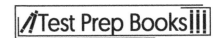

Methods Used to Clarify the Benefits and Limitations of Resources with Clients

Counselors must help clients understand their needs versus the services and resources available to them. Workers must be knowledgeable of the services available at their agency and in the communities in which their clients live. It is the role of the worker to assist clients in obtaining resources, but also to help clients understand their options and their right to choose or refuse which resources to access. Clients should receive assistance in identifying the pros and cons of each resource. They should also be involved in identifying and seeking resources as much as possible to foster the development of self-determination and empowerment.

Writing and Maintaining Client Records

Counselors must document their practice with the client. Counselors document sessions with clients as well as client legal mandates, such as visitation with minors in state custody. Documentation may be a combination of narrative and quantitative descriptions, depending on agency requirements. Records should be kept confidential either electronically or in a physical location. New laws require that all records be electronic, and they are called electronic health records. These records must be confidential as stated in the Health Insurance Portability and Accountability Act of 1996 (HIPAA). It is crucial for the counselor to maintain accurate documentation.

Elements of Client Reports

Elements of client reports may include developmental history, family history, substance use information, medical history, presenting problem, and recommendations. There are a variety of elements of client reports that may be required by the agency. With the advent of electronic records, client reports are often built into the software that the agency uses. Client reports may also be in DAP (data, assessment, plan) format or in the model of SOAP notes (subjective, objective, assessment, and plan). Reports are at the agency's discretion and the counselor should use the format that is required by the agency to develop client reports.

Written Communication Skills for a Variety of Professional Responsibilities

Counselors are required to be proficient in a variety of written and oral communication skills in order to fulfill their duties. They should be proficient at narrative writing skills for their client records. Counselors must also be able to quantify their work with clients so that they offer a variety of written skills to their practice and can communicate evidence-based engagement. They may need to be adept not only at practice notes, but also in legal writing, such as when they are required to write an affidavit on behalf of the client. Counselors should practice these written communication skills under the direction of superiors until they are certain of their proficiency.

Developing Reports for External Organizations

Counselors often receive requests to provide reports to the courts and other organizations that may be making decisions regarding the client's life and future. Reports must be written thoughtfully, in a professional and objective manner, and should be drawn from the counselor's notes and observations regarding the client. Reports for external organizations must provide detailed and relevant data and be clear and concise so they can be easily understood. Counselors do not need to provide information beyond what has been requested by a court order, and only in the case of a court order should information be released without the client's prior consent. Even if information must be legally released, the client should be informed of the situation and be aware that the information is being submitted to

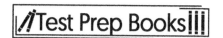

the external organization. A helpful habit for counselors is to take regular, comprehensive progress notes about visits and interactions with clients. If client records are already available, it is easier to compile a summary report with factual observations and the counselor's professional opinion.

Developing Administrative Reports

The administrative side of counseling involves writing a plethora of reports related to funding and programs. All types of reports must be detailed, factual, statistically accurate, and proofread to detect any grammatical errors that may detract from the professionalism of the document.

Grant reports must be compelling and persuasive to show that a particular program or organization should receive a grant. The report must include extensive but concise information about program services, including stated objectives and results, lessons learned and future plans, as well as detailed financial reports. Part of grant reports and other documents are outcomes and evaluations, which help organizations to set and achieve measurable goals. The field of counseling can appear subjective, but it is important to provide evidence-based research and to quantify progress and effectiveness through outcomes and evaluations, especially when attempting to obtain funding. In order to begin new programs, it is also necessary to write program proposals, which outline the specific need for the program. Good administrative writing provides sustainable funding, which will lead to better programs and help organizations provide more services for a greater number of people.

Recording and Monitoring Assessments and Service Plans

Accurate case recording is an integral part of counseling. It is necessary to accurately document clients' information for effective treatment and protection of confidentiality. It is also required to protect the agency from possible legal ramifications and to ensure reimbursement from funders. Client records should be kept up-to-date, objective, and completed as soon as possible to ensure accuracy of information. Counselors should assume it is always possible that records may be requested as part of legal proceedings. Treatment notes should always be clearly written and only include information necessary to the client's treatment to protect confidentiality as much as possible. Counselors must also adhere to any state or federal legal requirements related to storage, disclosure of information, release of client records, and confidential information.

Obtaining and Recording Service-Related Forms

Organization and storage of client information varies greatly depending on the practitioner, the institution, and the requirements of any external funding sources. Information may be stored electronically in online systems or on paper. Important components of information in counseling include: intake forms; personal, medical, and demographic information; assessments and reviews; any diagnoses, intervention, and treatment outlines with measurable goals; and discharge plans or paperwork. Since this is all highly sensitive and confidential information, practitioners should be mindful to keep all information updated, accurate, and stored securely.

Because of legal and ethical issues surrounding privacy and informed consent, which are a means of maintaining a client's self-determination and dignity, it is critical that counselors always complete the appropriate forms when information is being shared about the client or decisions are being made on their behalf. Foundational to service provision is to first get written informed consent from the client to participate in services. Clients must fully understand the services being offered and agree to participate before treatment begins. Because it is often valuable for counselors to collaborate with other providers

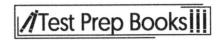

and professionals, it is important to obtain the Consent for Release of Information form before sharing any information with other providers. Clients must also be made fully aware of the reasons for this collaboration and information sharing and be told what information will be shared. Even if the client consents to having information released, the counselor should share only the relevant information with other providers, being careful to still maintain the client's confidentiality and privacy.

In the case of clients who are terminally ill or elderly, counselors play a supportive role in encouraging them to prepare end-of-life forms, such as advanced directives and Do Not Resuscitate orders (DNRs), in conjunction with the appropriate legal and medical authorities. An advance directive is a document that outlines the client's medical treatment wishes in the event that they become unable to make those decisions. Do Not Resuscitate (DNR) is written by the doctor, with the consent of the patient, dictating that if the patient's heart or breathing stop, attempts will not be made to resuscitate. Counselors must empower clients to make decisions that they feel comfortable with and be careful not to impose their own personal biases.

Legal and Ethical Issues Regarding Documentation

Keeping accurate client records has many purposes, such as documenting the history and treatment of a client, getting insurance reimbursement, and providing counselors a historical account of client sessions. The information contained in a client record can also be used to evaluate the effectiveness of services. Client records, when combined with other evaluation tools (e.g., client satisfaction surveys, reactions to treatments, accomplishments of goals), can be an effective method of evaluating treatment progress. Supervisors may review client records to evaluate the effectiveness of the treatment process, counselor performance, and client progress, or to ensure documentation is being completed accurately and on time. When reviewing client records for evaluation, ethical standards must always be upheld.

The NBCC Code of Ethics specifically addresses guidelines for using client information for evaluation, including:

- Protecting confidentiality to the fullest extent possible
- Accurately reporting information
- Protecting clients from harm
- Obtaining required client consent for all uses of their information (e.g., supervisory review, reimbursement)
- Making clients aware that the consent can be withdrawn without punishment

Services and Client Needs

Assessing the Client's Needed Level of Care

Practitioners should work with individuals to identify service needs. The methodology for doing so may include:

- Discussion with the individual and/or support system to determine goals for treatment or collaboration to shape goals

- Prioritizing goals and setting clear, measurable objectives

- Determining what a successful outcome of treatment should look like and how this will enrich the individual's quality of life

- Assessing the individual's strengths and available resources, and highlighting these throughout treatment rather than focusing on challenges; using these strengths to determine how the individual can be self-sufficient and involved in the process

- Ensuring confidentiality across all interactions and documentation

The level of care an individual requires is an important component of the service delivery plan. The practitioner may note the following details:

- Is care medically necessary?

- Can the individual continue to live in their current residence, or is relocation necessary?

- What level of physical support or assistance does the individual need at this time?

- What level of restriction is needed in care? (For example, more restrictive care would include inpatient treatment, while less restrictive care would include day sessions or community group meetings.)

Techniques Used to Evaluate a Client's Progress

Treatment evaluation is a necessary part of direct practice. Counselors should strive to exercise best practice techniques by using evidence-based practice evaluation. It is beneficial for clients to see the progress they have made, while simultaneously providing information to funders and insurance companies that typically require documentation and outcome measures for reimbursement of services. Other benefits include providing indicators that interventions should be modified or that treatment is complete and termination is warranted. Several factors are important in the evaluation of a client's progress, including identifying specific issues to be addressed; creating appropriate goals, objectives, and tasks; using effective and relevant techniques and tools to measure success; and routinely documenting progress.

Client progress may be measured using a quantitative or qualitative approach used in research. Quantitative measures relate to the rate of occurrence or severity of a behavior or problem. When performing quantitative evaluation, first establish a baseline, which is a measurement of the target problem, prior to intervention. Qualitative measures are more subjective and reflective of the client's experience (information is gathered largely from observation and different forms of interviewing) and provide a view of whether progress is being made.

Determining Which Individual, Family, Group, or Combined Modality Meets the Needs of Client Systems

Interventions matched to client problems are based on the biopsychosocial assessment information, empirical data, and research collected by the practitioner during sessions and during practitioner education. The components of the biopsychosocial assessment gather client factors that help guide the practitioner in applying a theoretical model that will work best in designing an intervention to treat the client's presenting issue effectively.

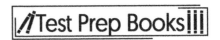

The specific objectives and strategies that will support the selected interventions are outlined in an **intervention or treatment service plan** for the client. The intervention plan for the client should be reviewed at the beginning of treatment, as well as periodically during treatment. This will ensure the goals remain aligned with the client's strengths, needs, progress, and interests. Additionally, at the conclusion of services, the interventions should be reviewed to clarify what was/was not met and whether or not additional interventions are needed.

Determining Which Community or Organizational Approach Meets the Needs of Client Systems

In order to determine which community or organizational approach will most effectively meet the needs of the client system, counselors must first establish what type of client system is involved and what challenges the client system is facing. If the client system consists of an individual or family, then the community intervention may involve connecting clients to resources available in their locality, such as literacy programs or financial assistance. A more macro approach, including program development or social advocacy, is needed for a client system that consists of more than one person or family, such as a community or organization.

Whether helping an individual or organization, the counselor must collect data and look at the resources and strengths of the client system, as well as the stated problems or needs. During this process, the organizational and leadership structure of the client system can be evaluated, as well as communication patterns and expectations. It is also important to explore the cultural and societal issues that are being faced, such as discrimination, poverty, social inequality, and inaccessibility to resources. Cultural awareness and sensitivity, thorough research, and support of client self-determination are all vital aspects of this process. Another aspect to assess is whether the client system needs crisis or long-term intervention. Once this type of assessment is accomplished, it is easier to determine what type of approach will best meet the needs of the client system, whether it involves social policy change, organizational or program development, funding crisis intervention, or connecting clients to the resources in their community.

Due to limited funding and resources and a rapidly growing demand for services, establishing service networks to maximize community resources has become a necessary part of counseling. Counselors and social service agencies frequently create partnerships, collaborations, or networks to bridge gaps in service and provide a comprehensive system of care for clients. These collaborations can be formal with the use of a comprehensive intake process and service or memorandums of agreements between programs. Partnerships can also be informal in which counselors routinely refer clients to specific providers. When establishing new community resources, counselors must first perform a community assessment, which involves examining existing resources, community needs, and demographics.

Limited resources in communities make community member participation in social change movements vital to the success of the community. Mobilizing community members is an important part of creating macro-level change. The community develops a sense of self-determination when it takes an active role in removing barriers, creating needed services and resources and advocating for the rights of its members. Members are encouraged to participate in problem identification, goal setting, and resource mobilization to create change. When community members become engaged in the change process, the overall sense of community empowerment increases. There are some challenges with community participation in which counselors can assist. Community members may lack necessary skills, or there may be barriers created by institutions that operate in the community. Counselors can serve the role of educator to help community members develop needed social organizational skills. The worker may also serve as an advocate to overcome barriers created by larger systems and institutions. Workers must engage a community and mobilize its strengths, resources, and support systems to create positive changes.

Effect of the Client System's Abilities on the Selection of an Intervention

The **ABCs of a problem** refer to the Antecedent, Behavior, and Consequences linked to a client's perceived problem. The discovery of these items allows the client to define the problem specifically and examine factors affecting emotional wellbeing.

Antecedents to a problem may be prefaced by the involvement of certain individuals in the client's life. It is important to gather understanding on how the client was involved with these individuals and how the client felt affected. Environmental antecedents may also be present.

The client may disclose interactions that lead to problematic **behaviors**, based on the aforementioned information in the evaluation of the antecedent. When addressing the behavior, it is important that practitioners gather information on what is said before, during, and after the maladaptive behavior takes place.

The **consequences** to a presenting problem are comprised of both cognitive (internal) and environmental (external) interactions with the behavior. The client and other identified participants linked to the problem will reveal their belief sets and values based on the role played in either sustaining the behavior or attempting to decrease it.

The client's coping skills should be evaluated to determine the type of mechanism they implement when the problem is present and whether or not it is an appropriate coping mechanism for the situation.

If the client presents with a heightened emotional reaction, as a consequence to the problem, it could parlay into another problem and create more complex issues for the client.

At this juncture, the information previously gathered on the client's legal and medical history is beneficial for practitioners to incorporate into the assessment process as it may have a significant impact on the factors shaping the client's problem and the resulting consequences.

Factors Used in Determining Client's Ability to Use Intervention/Treatment

Assessing the client's support systems and strengths can be utilized to hypothesize how the client will respond to treatment. Some of the factors that determine a client's success are listed here:

- Cognitive Skills
  - Rationalization
  - Intellectual capacity and abilities
  - Creativity and innovation
  - Drive and initiative
- Internal Supports/Interpersonal Skills
  - Problem solving
  - Ability to empathize
  - Confidence/sense of self
  - Relationship sustainability
  - Sense of purpose
- Coping Skills

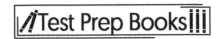

          Ability to multi-task
          Self-regulation
          Ability to navigate uncertainty
          Optimism
          Temperament
- Other Factors
          Income, associated socioeconomic status
          Physical health
          Community involvement
          External supports (church, family, and friends)

Psychopathology

Psychopathology in counseling is the study of mental illness and the contributing psychological, social, or genetic factors. Counselors must understand tenets behind the scientific and medical model for psychopathology in order to provide appropriate diagnoses of mental health disorders and render interventions and treatment accordingly.

Client System's Culture on the Selection of an Intervention

Counselors must be culturally competent to meet the needs of all clients. One way to do this is to have the staff demographics reflective of the community served. Workers must also recognize the differences in individuals of the same culture and not use a cookie-cutter approach to deal with people of the same demographic group. Counselors must also work to create agency policies that encourage culturally sensitive treatment and do not allow discriminatory practices. When choosing interventions, treatment methods, and evaluation techniques, counselors must also consider the appropriateness of the selection for the client's cultural background. According to the NBCC Code of Ethics, counselors must show multicultural competence and should not engage in counseling techniques that may discriminate against groups based on gender, ethnicity, race, national origin, sexual orientation, disability, or religion.

Cultural Awareness in Practice

Attitudes and Beliefs

Counselors need to be culturally aware in their attitudes and beliefs. This requires a keen awareness of their own cultural background and gaining awareness of any personal biases, stereotypes, and values that they hold. Practitioners should also accept different worldviews, be sensitive to differences, and refer minority clients to a practitioner from the client's culture when it would benefit the client.

Knowledge

Practitioners need to have the appropriate knowledge of different cultures. Specifically, practitioners must understand the client's culture and should not jump to conclusions about the client's way of being. Throughout their careers, counselors should be willing to gain a greater depth of knowledge of various cultural groups and update this knowledge as necessary. This includes understanding how issues like racism, sexism, and homophobia can negatively affect minority clients. Practitioners should understand how different therapeutic theories carry values that may be detrimental for some clients. Counselors should also understand how institutional barriers can affect the willingness of minority clients to use mental health services.

Cultural Skills

Counselors should be well versed in **cultural skills**. They must be able to apply interviewing and counseling techniques with clients and should be able to employ specialized skills and interventions that might be effective with specific minority populations. Practitioners need to be able to communicate effectively and understand the verbal and nonverbal language of the client. They also should take a systematic perspective in their practice, work collaboratively with community leaders, and advocate for clients when it's in their best interests.

Evaluation of Practice

Methods of practice evaluation are used to measure the effectiveness of treatment. Evaluation is a crucial part of counseling and improves treatment effectiveness, counselor skill, and overall agency management. Evaluation is often required by agency policy and can be a part of supervision. Some level of documentation and evaluation is also typically necessary for reimbursement. Evaluation of policies, programs, and interventions are outlined in the NBCC Code of Ethics. The code recommends the following:

- Counselors should know responsible evaluation procedures, report findings accurately, and use institutional review boards when appropriate.

- Clients must consent to evaluation and be notified of all uses of the information. Counselors need to ensure that clients know participation is voluntary and there are no penalties for refusal or withdrawal of participation.

- Counselors should ensure client confidentiality to the fullest extent possible and only include the information necessary to perform the evaluation.

When evaluating practice, the use of several types of evaluation tools are more likely to yield desired results. Also, the use of single-subject designs, surveys, scaling, and other tools can be combined to more effectively evaluate treatment. The following are types of evaluation tools:

Goal-Attainment Scaling
Identified problems are reframed as goals to be addressed. The goals are then given weights or ratings of importance by the client and then the outcomes for each goal are determined using scores.

Target Problem Scaling
Helpful when identified problems are difficult to quantify. The client identifies the severity of each target problem and then rates the changes in the problems as treatment progresses. An overall score is determined to evaluate progress toward all identified problems.

Task Achievement Scaling
Tasks related to an established goal are given ratings when completed to evaluate progress toward goal completion.

Surveys
This tool is used to rate and evaluate a client's feelings about services and may measure satisfaction or the impact of interventions on problems such as depression or anxiety.

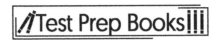

Indicators of Client Readiness for Termination

When clients have made significant progress on the treatment plan, goals, and objectives, the worker can begin planning for termination. Depending on the identified goals and objectives, a standardized assessment can be used to determine how much progress has been made. Counselor practices vary depending on what level of goal attainment should be completed before termination (i.e., some, most, all). Other options can be offered to the client for continued work and learning such as groups, workshops, and reading materials. In many instances, services are terminated due to limitations by insurance or other funding sources. It is extremely important in these circumstances that the worker assists the client in locating additional resources that can be used following service termination. When preparing clients for termination, counselors should discuss the following topics with the client:

- Initial reasons for requesting help
- What skills the client initially lacked that led to initiating services
- Skills developed as a result of treatment and how those new skills will help the client with future challenges
- Ways the client will continue to build on new skills development
- Counselor and client feelings about termination

Professional Communications

Relationship of Diversity and Communication Styles

Many large institutions, such as education facilities or workplaces, have become more diverse in the last twenty to thirty years. Cultural influences dictate how individuals communicate, conduct themselves at work, worship, dress, and develop relationships. Communication styles vary from culture to culture, not only in the words that are used, but also in eye contact, volume, and other nonverbal cues.

Leaders in the areas of education, politics, and economics need to understand these differences and be open and willing to learn how to address them. Persons in positions of authority must increase their understanding of cultural differences in order to better serve those from different backgrounds. Other professions in which an understanding of diverse forms of communication is mandatory include law enforcement, medicine, counseling, and those employed by government agencies, such as Child Protective Services. Being educated on diverse populations is crucial to increase understanding and avoid discrimination. While education can be helpful in learning to communicate effectively, it is also important to ask questions and clarify anything that may be confusing when communicating with someone from another culture. Counselors also should be aware and observant when communicating with a client to make sure that communication on both sides is fully understood.

Counselors should have basic understanding of the ways in which communication norms can vary across cultures. Counselors should exhibit cultural competence with regard to communication as demonstrated by the following:

- Their awareness of both nonverbal and verbal communication differences
- Their ability to use language that is appropriate and respectful to different cultures
- Their recognition of personal strengths and limitations in communication
- Their willingness to actively remove barriers that may inhibit effective communication with individuals from different cultures

Nonverbal communication can be a common source of misunderstanding in cross-cultural communication. Different cultures place different emphasis on these aspects of nonverbal communication:

- Levels of appropriate assertiveness
- Use of facial expressions and physical gestures
- Appropriateness of physical touch in communication
- Personal space and seating arrangements

There are cultural differences with regard to conflict as well:

- In the U.S., participants in a conflict are typically encouraged to resolve the conflict directly.
- In other cultures, conflict is viewed as an embarrassment that should be dealt with as privately and quietly as possible.

Disclosure of personal information and openness with regard to feelings are uncomfortable in some cultures, and it may be considered inappropriate to ask direct questions with regard to these topics.

Decision-making styles also vary across cultures:

- Delegating vs. making decisions
- Majority rule vs. consensus

Use of Verbal and Nonverbal Communication Techniques

Counselors use verbal and nonverbal communication techniques to engage clients in completing treatment goals. Verbal communication is vital to the counselor/client relationship, and counselors should be skilled at greetings, summarization, reflection, and the conveyance of new information to the client. The client may misconstrue a counselor's body language if it does not represent openness and trust. Likewise, the counselor needs to be adept at analyzing the client's body language in order to move forward. Clients use both verbal and nonverbal communication to convey their story to the counselor, and communication techniques used by the counselor can be modeled to teach the client improved communication. Clients should be instructed to recognize their own communication techniques in the context of the relationship with the counselor. Clients who are withdrawn or isolated may need especially sensitive communication with the counselor in order to better communicate verbally and nonverbally.

Identifying the Underlying Meaning of Communication

Clients use both verbal and nonverbal communication during treatment. Counselors must develop the ability to interpret communication congruency or develop the ability to assess both types of expressions simultaneously to understand client messaging accurately. Clients may use facial expressions, gesturing, eye contact, tone of voice, or other ways to express feelings nonverbally. Counselors must notice whether the nonverbal communication reinforces or conflicts with verbal messaging.

Use of Active Listening and Observation

Use of Active Listening Skills
Active listening is crucial to the relationship- and rapport-building stage with clients. Counselors must be fully engaged in the listening process and not distracted by thoughts of what will come next or

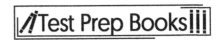

intervention planning. The worker must not only hear the audible language the client is offering but must also look at the nonverbal behaviors and the underlying meaning in the words and expressions of the client. Nonverbal behaviors include body language, facial expressions, voice quality, and physical reactions of the client. Other aspects of active listening include head nodding, eye contact, and using phrases of understanding and clarity such as, "What I hear you saying is . . . " or "You (may) wish to . . ." Workers may verify they understand the client's message by paraphrasing and asking for validation that it is correct (i.e., "What I hear you saying is . . .").

Use of Observation

Basic/Informal Observation

In order to complete a holistic client assessment, it is important that practitioners utilize observation to pick up on the nonverbal cues or surrounding environmental aspects. When meeting with a client outside of an office setting, the counselor should observe the condition and location of the client's home and/or work environment when possible.

Additionally, the client's physical characteristics should be observed, which includes some of the aforementioned nonverbal cues of posture, dress, and hygiene, in addition to identifying characteristics such as ethnicity and gender. After meeting with a client, the counselor should take some time to recall the interaction and document identifying information of items observed from the communication.

Observation of Behaviors

It may be necessary for a counselor to observe the client's behaviors, rather than solely relying on verbal reports. This is especially true when working with minors who have social and/or behavioral issues as their presenting problem, as well as adults with mental health diagnoses who are unable to contribute competently and verbally to their assessment and report.

A client may be observed in a common setting, such as a school environment or home, to allow the counselor to get a better understanding of how the client functions in a natural environment. The practitioner may casually observe how the client functions or may prompt those in the client's personal system to engage in known antecedents. This is done to trigger a particular behavior to gather more information on the client's response. Purposely targeting a behavior to occur in a pre-determined setting (home or office) is known as a **controlled observation**.

In addition to the controlled observation, there are other **formal observation** methods available, wherein specific data is collected on the client in a pre-determined setting. The data must be measurable and is generally used to identify behavioral patterns.

For example, a counselor may note the number of times a self-injurious behavior (like banging of the head) occurs within a setting, while writing down the events that occurred before the behavior (antecedent) and what took place afterwards (consequence). Observing the antecedents, behaviors, and consequences is known as a **functional analysis**.

Interviewing Techniques

Communication Techniques

There are several communication techniques beneficial to the counseling other than the basic interview process used to gather general demographic and presenting problem information. Here are several:

Furthering

A technique that reinforces the idea that the worker is listening to the client and encourages further information to be gathered. This technique includes nodding of the head, facial expressions, or encouragement responses such as "yes" or "I understand." It also includes accent responses, whereby counselors repeat or parrot back a few words of a client's last response.

Close/Open-Ended Questions

Depending on the timing or information the worker is seeking to elicit from the client, one of these types of questions may be used. Close-ended questions, such as "How old are you?" will typically elicit a short answer. Conversely, open-ended questions, such as "What are your feelings about school?" allow for longer, more-involved responses.

Clarifying and Paraphrasing

This is when counselors ask a client for clarification to ensure they understand the client's message. Clarifying also includes encouraging clients to speak more concretely and in less abstract terms to provide clearer messages. When paraphrasing, counselors should convey a message back to the client to ensure an understanding of the client's meaning.

Summarizing

This is similar to paraphrasing, but summarizing includes more information. It's frequently used to help focus the session and allow the worker to summarize the overall messages, problems, or goals of the client.

Active Listening

Using facial expressions, body language, and postures to show the worker is engaged and listening to the client. Workers should display eye contact and natural but engaged body movements and gestures. An example would be sitting slightly forward with a non-rigid posture. As with all communication techniques, counselors should be aware of cultural differences in what is appropriate, especially related to direct eye contact and posturing.

Methods of Summarizing Communication

Counselors may paraphrase and echo clients' verbal statements to acknowledge their feelings. Summarizing may involve reflecting back the statements made by the client to clarify what the client has said. Counselors also must summarize communication in order to provide sufficient records of the session. Further, during the end of the session, the counselor may wish to clarify goals and homework assigned for the next week so that the client is clear on the changes that need to take place.

Methods of Facilitating Communication

Counselors may facilitate communication with the client by verbally encouraging communication or by addressing the client with constructive information concerning the case. Counselors need to recall information concerning the client from session to session in order to facilitate communication and move forward with the client. Clarifying the client's feelings and statements helps to ensure the counselor understands what is being communicated as well as lets the client know that the counselor is engaged and actively listening. Development of trust with the client may facilitate additional communication, and counselors should be sensitive to the trust-building process because it is the cornerstone of the helping relationship. Counselors may provide clients with homework outside of a session that facilitates communication during the next session.

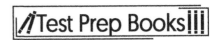

Mandated clients, including court-ordered clients or clients ordered to counseling from child protective services, may face challenges in communicating with the counselor because they do not choose to be in treatment. Developing trust with these clients to facilitate communication is especially important for progress to be made. It's helpful to acknowledge the client's feelings and possible frustration about the mandated treatment. Clients who require out-of-home placement need clear communication with the counselor to clarify what is happening and make appropriate psychological adjustments to their circumstances.

Eliciting Sensitive Information

Interviews are a critical component of counseling wherein clients provide verbal reports, accounts, or narratives that serve as the main source of information and data collected during the assessment process.

The basis of the interview is a verbal report that involves introductions between the practitioner and client. In some practice settings, the verbal report may be supplemented by an **information sheet** that provides client demographics and a brief overview of the **presenting problem**. Presenting problems are prevailing circumstances, symptoms, or difficulties that the client believes is a problem requiring psychotherapeutic assistance.

Principle: Practitioners Need to Establish Rapport with the Client

Providing a description of the services provided and what the client can expect during sessions is the practitioner's first opportunity to build rapport with the client. Rapport development impacts the thoroughness of the information provided from the client. If the level of rapport is limited, the client may not feel comfortable enough to provide sufficient information. The level of rapport also affects the type of impression the client wishes to make on the practitioner. Consequently, it is linked to the client's perception of self-awareness. Some key points to remember are as follows:

- The counselor's own personal characteristics (gender, race, age, etc.) may affect the level of client interaction, based on the client's cultural background.

- Clients may adjust their responses to questions based on how they perceive the counselor's characteristics.

- The counselor's demographics may also have an impact on how the client feels about disclosing sensitive information, such as domestic violence, sexual conduct, or child abuse.

Principle: The Basics of Social Work Practice Should be Used When an Interview is Conducted

Once the introductions have been made and an overview of services and interview processes provided, the client should be asked to explain why they came in for treatment.

Empowering clients to share their concerns and emphasizing the point of hearing things from their perspective provides the practitioner with an opportunity to gauge a client and start "where the client is" in the initial phases of the assessment process.

Technique
The use of encouraging, neutral phrases will help move the conversation forward and encourage the client to share, e.g., "What brings you in to see me today?"

While being encouraging to the client, it is important that practitioners are genuine and not phony. Practitioners should avoid overly complimentary statements, such as "I'm so glad you came in today!" If the client senses the interest is insincere, they may not wish to share.

Principle: The Practitioner Should Start Where the Client is.

After engaging the client, they should be allowed to open up, "vent," or speak freely for approximately fifteen minutes.

Technique

While the client is delving into any emotions, the practitioner should utilize active listening to keep the client engaged. Additionally, it is important to observe the client's **nonverbal cues** (posture, gestures, voice tone and pitch, and facial expressions) that lend to the emotional state. Once the client shares primary concerns, the practitioner can focus on what is important to the client.

The practitioner should observe the client's emotional state, allowing them to feel those emotions freely while providing the account of the problem. Demonstrating empathy is important when responding to the client's emotions. The emotion observed should be acknowledged. For example, if a client is crying, the practitioner can state, "You seem saddened about this," to demonstrate empathy. This practice can also hone in on an important area of the client's life that may be addressed later.

Once the client has been allowed to speak freely, the practitioner should utilize exploratory interviewing skills to delve into the specifics of topics that seemed particularly troubling for the client during the disclosure of the presenting problem.

After the client has revealed the presenting problem and the emotional state has been observed, the client should be asked to delve further into details about current life circumstances. This will provide an opportunity for the practitioner to gain additional information related to the context of the client's problem. It also allows the practitioner to uncover particularly troubling areas that can be explored later. Moreover, it may reveal certain boundaries for the client who is unwilling or unready to discuss certain details of their life.

Principle: It is Important to Engage the Client Verbally While Simultaneously Observing Nonverbal Cues

The practitioner should ask questions to provide clarification and deeper insight into the client's problems and level of functioning.

Question Techniques

Open-ended questions may provide more detail and allow the client to expand into other areas that can be explored later.

Closed-ended questions are ideal for fact-finding from a client.

Clarification questions should be asked whenever necessary. This may be done through active listening and reflective sharing on the counselor's part, to foster comprehensive communication and further build rapport.

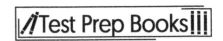

Note Taking Techniques
If the client has questions as to why notes are taken, the reasoning behind it should be explained, and a copy should be offered to the client to make them feel more comfortable and involved in the interview process.

Observation of client behaviors during the interview may be indicative of how the client behaves or reacts in settings outside of the session. Conversely, clients may act outside of their norm, due to the perceived pressure from the interview process. The aforementioned questions and nonverbal observations are essential to determine factors of the client's personality and the context of presenting issues.

Practitioners should also be aware that their interactions affect client behaviors and responses during the interview process. For example, the client may mimic rigid body language (folded arms, crossed legs, minimal eye contact) from the practitioner and become defensive in speech pattern, pitch, or tone.

Interviewing Clients with Communication Barriers

Sometimes there will be communication difficulties between the counselor and client, most notably with language or cultural differences that hinder straightforward communication. It is ethically imperative that all clients have access to adequate language assistance, including the option of a translator, so that those with limited English proficiency are still receiving the same level of care. The optimal situation is for clients to have a counselor who can speak to them directly in their first language, and this should be arranged whenever possible. However, this is not always feasible, and then a translator must be used. In cases where interpreters are necessary or are requested by the client, they should be professional and trained interpreters, rather than family members or non-professionals. They must also understand and agree to the rules of privacy and confidentiality. Counselors should make sure their communication is simple and easy to understand, and make sure to clarify what the client is saying if there is any confusion. Counselors should also familiarize themselves with the cultural backgrounds of the clients they work with to better understand their unique perspective and to minimize misunderstandings.

Using Bias-Free Language in Interviewing

When interviewing a client, a counselor must be careful to eliminate all personal bias from their language. This relates to all subtle negative phrasing related to race, ethnicity, socioeconomic status, gender, gender identity, life choices, disability, or psychological disorders. The job of the counselor is to support the client without bias, always promoting the client's self-identity. Phrases or expressions that demean or stereotype a particular group of people should never be used. Similarly, labeling someone can be hurtful, especially in cases where that label has a negative connotation or stigma attached to it. Sometimes it may even be appropriate for the counselor to ask the client how they wish to be identified or addressed. Inclusive and affirming language should be used when talking about all groups of people, and especially when talking to or about the client. Terms that are known to be offensive or degrading should always be avoided.

Responding to Clients' Resistant Behaviors

Clients may show resistance to treatment or to the counselor for a variety of reasons, including personality, misdirected anger, confusion, self-protection, fear, or anxiety. Many times clients show resistance when they have been required by a court or social services to cooperate with a counselor or have been pressurized in some other way to participate in services. Before making judgments about a client's resistance, it is important for the counselor to first try to understand them through active and empathetic listening. Before clients will listen to counselors, they need to be reassured that they have been fully heard. Counselors should acknowledge and validate the client's concerns. A relationship of trust needs to be built, which can be a slower process when clients begin with resistant behaviors, but this is the only way to ultimately overcome that resistance. No matter how skilled a counselor is, if there is resistance and a lack of trust in the relationship, then progress will be limited. Client engagement in services is vital, and it is only when the counselor helps empower the client to identify and work toward their own solutions that there will be real success. The goal is for the client and counselor to be on the same team, collaborating together to work towards the client's desired goals.

Methods to Obtain/Provide Feedback

There are several ways counselors can receive feedback. It can come in the form of evaluation by another counselor during supervision, or from a client during treatment. Obtaining feedback is an important means to improve a counselor's skill and ensure effective treatment for clients. Feedback from clients may be formal or informal. Clients may offer unsolicited feedback verbally or nonverbally during treatment, using words, body language, or tone of voice. Counselors must be sensitive to the messages clients are expressing to decipher how to interpret feedback that may not be clear.

When seeking feedback from a client, the counselor should ensure the method is appropriate to the skills, resources, and abilities of the client (i.e., in writing, by mail, text, in person, etc.)

Factors to consider when obtaining feedback from clients:

- Counselors may consider a client's progress toward a goal or lack thereof as a type of feedback. If treatment is not progressing as expected, the worker should evaluate and make adjustments as necessary.

- Always be clear why the information is needed and ensure client confidentiality to the fullest extent possible.

- Feedback can be sought at different times throughout the treatment process to ensure reliability and consistency.

- Workers should seek feedback regardless of whether it is expected to be negative or positive. All feedback should be viewed as a learning tool to enhance treatment and worker skill.

Factors to consider when receiving feedback during supervision/consultation:

- Counselors can benefit from feedback during supervision or consultation, especially with difficult clients/cases or at significant times in treatment, such as termination.

- When discussing cases, client confidentiality should be protected as much as possible, and client consent to release information should be acquired.

Obtaining Services

Considerations When Providing Counseling Services

Adults with Disabilities

Individuals with disabilities have additional challenges in the career planning process. Disabilities include physical limitations, learning disabilities, cognitive impairment, mental health issues, as well as veterans in the Wounded Warrior class. Fortunately, there are many resources available, including the Americans with Disabilities Act, the Job Accommodation Network (JAN), the Department of Labor Disability Employment Policy (ODEP), and many other national and community programs. Counselors can help clients to understand their legal rights and to learn how to educate employers about options during the application and interview process. Many employers can (and are required by law to) offer accommodations to assist with employment opportunity. In addition, most areas have service organizations that assist with career planning and can even offer on-the-job coaching.

Sexual Orientation

In recent years, there's been increased awareness and sensitivity to lesbian, gay, bisexual, and transgender (LGBT) individuals. However, like any minority group, they can be subject to discrimination and bias. For counselors, it's essential to be aware of LGBT issues in career development. Discrimination can occur in the interview process and on the job, and many states and countries don't provide legal protection to LGBT employees. An increasing number of employers value diversity in their workforce, and an April 2013 study shows that 88% of Fortune 500 companies enforce non-discrimination policies. Counselors working with LGBT individuals can utilize several strategies to increase the effectiveness of counseling. Making clients feel safe by demonstrating an understanding of LGBT culture is important, as well as avoiding stereotyping. Counselors should consult with other professionals as needed, use current resources on LGBT society, and refer out when necessary. Lastly, counselors should engage in open discussions about LGBT issues and help each client develop career goals unique to their personal situation.

Providing Case Management Services

Clients frequently experience difficulty navigating everyday life problems and systems. One of the roles of a counselor is to help link clients with needed services and resources. To perform this role effectively, counselors must have a thorough knowledge of available local resources to aid the client.

When acting in the case manager role, counselors help clients define, locate, and access needed services and resources. Additionally, counselors must often interact with other professionals, including external resources to ensure the client's needs are met. In the case management role, counselors also make referrals directing the client to the appropriate resource for needed services. The worker acts as a manager, following up with the client on a regular basis to ensure the client is following through with their case plan. Workers may also serve as an advocate in this role, working on behalf of the client if any barriers to resources are met.

Process of case management:

- Assessing needs and client engagement
- Creating an intervention plan of care that includes goals, needed services, and timelines
- Administering the plan

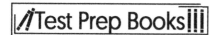

- Monitoring progress and reassessing the plan at fixed intervals
- Termination of services
- Evaluation and follow-up

Referring Client Systems for Services

Clients frequently need services or resources from multiple agencies. When there is a lack of careful coordination and follow-up, this can be a barrier to the client receiving care. Service coordination reduces the chances of service duplication, gaps in service provisioning, and clients dropping out of care. Furthermore, it improves the likelihood of client success.

Types of Coordination

Case management: Type of coordination in which the worker helps link the clients to services and manages client care throughout the process

Wraparound services: Type of inter-organizational collaboration where agencies form shared goals for client(s), but services remain separate

Service integration: Method of coordination where different types of services are provided simultaneously

Determining the Client's Eligibility for Services

A client's eligibility for services depends on the type of services desired. Many times, client eligibility involves proof of financial need. This is particularly true when attempting to obtain governmental financial assistance, or free psychological, psychiatric, or medical services. The counselor can play a significant role in helping the client to navigate websites, fill out necessary forms, and gather the appropriate documentation to prove eligibility for services. The process of determining service eligibility can be confusing and overwhelming for clients, and they may need the assistance of counselors in completing the process.

Diagnostic and Statistical Manual of Mental Disorders (DSM-5)

Neurodevelopmental Disorders

Intellectual Disability/Development Disorder

Intellectual disabilities are described in the DSM-5 as neurodevelopmental disorders starting in childhood and are characterized by intellectual difficulties as well as in several other domains of life, which include conceptual, social, and practical areas. The conceptual domain includes reasoning, memory, knowledge, and language skills. The social domain describes empathy, social judgment, and overall interpersonal skills. The practical domain focuses on areas such as personal self-care, professional responsibilities, and money management skills.

The DSM-5 diagnosis emphasizes the need to meet three criteria:

- Deficits in intellectual functioning that are confirmed by clinical evaluation and standard IQ tests
- Deficits in adaptive functioning that preclude the ability to conform to the standards necessary for independent functioning
- The onset of these deficits in childhood

The fifth edition of the DSM allows for a more comprehensive overview of the individual than the fourth. Intellectual developmental disorder replaces mental retardation in previous editions of the manuals. The substantial changes address the name of the disorder, how it impacts one's overall level of functioning, and improvements to diagnostic criteria to foster more comprehensive patient evaluation. In the DSM-5, all mental disorders will be on a single axis and allotted equal importance.

Communication Disorders

Diagnostic categories in the DSM-5 for **communication disorders** include the following:

- Language disorder
- Speech sound disorder
- Childhood-onset fluency disorder (or stuttering)
- Social (pragmatic) communication disorder
- Unspecified communication disorder

The diagnostic criteria for **language disorder** include an ongoing difficulty and deficit in language acquisition and production, whether written or spoken. Language abilities are also substantially lower than expected for one's age. The diagnostic criteria for **speech sound disorder** includes consistent trouble with sound production and a difficulty in verbally communicating coherent, intelligent speech. The diagnostic criterion for **childhood-onset fluency disorder** (or stuttering) include disruptions in fluent and temporal speech patterns, and the interferences are caused by an initial fear of communicating with others. The diagnostic criteria for **social (pragmatic) communication disorder (SCD)** include ongoing troubles with verbal and nonverbal communication such as deficits in interpersonal interactions, a mismatch between a conversation and the context in which it occurs, difficulties in following the rules of interpersonal discussions, and difficulties understanding direct yet abstract use of language. However, autism spectrum disorder is considered exclusionary criteria for this disorder. **Unspecified communication disorder** has no specific description, since symptoms do not meet criteria for any of the other listed disorders; however, this diagnosis is applied when the presence of a communication disorder is suspected.

Autism Spectrum Disorders

Individuals diagnosed with autism spectrum disorder (ASD) typically have communication deficits. They are sometimes unable to respond appropriately in conversations, misread nonverbal interactions, have difficulty developing age-appropriate friendships, are extremely dependent upon routines, are unusually sensitive to environmental changes, or are deeply focused on particular items. People previously diagnosed with a well-documented DSM-IV diagnosis of autistic disorder, Asperger's disorder, or pervasive developmental disorder not otherwise specified, should be included under the umbrella diagnosis of autism spectrum disorder. Those who have clear and obvious interpersonal communication deficits, but with symptoms not meeting the criteria for autism spectrum disorder, should be further evaluated for social communication disorder.

Attention-Deficit/Hyperactivity Disorder

Attention-deficit/hyperactivity disorder (ADHD) describes a continual pattern of inattention and hyperactivity that disrupts a person's functioning and overall growth and development. The criteria for ADHD consists of six or more symptoms related to inattention and hyperactivity up until age sixteen, or five or more for those up to age seventeen, that are present for upwards of six months and are inappropriate for one's level of development. The symptoms for inattention consist of not paying close attention to detail, difficulty holding attention for a task, not following through on instructions, trouble organizing, reluctance to putting in mental effort on long-term tasks, losing things often, getting easily distracted, and being forgetful. For impulsivity, the symptoms consist of fidgeting, trouble sitting still, restlessness, struggling to stay quiet, always on the go, excessive talking, answering incomplete questions, difficulty waiting their turn, and often intruding on others. In addition to this criteria, other conditions that must be met include several inattentive and hyperactive symptoms occurring before the age of twelve and in two or more settings. The symptoms interfere with daily functioning and the symptoms aren't better explained by another psychiatric disorder.

Three types of presentations can occur with ADHD, which consist of combined presentation, predominantly inattentive presentation, and predominantly hyperactive-impulsive presentation. **Combined presentation** is provided in the event that enough symptoms of criteria related to both inattention and hyperactivity-impulsivity have occurred in the past six months. **Predominantly inattentive presentation** is provided if enough symptoms related to inattention occurred over the past six months, but hyperactivity-impulsivity symptoms were not present. **Predominantly hyperactive-impulsive presentation** is provided if symptoms of hyperactivity-impulsivity occurred over six months, but symptoms of inattention were not present. A difference between ADHD in the DSM-IV and the DSM-5 is that in the former diagnostic manual, the age of onset was originally at the age of seven, not twelve.

Specific Learning Disorder

A **specific learning disorder (SLD)** is described as a neurodevelopmental disorder that interferes with a person's capacity to learn or use specific skills such as reading, writing, or arithmetic. These skills are regarded as the foundation for academic learning as a whole. SLD isn't synonymous with learning disability as defined by the educational system; however, those with a DSM-5 diagnosis of SLD would be required to also meet the criteria for learning disability set by the educational system.

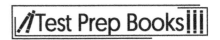

The DSM-5 diagnostic criteria for SLD include one category of SLD with *specifiers* to illustrate the specific displays of learning difficulties during an evaluation within the three aforementioned major academic domains, and the exclusion of the IQ-achievement discrepancy requirement, which is replaced with four criteria that must be met. **Criterion A** describes that at least one of six symptoms related to learning difficulties have continued for upwards of six months despite receiving additional assistance. **Criterion B** describes the measurement of the affected academic skills being significantly lower than those expected for age five and result in a dysfunction in academic, professional, or daily activities. **Criterion C** describes the age of onset when the problems started occurring, usually during school years or adulthood in some cases, and **Criterion D** specifies which other psychiatric or neurological disorders must be ruled out before a diagnosis of SLD can be substantiated and rendered.

Motor Disorders

In the DSM-5, **motor disorders** refer to a nervous system disorder resulting in abnormal or involuntary movements. These disorders include developmental coordination disorder, stereotypic movement disorder, and tic disorder. **Developmental coordination disorder** (or dyspraxia) is a long-term neurological disorder starting in childhood that affects planning of bodily movement and coordination due to brain messages not being accurately transmitted to the body. Impairments in skilled motor movements per a child's chronological age interfere with activities of daily living. The diagnostic criteria for dyspraxia consist of below average coordinated motor skills, persistent interference in daily activities, onset of symptoms in early development, and motor skill deficits that aren't better explained by an intellectual disability. **Stereotypic movement disorder** describes motor behavior that is often repetitive and purposeless, such as hitting, rocking, and shaking oneself. The age of onset is early development. **Tic disorder** describes rapid, sudden, and nonrhythmic movements. The DSM-5 classifies Tourette syndrome and tic disorders as motor disorders under the neurodevelopmental disorder category.

Schizophrenia Spectrum and Other Psychotic Disorders

Schizophrenia is a severe and long-term mental illness typified by symptoms involving disturbances in behavior, perception, and thought that are adversely affecting social or occupational functioning. The DSM-5 outlines five key features of psychotic disorders, which includes delusions, hallucinations, disorganized speech, disorganized or catatonic behavior, and negative symptoms. In the DSM-IV, two out of these five symptoms were required to render a diagnosis, though clinicians only required one of five symptoms if an individual suffered from bizarre delusions, if hallucinations entailed a running description of their thoughts or behavior, and/or auditory hallucinations involved two or more voices. However, due to poor reliability and in general being too broad, this exception was removed. In the current edition of the DSM, diagnosis only requires two of these five symptoms, with at least one symptom being one of the first three criteria. But the most significant change to this diagnostic category is removing subtypes (catatonic, disorganized, paranoid, residual, and undifferentiated). The reasons for doing this have to do with these subtypes not being considered stable conditions, not having any real clinical usefulness, and not having any scientific validity or reliability. However, a catatonic specifier is included and may be used with other psychotic disorders. Catatonia can occur across several diagnostic categories without necessarily indicating psychosis. With **schizoaffective disorder**, which creates a connection between mood and psychosis, any mood episode persists throughout the majority of the illness. This change was to help improve the reliability, stability, and validity of the disorder. For **delusional disorder**, the requirement that delusions only be non-bizarre has been eliminated, while a 'bizarre-type' delusion specifier is present. However, shared delusional disorder no longer remains a separate disorder, for it simply exists under the umbrella term of delusional disorder.

Bipolar and Related Disorders

Bipolar and related disorders are distinct categories that include the following:

- Bipolar I
- Bipolar II,
- Cyclothymic disorder
- Substance/medication induced bipolar and related disorder
- Bipolar and related disorder due to another medical condition
- Other specified bipolar and related disorder
- Unspecified bipolar and related disorder

For **bipolar I disorder**, criteria include the following:

- Requirement of at least one manic episode
- Psychotic episodes
- The occurrence of mania or a major depressive episode cannot be accounted for by the existence of another psychiatric disorder.

Mania is characterized as an unusually high level of arousal and overall energy, including changes in mood or emotion. For example, someone with bipolar disorder might suddenly leave their job or undertake risky behaviors that bring about momentary feelings of pleasure, such as having sex with multiple partners.

In **bipolar II disorder**, the criteria include the following:

- Occurrence of at least one hypomanic episode
- Occurrence of at least one depressive episode

Hypomania describes a consistent mood elevation with atypical behavior that occurs when depression is absent. For example, someone makes inappropriate sexual advances or spends more money than usual. Also, with bipolar II disorder, the client must never have experienced mania, the symptoms cannot be accounted for by the presence of another psychiatric disorder, and depressive symptoms, as well as those of unpredictable behavior, resulting in a frequent shift between hypomania and depression cause clinically significant distress or functional impairment.

With **cyclothymic disorder**, the criteria include the following:

- Existence of hypomania that does not meet all criteria for hypomanic episodes
- Depression that does not meet all the criteria for depressive episodes for anywhere between one to two years
- Hypomania and depression have each been present for roughly half the time
- The criteria for depression, mania, or hypomania has never been met

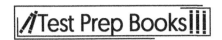

Further, symptoms aren't better accounted for by the existence of other psychiatric disorders, aren't the result of substance abuse or another medical condition, and cause clinically significant distress and functional impairment.

For **substance/medication induced bipolar and related disorder**, criteria include the following:

- Ongoing mood disturbance and instances of elevated mood with or without depression
- Anhedonia (lack of pleasure)
- Occurs as a result of exposure to substances or medication
- Symptoms aren't the result of another psychiatric disorder and are causing clinically significant distress, as well as functional impairment.

With **bipolar and related disorder due to another medical condition**, which has been changed from general medical condition, the diagnostic criteria consist of the following:

- Causing clinically significant distress and functional impairment
- Warrants hospitalization
- The presence of psychotic features

By adding both **other specified bipolar and related disorder** and **unspecified bipolar and related disorder**, the DSM-5 has removed the diagnosis of mood disorder not otherwise specified. Either of these diagnoses are suggested when bipolar symptoms cause clinically significant distress or functional impairment, but do not meet criteria for any of the other diagnostic categories.

Depressive Disorders

Disruptive Mood Dysregulation Disorder

Disruptive mood dysregulation disorder (DMDD) is a relatively recent addition to the DSM. DMDD describes a disorder occurring in early childhood that consists of frequent anger or irritability. Symptoms of DMDD include frequent aggressive outbursts combined with an angry or irritable mood on days without any such aggressive behaviors. These eruptions tend to happen approximately three times per week and at two different settings, such as at school and in the home, and the majority of people in the affected child's life will notice this behavior. The age of onset for DMDD is prior to age ten, specifically between ages six to eight. The tantrums must be inappropriate to their age of development and persist for at least one year before a diagnosis of DMDD can be rendered. DMDD is common to other disorders such as bipolar disorder and conduct disorder, and comorbidity is fairly common. For instance, children with DMDD tend to also meet criteria for disorders related to attention, behavior, and emotion. Children diagnosed with DMDD are also at an increased risk of developing self-harm and suicidal behaviors. Thus, DMDD is typically common with children already being treated for a psychiatric disorder, although the prevalence is usually lower among the general population.

Premenstrual Dysphoric Disorder

Premenstrual dysphoric disorder (PMDD) is an extreme and debilitating form of premenstrual syndrome. While the symptoms of PMDD can be emotional or physical, mood symptoms must be present in order for a diagnosis of PMDD to be rendered. Anxiety and mood disorders are common in those suffering from PMDD. Criteria for PMDD consists of the following:

- Mood swings
- Irritability

- Depressed mood
- Anxiety
- Decreased interests
- Trouble focusing
- Lethargy
- Changes in appetite
- Sleep difficulties
- Feeling overwhelmed
- Tenderness
- Pain
- Bloating sensation
- Anger
- Feeling hopeless
- Self-deprecating thoughts
- Tension
- Increased social conflicts
- General fatigue

These symptoms must interfere with daily functioning and cause clinically significant distress and are not the result of other preexisting issues such as anxiety, depressive disorders, substance abuse, or a medical condition. When pregnant, women diagnosed with PMDD tend to notice their symptoms disappear; however, after pregnancy, PMDD symptoms can be exacerbated. Suicidal thoughts are also fairly common in women suffering from PMDD. Not unlike premenstrual syndrome, PMDD tends to follow a predictable, cyclical pattern. And while a higher rate of postpartum depression is expected among those with PMDD, research shows that women with PMDD did not have a higher occurrence of it than control groups.

Persistent Depressive Disorder

Formerly known as dysthymic disorder, **persistent depressive disorder (PDD)** describes a depressed mood that occurs most of the time, on more days than not, and has been occurring for upward of two years, as suggested by either one's own personal account or via the observation of others. During this two-year disturbance, the affected individual has never been without symptoms for more than sixty days at a time. Symptoms include the following:

- Poor appetite or overeating
- Poor focus or decision-making abilities
- Feelings of hopelessness
- Low self-esteem
- Low energy or fatigue
- Insomnia or hypersomnia

The depressed client must have two or more of these symptoms before a diagnosis of PDD can be rendered. Also, to be diagnosed with PDD, the client must never have met the criteria for mania, hypomania, a mixed episode, or cyclothymia; and the symptoms are not better accounted for by psychotic disorder and are known to cause clinically significant distress or functional impairment. This disturbance in mood must also not be the direct physiological effects of a substance or medication, or a general medical condition. And if criteria for major depressive disorder is present for two years, clients can be given comorbid diagnoses of both PDD and major depressive disorder.

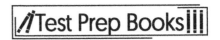

Anxiety Disorders

Specific Phobia

Specific phobia describes a pervasive fear of a certain stimulus and typically occurs in the presence of an object or situation. Common examples of feared stimuli are animals, heights, flying, seeing blood, or receiving an injection. Individuals almost always express a pronounced fear or anxiety in response to the stimuli. Additionally, the fear or anxiety is considered within the context in which it occurs. If the fear does not align with any actual threat caused by the stimuli, then it can be considered a specific phobia. The feared object or stimuli is consistently avoided by the individual or endured with intense discomfort and fear. The anxiety, fear, or avoidance of the stimuli creates significant clinical distress within the individual or severe impairment in areas of functioning. The fear is persistent, lasting at least six months or more to be considered a clinical diagnosis. In order to diagnose a specific phobia, the anxiety caused by the stimuli cannot be better explained by the symptoms of another disorder such as panic disorder, obsessive-compulsive disorder, post-traumatic stress disorder, separation anxiety disorder, or social anxiety disorder. Specific phobias can be classified by the type of the phobic object: animal, natural environment, blood/injection/injury, situational, or other (for unspecified specific phobias).

Previously, the DSM-IV required that individuals with specific phobia had to be able to recognize the irrationality of the anxiety and it must endure for at least six months if the individual is under the age of eighteen.

Social Anxiety Disorder

Social anxiety disorder (SAD) is characterized as an intense fear or anxiety when in a situation that involves being observed by others. Examples of these situations may include social gatherings, public speaking, or even having a conversation with somebody. For children, the anxiety must also be presented when engaging with peers and not just adults. These social situations do not put the individual at risk in any way other than significant emotional distress. As a result, individuals may consistently avoid these types of instances or endure them with severe anxiety. The fear or anxiety disrupts the individual's daily functioning in a significant way as well as social life. To be confirmed as a diagnosis, the anxiety must last for at least six months, cannot be induced by a substance, and cannot be explained by a symptom of a different mental disorder (panic disorder, agoraphobia, body dysmorphic disorder, etc.). SAD may also be specified as performance only social anxiety disorder, meaning that the anxiety is only present in public interactions.

Separation anxiety disorder

Separation anxiety disorder presents itself as excessive fear or anxiety when an individual is separated from their attachment figures (e.g., parents and close relatives). This anxiety is not developmentally appropriate for the individual's age. The anxiety about the separation can manifest in a variety of ways, all of which are representative of impairment in functioning and of clinical significance. People diagnosed with separation anxiety disorder may experience intense distress when anticipating separation from their attachment figures, excessively worry about losing the attachment figures, or even worry about the possibility of an event that would cause the separation. Additionally, individuals with this disorder may avoid leaving their attachment figures and refuse to leave home or go to school. When these individuals are left at home, they may also have excessive fear about being alone. Sleep patterns may also be disrupted in these individuals, as the time spent away from attachment figures can occupy their minds. Nightmares and physical symptoms of illness, like headaches, may occur when separation occurs or is anticipated. For children, the anxiety needs to persist for at least four weeks for a diagnosis to be rendered. In adults, the anxiety must persist for six months or more.

Selective Mutism

Children diagnosed with **selective mutism** exhibit failure to speak in specific situations. The individual is able to speak in other social interactions and settings, but there is something about being in one environment that prevents the individual from giving auditory information. For example, a child with selective mutism may speak in their home with their nuclear family, but not at all at school or in front of their grandparents. It is vital to understand that selective mutism may greatly impact educational or occupational progression. Teachers may find it extremely difficult in prompting a child to speak and formulate meaningful lesson plans for essential skills, like reading or writing. In addition to the impact on learning, the failure to speak should not be explainable by a lack of knowledge of appropriate linguistics or spoken language needed for oral participation. In order to be classified as a clinical disorder, the disturbance must occur for at least one month.

Selective mutism can only be an accurate diagnosis when the symptoms are not descriptive of a communication disorder and do not occur during the course of autism spectrum disorder, schizophrenia, or any other psychotic disorder.

Obsessive-Compulsive and Related Disorders

Hoarding

Obsessive-compulsive and related disorders cover a variety of mental illnesses that involve obsessions and compulsions, or urges and repetitive behaviors that significantly impair the individual's daily life. In individuals with **hoarding disorder**, there is extreme difficulty parting with possessions, regardless of any actual value attached to them. This results in their living spaces being overly cluttered, often to the point where objects need to be moved in order to get from one room to the next. Hoarding differs from collecting in that the compulsion causes significant distress and impairment for the individual. To diagnose this disorder, the hoarding cannot be due to another medical condition or be better explained by the symptoms of another mental disorder.

Excoriation

The act of **excoriation** involves picking at the skin, often resulting in scars, wounds, or lesions. Excoriation is presented as a compulsion and causes the individual extreme distress in areas of functioning. The compulsion is not due to the physiological effects of a substance, another medical condition, or a symptom of another mental disorder (e.g., tactile hallucinations from a psychotic disorder, attempts to improve a flaw in physical appearance, or a manifestation of non-suicidal self-injury). Individuals with this disorder have made attempts to stop picking their skin, but the compulsion is so strong and ingrained into their reactive tendencies that they manage to engage in this behavior again after a hiatus.

Substance-/Medication-Induced Obsessive-Compulsive and Related Disorder

When there is history of substance or medication use in the individual, combined with obsessions and compulsions, a **substance/medication-induced obsessive-compulsive and related disorder** can be diagnosed. This diagnosis is only applicable when there is evidence that obsessions and compulsions developed after taking a substance and the individual has experienced withdrawal or has been exposed to a medication. The disturbance cannot be better explained by any other obsessive-compulsive disorder and does not occur within the course of a delirium. Clinically significant distress and impairment in areas of functioning are present within the individual as a result.

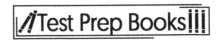

Obsessive-Compulsive and Related Disorder Due to Another Medical Condition

This disorder can be taken in the same regard as the previous one. Obsessions and compulsions have the propensity to be symptoms of other medical conditions. For this diagnosis, a pre-existing medical condition is required and serves as the root cause for obsessions and compulsions. There must be evidence from medical records containing information about how the obsessions and compulsions are the result of another medical condition, and it cannot be better explained by any other mental disorder. The disturbance is not present exclusively throughout the course of a delirium and causes significant distress and impairment of functioning.

Trauma- and Stressor-Related Disorders

Reactive Attachment Disorder

While post-traumatic stress disorder is one of the more identifiable trauma- and stressor-related disorders, there are others that are important to consider in order to make an accurate clinical diagnosis. **Reactive attachment disorder (RAD)** describes a consistent pattern of emotionally withdrawn behaviors toward adult caregivers. As the clinical features of this disorder begin to manifest between the ages of nine months and five years, children demonstrate emotionally withdrawn behavior by minimally seeking or responding to comfort when they are distressed. Additionally, a persistent emotional disturbance is presented through minimal responses to others, limited positive affect, or episodes of agitation even in non-threatening situations with adult caregivers.

The child must also have experienced a pattern of developmental intrusions as a result of insufficient care. Social neglect, repeated turnover of caregivers, or being raised in environments where children are not able to form meaningful attachments are all representative of the criteria that identifies insufficient care for this disorder. Autism spectrum disorder must be ruled out in order to be diagnosed with reactive attachment disorder.

When confirming a diagnosis of reactive attachment disorder, clinicians must understand and be able to differentiate it from autism spectrum disorder (ASD). Many of the symptoms of ASD and RAD are similar; they both involve a lessened positive expression of emotions, cognitive and language impairments, and difficulty with social interactions. What separates these two disorders from each other is that children with RAD must experience the component of severe social neglect, while children with ASD are less likely to have a history with this. Additionally, ASD presents individuals with difficulty in having intentional communication (deliberate, goal-directed language) while RAD still allows children to have social communication levels representative of their intellect.

Disinhibited Social Engagement Disorder

Another trauma- and stressor-related disorder is disinhibited social engagement disorder (DSED). The features of this disorder involve children who are actively interactive with unfamiliar adults, violating social and cultural boundaries. This can be represented by reduced shyness when interacting with strangers, overly familiar physical behavior, lack of attention directed toward actual caregiver, or willingness to accompany an unfamiliar adult with no hesitation. These behaviors are not exclusively due to impulsivity and appear to be socially disinhibited behavior.

The criteria of this disorder also include that of reactive attachment disorder; a history of social neglect, changing caregivers, or maladaptive attachment environments. In order to be diagnosed as a clinical disorder, the child must at least be nine years of age. This age requirement exists because of the fact that DSED cannot be considered as a diagnosis until a child is mature enough to form selective attachments.

While this disorder has an unknown prevalence rate, research shows that it does appear to have rare occurrences. Of the children that are severely neglected and placed within the foster care system, only about 20% meet the full criteria for DSED. Although it is not a common mental disorder, the impairments of social functioning highlight how impactful an unstable and detached rearing environment can have on a child.

Often, children who have DSED are misdiagnosed with attention-deficit/hyperactivity disorder (ADHD) because of the impulsivity they may present when interacting with strangers. Children with DSED can be distinguished from those with ADHD by not showing difficulties with concentration, attention, or hyperactivity. It is, however, possible for the two disorders to occur concurrently within the same child if they do present issues regarding inattention, hyperactivity, or both combined as well as the rest of the criteria with ADHD and DSED.

Dissociative Disorders

Dissociative disorders are a classification of mental illness that are centered around identity disturbances, an aberrant construal of consciousness, and interruptions related to memory, emotion, perception, motor control, and behavior. When an individual is diagnosed with a dissociative disorder, all aspects of psychological functioning are severely impacted. The DSM-5 contains dissociative identity disorder, dissociative amnesia, depersonalization/derealization disorder, other specified dissociative disorder, and unspecified dissociative disorder within this section.

Symptoms of dissociation can be experienced as intrusions that alter reality and awareness, causing the individual to have significant difficulty in rationalizing what is real and what is not. Symptoms can also present as an inability to access information that they normally would be able to have access to. For example, if someone is experiencing amnesia manifested by a dissociative disorder, they may not have the ability to recall events that had happened that day.

Frequently, dissociative disorders develop from the result of trauma that has been inflicted upon the individual. Many of the symptoms of dissociation are determined by trauma, such as the tendency to feel embarrassed or confused by the symptoms or even a desire to conceal them from people. For this reason, dissociative disorders are placed right next to the section of trauma- and stressor-related disorders. Many trauma disorders, like post-traumatic stress disorder and acute stress disorder, include dissociative symptoms (e.g., amnesia, flashbacks, numbing, depersonalization/derealization).

Somatic Symptom and Related Disorders

This category of mental disorders, **somatic symptom and related disorders**, is a novel section of the DSM-5. All of these disorders involve physical symptoms that are brought about from mental distress. The diagnoses within this section represent a newly organized version of the somatoform disorders as described in the DSM-IV. The disorders mentioned in this section include somatic symptom disorder, illness anxiety disorder, conversion disorder, factitious disorder, other specified somatic symptom and related disorder and unspecified somatic symptom and related disorder.

Somatic symptom disorder, the most common diagnosis from this area, focuses on the nuances of discomfort in both physical and emotional measures. While physical pain can cause distress, it is imperative to consider how the individual perceives the pain as well. Individuals with somatic symptom disorder often have extremely high levels of worry. Health concerns may take over the person's life; always seeking treatment and care results in significant impairment in functioning and distress. These

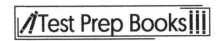

individuals think the worst about their health, and may describe how it affects other aspects of their lives instead of just their physical discomfort.

It is clear how somatic symptom disorder greatly affects an individual's lifestyle on physical and emotional levels. Cognitive features of this illness include centering their attention on their illness, attributing normal body functions to the illness, interpreting normal body functions as catastrophic or worrisome, and fearing that physical activity may damage their body even further. These individuals may engage in behaviors like constantly checking their bodies for irregularities, constantly seeking medical assistance, and avoiding exercise of any kind. When doctors reassure them that what they are experiencing is mild, people with this disorder will believe that they are not being taken seriously. Due to the physical manifestation of this disorder, people often seek general medical help rather than mental health services. When referred to a mental health service, these individuals may refuse to go in for an initial intake interview with a therapist entirely.

Another disorder within this section is known as **illness anxiety disorder**. This disorder specifically describes clinically significant anxiety about having or possibly contracting a serious illness. These individuals are extremely preoccupied with these thoughts and often seek medical attention. The somatic symptoms that are present, in actuality, are mild or not present at all. The individual is particularly vigilant about their health status, worrying for and caring to any bodily sensation perceived as negative. The preoccupation of the illness must occur for at least six months.

Even after testing negative for serious illness or being reassured by doctors, individuals with illness anxiety disorder still maintain a constant worry or fear related to their health. Illness becomes a prominent feature of their personality and lifestyle. They will often seek out assistance from several medical providers for the same problems that have already been scrutinized by professionals. They examine themselves repeatedly and perform excessive research on medical illnesses they are worried about. The social and family environment becomes extremely at risk for impairment in these individuals as it may prevent them from going to significant events, family gatherings, visiting sick relatives, etc. Environmental stressors may serve as a catalyst for this disorder, considering research suggests that childhood abuse or serious childhood illness may give the individual a predisposition to the development of this disorder as they get older. Illness anxiety disorder is a revised interpretation of hypochondriasis as stated in the DSM-IV.

Feeding and Eating Disorders

Feeding and eating disorders are delineated as a persistent disruption in eating or eating-related behavior. The behavior that results from these disorders involve altering food consumption or digestion that affects individuals on a social, cognitive, and emotional level. The disorders covered in this section are pica, rumination disorder, avoidant/restrictive food intake disorder, anorexia nervosa, bulimia nervosa, and binge-eating disorder.

The diagnostic criteria for rumination disorder, avoidant/restrictive food intake disorder, anorexia nervosa, bulimia nervosa, and binge-eating disorder are mutually exclusive. This describes how an individual can only be diagnosed with one of these disorders based off of what has occurred in their behavior. The explanation for this is despite commonalities that may be depicted in individuals with these disorders, the disorders greatly differ from one another in terms of presentation, clinical prognosis/course, outcome, and types of treatment. The exception is that pica may be diagnosed simultaneously with any other feeding and eating disorder.

Pica describes the act of persistently eating substances that are not food for at least one month. Developmental level is considered for this diagnosis, as young children may often accidentally eat objects other than food, and is required that the consumption must be disproportionate to an individual's age. The behavior is abnormal when considering the context of the individual's culture. **Rumination disorder** is when an individual repeatedly regurgitates food for over a period of one month. The regurgitation behavior is not attributable to a gastrointestinal issue or any other medical condition. This disturbance does not only occur within the course of anorexia nervosa, bulimia nervosa, binge-eating disorder, or avoidant/restrictive intake disorder.

Avoidant/restrictive food intake disorder is an eating disturbance in which the individual consistently fails to meet nutritional needs. This can be presented as significant weight loss, serious nutritional deficiency, dependence on oral feeding supplements, or severe interference in social and psychological functioning.

Anorexia nervosa, one of the most commonly-known eating disorders, is when the individual restricts their intake of food relative to what their body requires. This leads to a significant low body weight that is less than minimally normal or expected with age, sex, developmental trajectory, and physical health. Individuals have a predominant fear of gaining weight or becoming fat even though they are at an incredibly low weight. Individuals also experience a disturbance in perceiving their body for how it actually looks or denounce the seriousness of the significantly low weight.

Bulimia nervosa is clinically presented as recurrent episodes of binge eating followed by inappropriate compensatory behaviors to prevent weight gain. Some of these behaviors involve self-induced vomiting, misusing laxatives, fasting, or exercising excessively. The binge eating and compensatory behaviors both occur at least once a week for three months. Unlike anorexia nervosa, people with bulimia nervosa often present as average or overweight. It is not uncommon for individuals' behavior to be described as switching off between the two disorders.

Lastly, **binge-eating disorder** is another mental disorder within this section of the DSM-5. This disorder is characterized by recurrent episodes of binge eating and are associated with eating faster than normal, until uncomfortably full, eating large amounts of food when not physically hungry, eating alone due to embarrassment of how much they ate, and feeling disgusted with oneself afterwards. Marked distress occurs from this disorder and the behavior occurs at least once a week for three months.

Elimination Disorders

Unlike other classes of disorders, the **elimination disorders** section in the DSM-5 is particularly succinct. It contains disorders that involve issues with excreting urine and feces from the body. While it is extremely common for young children to have "accidents" when they are young, this problem has the potential to develop into a disorder if it persists past the age of five for more than three months. **Enuresis** describes the repetitive tendency to release urine in places other than a bathroom. The most common type of enuresis that occurs at night is bed-wetting. **Encopresis**, the other type of elimination disorder, involves the process of excreting feces instead of urine. These behaviors may or may not be done on purpose.

Children with this disorder may experience other symptoms of these disorders such as loss of appetite, abdominal pain, watery bowel movements, lessened interest in physical activity, withdrawn around friends and family, or even displaying secretive behavior related to bowel movements. The effects caused by an elimination disorder that may impact a child's life can range from mild to severe

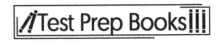

depending on the symptoms. It is essential for clinicians and caregivers to approach children with this disorder with warmth and comfort in order to ease any negative feelings they may have about their symptoms.

Sleep-Wake Disorders

A healthy sleep pattern is a major factor when it comes to psychological functioning. For many, inadequate sleep serves as the root cause of their negative affect. The **sleep-wake disorders** section of the DSM-5 covers all mental disorders that involve issues related to sleep. Insomnia disorder, hypersomnolence disorder, narcolepsy, breathing-related sleep disorders, circadian rhythm sleep-wake disorders, non-rapid eye movement (NREM) sleep arousal disorders, nightmare disorder, rapid eye movement (REM) sleep behavior disorder, restless legs syndrome, and substance/medication-induced sleep disorder are all included within this distinction.

Individuals with sleep-wake disorders mainly present with problems related to inadequate sleep in terms of quality, timing, and amount. All of these areas of sleep will determine how an individual acts in the daytime. Both physical and emotional problems can be attributable to sleep-wake disorders, meaning that clinicians must be able to differentiate if the sleep is being affected by symptoms of other mental disorders or a pre-existing medical condition.

The most common sleep-wake disorder is **insomnia disorder**. People with insomnia have a very difficult time falling asleep or staying asleep. While one-third of adults experience insomnia symptoms, only 6–10% meet all of the criteria for insomnia disorder. Symptoms include difficulty falling asleep, staying asleep, or waking up early and having the inability to fall back asleep. The sleep difficulty must persist for three months and occur at least three nights per week in order to fully disrupt functioning on social, academic, or occupational levels.

Sexual Dysfunctions

Genito-Pelvic Pain/Penetration Disorder

For women, penetration during sex has the potential to be painful if not properly operated. However, some individuals with persistent problems related to sexual penetration can be diagnosed with **genito-pelvic pain/penetration disorder**. People with this disorder may experience difficulties with vaginal penetration, intense vulvovaginal or pelvic pain during intercourse, anxiety related to the pain or anticipation of pain, or severe pelvic muscle tension during attempted vaginal intercourse. These symptoms must persist for at least six months and cause great distress to the individual in order for the issue to be classified as a disorder.

Individuals primarily seek treatment for this disorder or just these symptoms in medical settings. The course for this diagnosis is unclear, but there are a few signs that may indicate issues with this disorder that the individual may not be aware of. For example, avoiding the use of tampons persistently has been shown by research to be a common indicator that there may be some issues of discomfort when it comes to vaginal penetration. Additionally, clinicians must be able to differentiate this disorder from another medical condition. Lichen sclerosus, endometriosis, pelvic inflammatory disease, and vulvovaginal atrophy are commonly diagnosed in these individuals who actually have genito-pelvic pain/penetration disorder. If a marked fear or anxiety of intercourse is present, then the possibility of this diagnosis must be considered.

Sexual Dysfunction Subtypes

Within individuals diagnosed with a sexual disorder, it is imperative to specify the onset of when the difficulty occurred. This is mainly because the timing of when the issue occurs may determine the course of the treatment, and the cause for what made the dysfunction apparent in the first place. These specifications are demonstrated through four subtypes within sexual dysfunctions.

The lifelong subtype specifies that the sexual problem has been present since the individual's first sexual experiences. If someone who is diagnosed with erectile disorder is placed in the lifelong subtype, then that would specify how the difficulty in obtaining or maintaining an erection has been present ever since the individual became sexually active.

The next subtype is referred to as the acquired subtype. This subtype notes that the sexual disturbance has developed after a period of normal sexual functioning. Individuals within this subtype may be more likely to seek treatment because they may be able to recognize the disturbance when it occurs or notice a bodily-related abnormality. Individuals either fall within the lifelong or acquired subtype when specifying the onset of the difficulty.

The generalized subtype characterizes how the sexual disturbance is not limited to certain types of stimulation, situations, or partners. In contrast, the situational subtype describes how the difficulty is only present within those parameters. If someone is diagnosed with erectile disorder and is placed within the situational subtype, then this offers insight on when the disturbance becomes present. Often, sex therapists work with couples who are experiencing problems related to their sexual relationship. While medical attention may be necessary for some of these disorders, interventions used by therapists to allow open communication of feelings and thoughts about sexual pleasure between partners has the ability to enhance sexual performance as well as satisfaction with their relationship in general.

Gender Dysphoria

Gender dysphoria encapsulates an entire section within the DSM-5 in addition to being labeled as a mental disorder. When individuals develop an awareness of incongruence in the gender identity that is associated with the sex they were assigned with at birth, they may experience **gender dysphoria**. The incongruence may be accompanied by severe distress in terms of how the individual should not only express themselves physically, but also how they perceive themselves internally with regard to the cultural context. Experiencing gender dysphoria typically manifests in those who identify as transgender, an individual who identifies with a gender or other identity that is different from the sex they were assigned at birth. The diagnostic criteria for gender dysphoria are different for adults, adolescents, and children.

In children, one of the indicators for gender dysphoria is a strong insistence that they are the other gender (male or female) or some alternative identity that is different from the assigned one. Young boys experiencing gender dysphoria may prefer to dress in female attire, whereas young girls may prefer to present as more masculine. Often, young children engage in fantasy play and taking on the role of a different gender during this may also serve as an indication for gender dysphoria. The DSM-5 emphasizes that children strongly prefer the objects, roles, and characteristics of an opposite gender for a period of six months or more.

Gender dysphoria is not only presented in children. For many, adolescence and adulthood are when the incongruence becomes more apparent. The course for this disorder will present differently from person to person as everyone's relationship with gender and identity is different. The indicators for adults are essentially the same as they are in children but are more conceptualized as a fully developed awareness. Individuals must have a strong desire to be a different gender, to be treated/referred to as a different gender, and embody the typical feelings and reactions of the gender they truly identify as.

People who experience gender dysphoria are considered sexual minorities as they are often discriminated against on many different scales in a variety of social, occupational, medical, and institutional environments. With this in mind, clinicians must be properly educated on the concept of sexual identity as well as develop competency with this population in order to prevent their internal biases from violating proper treatment protocols.

Disruptive, Impulse-Control, and Conduct Disorders

This section of the DSM-5 characterizes issues related to self-control in expressing emotions and behaviors. Specifically, disruptive, impulse-control, and conduct disorders address problematic behaviors that can be directed onto another person (e.g., destruction of property, vandalism, aggression, etc.). What causes these behaviors are issues stemming from emotional reactivity and self-regulating abilities.

The first disorder within this section is **oppositional defiant disorder**. This disorder presents a pattern of angry/irritable moods in addition to defiant behavior. Emotional symptoms include losing temper often, being easily annoyed, or often angry and resentful. Behavioral criteria consist of arguing with authority figures or caregivers, refusing to comply with direction from mentioned figures, annoying others on purpose, or blaming others for their mistakes. A spiteful or vindictive behavioral pattern must occur twice within the past six months. Additionally, these behaviors are directed towards individuals other than immediate family members (parents, siblings, etc.).

Intermittent explosive disorder is the next listing in this section. Verbal aggression, in addition to three instances where the individual damages property or physically assaults another person/animal occurring within a twelve-month period, is what is required for a diagnosis of this disorder. The person must be at least six years of age with the outbursts resulting from anger alone. The situation at hand would normally never elicit an outburst from the average person.

Conduct disorder describes the persistent pattern of violating basic rights and rules of others. This disorder typically develops during the course of childhood and adolescence. This population is highly aggressive and often seen starting physical fights, bullying others, destroying property, conning others, or running away from home. This is the kind of person who will show little to no concern for other people and feel comfortable using them in order to get what they want. Conduct disorder is a necessary prerequisite for children who are later diagnosed with antisocial personality disorder. The other disorders within this section include pyromania, kleptomania, and other specified and unspecified disruptive, impulse-control, and conduct disorders.

Substance-Related and Addictive Disorders

The ten classes of drugs that are covered in this section are alcohol, caffeine, cannabis, hallucinogens, inhalants, opioids, sedatives, hypnotics, stimulants, and tobacco. While these classifications are not fully distinct from one another, each one is still capable of chemically altering the brain's reward pathway. These drugs activate neurotransmitters within the brain to create pleasant feelings or "highs." When abused, these drugs inhibit the brain from naturally producing these neurotransmitters which can serve as a catalyst for dependency and problems with functioning in all areas of life. This section of the DSM-5 includes gambling disorder, as the behavior associated with gambling is known to activate the reward system in a similar way. Other behavioral addictions such as internet gaming, sex addiction, or shopping addiction are not covered within this section due to the lack of peer-reviewed empirical evidence.

Diagnostic criteria are similar across all of the drug classifications. An individual with a **substance-related addiction** generally displays taking the substance in large amounts or more than was intended, attempting to cut down drug use but consistently failing, spending a great deal of time obtaining substances or recovering from its effects, and a strong craving or desire to use the substance. People with substance abuse disorders may spend the majority of their time interacting with a substance or being in its presence. As a result, significant impairment in functioning, interpersonal issues, and a decrease in responsibilities or recreational activities may occur. Risky use is another factor of substance abuse as it explains how this population may still use the substance in situations that are physically dangerous (e.g., while driving) or even when knowing that the substance is the cause of a current physical or psychological problem.

Tolerance and withdrawal symptoms are also indicators of substance abuse. Tolerance is defined as requiring an increased dose of the substance in order to achieve its desired effects. People with substance-use disorders may develop tolerance rather quickly depending on the type of substance and pre-existing brain chemistry. Tolerance needs to be distinguished from the variety of bodily responses that someone taking a substance for the first time might experience. For example, someone who smokes marijuana for the first time may feel little to no effect, while individuals that have the same physical characteristics and ingest the same amount feel the effects at a significant rate. Withdrawal symptoms are the body's physical responses to using the drug continuously and then not at all. When heavy drug use is maintained, the blood and tissue concentrations of the body become affected. This can be dangerous and potentially life-threatening to the individual because they may take more of the substance in order to alleviate the withdrawal symptoms. Withdrawal symptoms are specified for each of the drug classes because each substance affects the body differently.

Neurocognitive Disorders

What distinguishes the neurocognitive disorders section from other disorders of the DSM-5 are issues with cognitive functioning that have been acquired instead of developed. Developmental cognitive disorders like ADHD and autism spectrum disorder are instead classified as neurodevelopmental disorders. **Neurocognitive disorders** represent an impairment in functioning that has increased throughout time, and thus the reasoning for the abnormality can be determined. Neurocognitive disorders in the DSM-5 are organized by being major or mild, along with a pre-existing medical condition. Delirium is the only neurocognitive disorder that is not classified this way. Cognitive functioning is measured by six domains: complex attention (selective attention, processing speed), executive functioning (decision making, planning), learning and memory (short- and long-term), language (processing, expression), perceptual-motor, and social cognition (recognizing emotions, theory of mind).

Delirium can be most simply described as an impairment of attention and awareness. People who experience delirium have extreme difficulty focusing their attention, remembering things, and processing language. Episodes of delirium typically last hours to a few days and may become more or less severe depending on the time of day. Delirium can be caused by substance withdrawal, a side-effect from medication, or another medical condition.

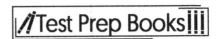

What separates a major neurocognitive disorder from a mild one is the severity of impairment related to cognitive functioning. In major neurocognitive disorders, individuals experience a severe decline in performance of one or more cognitive levels (e.g., language, memory, social cognition). This is based on the level of concern from the individual themselves, an informant, or a clinician. Documentation of cognitive decline or a cognitive assessment is required for the diagnosis as well. This decline in functioning does not exclusively occur during an episode of delirium and at minimum impacts the individual where they cannot live on their own without assistance. On the contrary, a mild neurocognitive disorder does not interfere with the responsibilities of daily living but contains the same criteria for a major neurocognitive disorder. People with mild neurocognitive disorders are able to fully function on their own.

Personality Disorders

When patterns of behavior, emotional responses, and cognition become ingrained within an individual, then it is possible for them to have developed a **personality disorder**. People with personality disorders engage in problematic behaviors and tendencies that are not normally accepted within the cultural context. Past research has shown that personality disorders develop in early childhood and adolescence. For organizational purposes, the DSM-5 separates personality disorders into three clusters: cluster A, odd and eccentric; cluster B, dramatic and erratic; and cluster C, fearful and anxious.

The cluster A personality disorders are paranoid personality disorder, schizoid personality disorder, and schizotypal personality disorder. Individuals with any of these disorders exhibit behavior that is considered odd or eccentric with significant deviation from what is normally accepted. **Paranoid personality disorder** is quite self-explanatory in that this population has extreme difficulty trusting other people and views their motives as evil or harmful. The paranoia is generalizable, leaving these individuals with a very solitary lifestyle. The **schizoid personality disorder** population does not care for social relationships or responsibilities and often have a limited display of emotion. These individuals have no interest in maintaining relationships on any level and do not elicit any warm emotions. People with **schizotypal personality disorder**, on the other hand, are not able to form interpersonal relationships because of their social deficits. These individuals present odd thinking and speech, magical thinking, ideas of reference, and more that prevent them from building relationships with others. These people may physically appear odd through choice of clothing or other stylistic decisions.

Cluster B personality disorders include antisocial personality disorder, borderline personality disorder, histrionic personality disorder, and narcissistic personality disorder. Individuals within this cluster have a difficult time maintaining interpersonal relationships because of their erratic and dramatic emotional reactivity. People with **antisocial personality disorder** have a complete disregard for others and often use other people for their own personal gain. Conduct disorder during childhood is a requirement for a diagnosis of antisocial personality disorders. **Borderline personality disorder** describes those who have unstable personal relationships and intense levels of impulsivity. Common indicators of this disorder include self-harm and black-and-white thinking. These individuals will go to great lengths in order to keep those around them because of their tendency to associate their self-worth with their relationships with other people. Similarly, **histrionic personality disorder** involves a pattern of attention-seeking behavior. People with histrionic personalities may use their physical appearance to gain attention, have rapid shifts in emotion, and are uncomfortable when they are not the center of attention. Lastly, **narcissistic personality disorder** is diagnosed in those who display a grandiose sense of self, needs constant validation or admiration, and has a strong sense of entitlement. The basis for this disorder is that these people thrive off of their feelings about themselves and need reinforcement of their grandiosity from others.

The fearful and anxious personality disorders of cluster C are avoidant personality disorder, dependent personality disorder, and obsessive-compulsive personality disorder. The fear or anxiety within these personality types prevent individuals from forming meaningful relationships, inhibit the development of independence, or become too preoccupied with behavioral tendencies that they cannot live a substantial, healthy lifestyle. When someone is diagnosed with **avoidant personality disorder**, this means that they have an intense fear of interpersonal communication. The fear of rejection or criticism prevents them from taking risks to meet new people and is so ingrained that they believe they are socially incapable of healthily interacting with others. **Dependent personality disorder** represents those who have a pervasive need to be taken care of. These people cannot make decisions by themselves, will not create conflict out of worry that their caretaker may leave them, feel extremely uncomfortable being alone, or goes to great lengths in order to keep someone around to take care of them. These individuals may feel extreme discomfort or distress when having to move out of their parents' house or going through a breakup with their partner to the point where they do not know what to do with themselves. The last of these disorders, **obsessive-compulsive personality disorder**, emphasizes the pattern of being a perfectionist with no flexibility for mistakes on their own part or those involved in their life. These individuals are unable to complete tasks because they are so caught up in the details. When offered a different perspective on a situation, someone with this personality type would reject it and show stubbornness when working with others. What differentiates this disorder from obsessive-compulsive disorder (OCD) is that the person will not have obsessions and compulsions to the same extent as those with OCD.

Paraphilic Disorders

Patterns of urges, fantasies, or taboo sexual acts that cause distress within an individual are known as **paraphilic disorders** within the DSM-5. These acts may include inanimate objects, children or nonconsenting adults, suffering and humiliation of a sexual partner, or even the person themselves. Paraphilic disorders include voyeuristic disorder, exhibitionistic disorder, frotteuristic disorder, sexual masochism disorder, sexual sadism disorder, pedophilic disorder, fetishistic disorder, and transvestic disorder.

The main idea surrounding these disorders is that despite the pleasure that may be gained from engaging in these acts, individuals with paraphilic disorders still manage to cause severe distress and harm to themselves or other people. Having a paraphilia, an intense sexual interest in something or someone that is not a physically normal, mature, consenting human partner, does not immediately indicate that someone has a paraphilic disorder. A major component of paraphilic disorders is the occurrence of distress as a result from the sexual interest.

Section III (Emerging Measures and Models)

Cross-Cutting Symptom Measures for Adults and Children

Assessing the symptoms of psychiatric illness is one of many central responsibilities psychologists and other mental health professionals engage in. In order to conduct this process in an accurate and organized way, the DSM-5 created the cross-cutting symptom measures (CCSM) with separate versions for adults and children. The first level of the CCSM is used to aid psychiatric professionals in determining areas of functioning that may have an impact on treatment and prognosis.

For adults, the measure consists of twenty-three questions that address thirteen psychological areas of functioning. The thirteen domains included within the assessment are depression, anger, mania, anxiety,

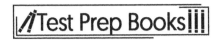

somatic symptoms, suicidal ideation, psychosis, sleep problems, memory, repetitive thoughts/behaviors, dissociation, personality functioning, and substance use. One to three questions are designated for each domain, measuring how impacted the individual is by the symptom for the last two weeks. For children, the measure is typically completed by a parent or guardian and consists of twenty-five questions that address most of the same domains, with the addition of irritability and inattention domains and excluding personality functioning, dissociation, and memory. For older children and adolescents, ages eleven to seventeen, the clinician may also have the child complete the child-rated version of the measure.

Scoring the CCSM is relatively similar for both the child and adult version. For the adult version, each item is measured on a scale from zero to four, with zero indicating none/not at all while four indicates severe/nearly every day. A rating of two or more on each item within a domain may signify that the CCSM level two, a more detailed measure, might be necessary in order to gain a better understanding of an individual's symptomology. The child version is also measured on the same five-point scale as the adult version; however, suicidal ideation items are rated on a "yes, no, or don't know" scale. As mentioned before, the CCSM level two provides another way of receiving more information on domains that the individual was highly rated on so the clinician has an even more in-depth comprehension of the patient's clinical formulation.

Clinician-Rated Dimensions of Psychosis Symptom Severity

Dimensional measures are used by clinicians in order to assess the severity and course of mental illness. The clinician-rated dimensions of psychosis are designed to be used in this way, as they measure the main symptoms of psychosis: hallucinations, delusions, disorganized speech, abnormal psychomotor behavior, and negative symptoms of psychosis (e.g., anhedonia and lack of cognitive input). Depending on how the individual responds to these measures, clinicians are able to conceptualize the prognosis for their mental illness as well as the treatment methods. The assessment consists of an eight-item measure that allows the clinician to rate the severity of each psychosis symptom of the individual within the past seven days.

WHODAS 2.0

The World Health Organization Disability Assessment Schedule 2.0 (WHODAS 2.0) is an assessment conducted by clinicians that analyzes any indication of disability in individuals that are eighteen years of age or older. The six domains it covers include understanding/communicating, getting around, self-care, getting along with people, life activities, and participation in society. The WHODAS 2.0 is completed by the individual themself and asks them to rate the difficulty in each specific domain within the last thirty days on a thirty-six-item questionnaire.

There are two versions of the WHODAS 2.0, simple and complex, that clinicians use. They differ in their scoring. The simple version allows for the individual to rate the difficulty on a scale from one to five, one being none and five being extreme. These methods are then summed across all of the domains and that determines the degree of impairment in functioning. This version can be scored by hand, making it more preferable for clinicians in a busy environment. The complex version, on the other hand, does not use this simple scoring technique. Instead, it uses item-response-theory- (IRT) based scoring. IRT-based scoring involves weighing individual items within each domain. This process is completed via computer and the resulting score is represented on a scale from zero to one hundred, where zero represents no disability and one hundred is full disability.

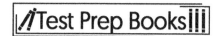

Cultural Formulation

Culture

Cultural context is an essential factor when diagnosing, assessing, or treating individuals with mental illness. **Culture** is defined as the systems of knowledge, concepts, rules, and practices that are learned and passed on throughout generations. Culture is often used as an umbrella-term that encapsulates language, religion/spirituality, family structures, life-cycle stages, ceremonies, customs, and both moral and legal systems. Cultures are considered to be dynamic networks because they change so much over time. Individuals, more often than not, experience different cultures intersecting at once which allows them to gain a more specific understanding of their own identity. This conceptualization of identity then leads to the formation of other beliefs that extend to other areas of life such as relationships, career choices, and education. Due to the importance of culture and how it interacts with our experience as human beings, it is imperative for clinicians to evaluate cultural factors when working with people in their practices and not fall into stereotypic or generalizable thinking.

Culture also includes the concepts of race and ethnicity, which are commonly mistaken to be the same thing. Race is a category of identity that differentiates individuals based on physical traits and biological characteristics. Racial categories vary across cultural societies. On a social basis, race is a construct that serves as a catalyst for racism, discrimination, and isolation. Existing empirical evidence demonstrates how racism can worsen the effects of mental disorders and racial biases impact diagnostic psychological assessment. Racial minorities are subject to these realities outside of clinical settings, so proper education and cultural competency is required in clinicians in order to not emulate these concepts within the therapeutic relationship.

Ethnicity specifies an individual's community or group. They can exist across a common historical, geographical, linguistic, or religious domain. Ethnicity is able to be self-assigned or attributed by other people. In the essence of culture, ethnicities have evolved to intersect and introduce new variations of ethnic identities.

DSM-5 Cultural Formulation Interview

How individuals think about their symptoms or mental illness is greatly influenced by their cultural context. The **Cultural Formulation Interview (CFI)** is designed to evaluate these perspectives in order to gain a comprehensive understanding of the individual's specific experience. It consists of a set of sixteen questions that are typically asked when first meeting a new client during an initial interview. The CFI covers four domains of cultural assessment: cultural definition of the problem; cultural perceptions of cause, context, and support; cultural factors affecting self-coping; and past help seeking.

When obtaining cultural information about the client, clinicians should do so in an inviting and welcoming manner. The CFI emulates a person-centered process, meaning that clinicians encourage clients to explore their thought processes and experience. By using this approach, the diagnostic assessment becomes more valid and the individual becomes more engaged in the process. Stereotypic thinking is also controlled for as much as possible by this interview because clinicians have the ability to understand how the client's particular culture affects their clinical presentation. Other variations of the CFI have been developed in order to assess certain populations such as children and adolescents, the elderly, immigrants, and refugees.

The CFI is such a vital part of diagnostic assessment as it provides extraordinary emphasis on the way mental illness is perceived through a cultural lens. Level of distress, one of the main indicators of psychological illness, can vary in the way it is expressed from culture to culture in how it is

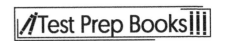

communicated (if at all), understood, or felt. A specific psychological experience that is shared among individuals in certain cultural groups, known as a cultural syndrome, may be presented through the CFI. Additionally, cultural idioms of distress and cultural explanations are able to be highlighted and understood through the process of the CFI. Culture will always affect the way in which mental illness presents. By extracting information about the client's experience in this context, clinicians can avoid misdiagnosis, obtain useful clinical information, improve rapport and client engagement, guide clinical research, and possibly clarify cultural epidemiology.

Alternative DSM-5 Model for Personality Disorders

Overview of model/general differences from current model (how DSM-5 currently classifies personality disorders)

There are seven existing components in the DSM-5 that describe the validity of a personality disorder. These disorders involve significant impairment in personality functioning. When individuals have patterns of unstable relationships or identity issues, this impairment in function demonstrates great consequences in terms of personality functioning. Inflexibility and pervasiveness are essential criteria for diagnosing personality disorders. The client's thought patterns are stable throughout a variety of contexts and can be generalized to everyday interactions. Additionally, these thought patterns are able to be linked back to behavioral traits that have been represented in childhood. Like other mental disorders, personality disorder symptoms cannot be attributable to substances, a different mental disorder, and cannot be considered normal given the cultural context.

Level of Personality Functioning

Personality functioning is measured within four critical domains: identity, self-direction, empathy, and intimacy. As one can tell, personality functioning occurs on both an interpersonal and intrapersonal level. When an individual expresses great difficulty in identifying with these concepts of personality functioning in their behavior, it is possible that they are exhibiting traits of a personality disorder. For example, some of the criteria for borderline personality disorder mentions identity disturbances, turnover within their relationships, and marked impulsivity. All of these symptoms are indicative of a personality disorder in this way and represent how personality functioning plays a role in the diagnosis.

Pathological Personality Traits

Much like levels of personality functioning, pathological personality traits are also divided into five domains. Negative affectivity, detachment, antagonism, disinhibition, and psychoticism represent these categories. Within these domains, several key traits have been identified within the DSM-5 that highlight specific thought patterns, attitudes, and behaviors that individuals with pathological personality traits exhibit. For example, within the negative affectivity domain, there are six key traits that make up this category: emotional lability, anxiousness, separation insecurity, submissiveness, hostility, and perseveration. Each one of these traits are indicative of one personality disorder or more. The five domains also lay the foundation for the personality trait model that is used to evaluate problematic personality traits in a multidimensional way.

Pervasiveness and Stability

In order to be officially classified as a personality disorder, the criteria specifying behaviors and symptoms must be relatively persistent throughout the individual's life. These traits and symptoms are generalizable across multiple contexts and environments, leading to disruptions and impairments within the social and occupational features of their life. The traits associated with a specific disorder can automatically and easily be associated with an individual. This demonstrates just how inflexible and stable the personality traits must be in order to be diagnosed with a personality disorder.

Differential Diagnosis

When understanding personality disorders, it is important to comprehend how it can be mistaken for other disorders and impact other possible comorbid disorders. When assessing for a personality disorder, clinicians need to be able to have a thorough understanding that the personality traits and behaviors associated with a personality disorder are not solely because of another existing mental disorder. An example of this is if someone experiences obsessions and compulsions with repetitive behaviors/rituals, then they would be classified with obsessive-compulsive disorder and instead of obsessive-compulsive personality disorder. Typical features of each personality disorder are listed in the previous section as well as the DSM-5 for further review.

Personality Trait Model

By examining personality traits in a multidimensional way, clinicians have the propensity to determine treatment style, prognosis, course of illness, and the severity of impairment in psychological functioning. Within the personality trait model, five domains are used to assess the nuances within an individual's personality. These five domains include negative affectivity, detachment, antagonism, disinhibition, and psychoticism. When an individual presents these domains in their everyday behavior, or if they severely impact everyday aspects of their lives, then clinicians are then able to consider the diagnosis of a personality disorder. These five domains are commonly referred to as the "Big Five" or Five Factor Model of Personality (FFM).

- **Negative affectivity** presents as consistent negative feelings and attitudes. These negative emotions can be expressed as sadness, anxiety, guilt, shame, anger, etc. Sometimes, those with negative affectivity are drawn to behavioral tendencies to cope with these negative emotions (e.g., self-harm). The personality disorders associated with negative affectivity include borderline personality disorder, obsessive-compulsive personality disorder, dependent personality disorder, and paranoid personality disorder.

- **Detachment** describes the lack of interest in emotional experiences with other people. Detached individuals will have little emotional expression and often find themselves engaging in activities that further isolate themselves, much like those who exhibit symptoms of schizoid personality disorder.

- **Antagonistic** people are often perceived as manipulative, exploitative, and deceitful as their primary traits. Never thinking of others, antagonists are always looking for ways to benefit in any aspect of life by using other people. Antisocial personality disorder, narcissistic personality disorder, and histrionic personality disorder characteristics may fall under this domain.

- **Disinhibition** reflects the lack of thought that goes into someone's actions. Disinhibited people do not think ahead of time nor are they typically prepared to face the consequences of their actions. Irresponsibility, impulsivity, distractibility, risk-taking, and rigid perfectionism are the facets within this domain. As one can tell, borderline personality disorder, obsessive compulsive personality disorder, histrionic personality disorder, and avoidant personality disorder may serve as examples of how this trait can impact people's lives so severely.

- Lastly, **psychoticism** is a trait that prevents people from experiencing the world for how it actually exists. Their perception, cognitions, and behavioral tendencies do not reflect the norms of the culture in which they live in and do not operate in a way that allows them to perceive reality.

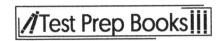

Hallucinations, dissociative experiences, and unusual beliefs occur within this population very frequently. Schizotypal personality disorder encompasses how psychoticism can influence a person's behavior on a personal level.

While these problematic qualities are found in individuals with personality disorders, psychologists and researchers have identified five polar opposites of these factors that exhibit healthy functioning: emotional stability, extraversion, agreeableness, conscientiousness, and lucidity. The appearance of these conditions can greatly affect the presentation and development of multiple mental disorders, not just personality disorders. Research within the DSM-5 has also extracted information from professionals of trauma (both psychological symptoms and physical injuries) that shed light on how these five traits allow the individual to cope in a healthy manner and regulate their emotions.

The personality trait model, in addition to other psychological principles, is present within the tools that psychologists and other clinicians use to assess for mental disorders. This process is completed by psychological assessment, a process by which a mental health professional combines counseling theory and measurement techniques in order to compile information that can be used to examine psychological constructs. Personality assessment is commonly completed by psychologists who are presented with patients who exhibit the FFM in their mannerisms.

The most renowned personality assessment tool is the Minnesota multiphasic personality inventory (MMPI). With 567 true/false questions, the MMPI-2 has been formulated by psychologists in order to assess personality in its most accurate form because it specifically addresses the domains of the FFM. Once completed, a computer is used to score the items numerically, and then a psychologist interprets these scores in relation to the individual's concerns and history in order to create a personalized document for the person seeking treatment. The assessment can then be entered into the client's medical records and can be distributed to psychiatrists or other doctors in reference for symptom treatment. The MMPI can be utilized to diagnose all types of mental disorders, including personality disorders.

Conditions for Further Study

These next mental disorders or mental health conditions are not officially allocated within their respective domains in the DSM-5 because they still require more research in order to become valid diagnoses. By evaluating these areas of future study, clinicians have access to current mental health literature and discussions that will likely be presented within newer versions of the DSM as time progresses.

Attenuated Psychosis Syndrome (APS)

Attenuated Psychosis Syndrome (APS) is a comparable mental disorder to psychosis, although the diagnosis is not representative of a fully developed psychotic disorder. For this diagnosis, individuals must experience at least one of the following symptoms: delusions, hallucinations, or disorganized speech. The symptom(s) must appear at least once per week during the past month and have worsened within the last year. The criteria for a psychotic disorder must not be met and the effects of APS cause a sufficient amount of distress within the individual. The initial symptomology of APS may often resemble that of brief psychotic disorder. However, since reality testing/insight is still accurate, a diagnosis of brief psychotic disorder would be considered incorrect.

This diagnosis differs from brief psychotic disorder because the effects the person experiences are not as clinically severe as someone who would experience psychosis. This can be explained by the duration of the symptoms. For fully developed psychosis, an individual must experience an episode for at least one day but less than one month. As mentioned before, attenuated psychosis symptoms only occur once per week during the last month, with a sense of reality still in-tact. If someone with APS is having delusions, the individual may not believe them as strictly and with such conviction as they would with brief psychotic disorder. This also applies to hallucinations, considering APS hallucinations are not as frequent or vivid. Psychologists are still debating over the legitimacy of APS because not enough research is available for it to be officially considered a separate mental disorder given its closeness in symptomatology to brief psychotic disorder and other disorders. Schizotypal personality disorder, depressive and bipolar disorders, anxiety disorders, and borderline personality disorders all contain aspects of their symptomology that may resemble APS.

Depressive Episodes with Short-Duration Hypomania

Depression manifests differently in individuals of all cultures, communities, and identities. For some people, depression may consist of a combination of depressive episodes in addition to hypomanic episodes. **Hypomanic episodes** are brief episodes of mania in which a person may feel unusually elated, energized, or impulsive. If someone experiences at least one depressive episode in addition to at least two hypomanic episodes in their lifetime, then they may meet the criteria for depressive episodes with short-duration hypomania.

In order to understand this diagnosis, one must be able to differentiate hypomania from mania. The difference between the two exists in their time duration. Hypomanic episodes last at least four days, while manic episodes last at least one week. These elevated feelings of happiness and productivity are present for the majority of the time frame for both hypomania and mania. For this specific diagnosis, someone is experiencing hypomanic episodes for only two days when they occur, hence the term "short duration." The episodes still resemble all of the thoughts and feelings that are associated with hypomania, they just do not meet the time duration requirement of four days. Additionally, bipolar disorder is separated into two distinct disorders: bipolar I and bipolar II. Bipolar II entails the experience of hypomanic episodes in addition to depressive episodes, while bipolar I includes depressive episodes in addition to manic episodes. What separates bipolar disorders from depressive episodes with short duration hypomania is the time duration, as the episodes do not meet the time duration requirements for a definite manic or hypomanic episode.

Short-duration hypomania occurs in 2.8% of the population, while hypomania or mania occurs in 5.5%. The reasoning for including this condition in this section of the DSM-5 is that it may just serve as the onset for bipolar II disorder. If the hypomanic episodes reach the four-day time duration requirement as the condition progresses, then bipolar II would serve as the most accurate diagnosis. In actuality, there is not enough empirical evidence or research to determine if this condition should be considered separate from bipolar disorders or not.

Persistent Complex Bereavement Disorder

Persistent complex bereavement disorder (PCBD) is a mental disorder that may develop after a person experiences a death of someone they were close with. Persisting more than one year after the death, or six months in children, individuals may experience severe longing for the deceased, intense sorrow and emotional pain, preoccupation with the deceased, or preoccupation with how the death occurred. People with PCBD must experience at least six symptoms of reactive distress to the death or social identity/disruption that manifests in the following ways: difficulty accepting the death, disbelief, bitterness, a desire to die to be with the deceased, untrusting of others, feeling that life is meaningless, or confusion about one's sense of identity. People with PCBD have also reported experiencing difficulty

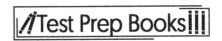

in positively reminiscing the deceased, being emotionally numb, blaming themselves, avoiding reminders of the loss, feeling alone or detached from others, and being unwilling to pursue relationships or goals after the loss. It is important for clinicians to be able to identify someone with PCBD rather than someone who is experiencing normal grief, a depressive disorder, or post-traumatic stress disorder. Normal grief would not surpass a year-long period, and the loss of someone is central to symptoms of depressed mood. Individuals with PCBD and PTSD are able to develop both disorders, although PTSD is based on the traumatic event itself where PCBD focuses on the nuances of the relationship with the deceased.

Referring to the symptoms of this disorder, one might be able to imagine the difficulty this population may have in daily functioning. These individuals have expressed the inability to move on from this difficult event in their lives. Taking care of themselves, fulfilling work-related duties, and maintaining friendships and relationships becomes too much for them handle all at once because of the loss of someone they care about. It is not uncommon for these people to be forced to resign from their jobs or be admitted by someone else into an inpatient mental health facility. As explained by the title of the diagnosis, this grief is persistent and complex as it has the potential to skew their perception of themselves and the world around them.

Caffeine Use Disorder

While caffeine is not considered a dangerous substance, it still has the potential to cause people to develop an addiction that may result in distress or impairment in functioning. Like other substance use disorders, **caffeine use disorder** consists of an unsuccessful effort to cut down consumption, continued use despite problems that develop from it, withdrawal, tolerance, accidental consumption of larger amounts, interfering with responsibilities, or spending a great deal of time consuming caffeine or recovering from its effects. Many people consume caffeine daily and future research will allow clinicians to determine if it should be categorized as a mental disorder or not.

Research regarding this topic has shown that about 75%–80% of the American population consumes caffeine. Of these individuals, about 30% may have met the criteria for dependent use. These statistics explain how predominant and normalized caffeine use has become. On a physical level, caffeine use disorder can facilitate withdrawal symptoms that reinforce its consumption as well as heart, stomach, and urinary problems. Mentally, consuming excessive amounts of caffeine over a period of time can cause individuals to develop anxiety, depression, insomnia, irritability, and problems related to cognitive processes. Individuals with this disorder are unable to work or complete daily tasks without consuming caffeine and consume even larger amounts in anticipation of a busy day or week. Like any stimulant, what draws people to caffeine is the energy they receive as a result. When it becomes clear to individuals that energy can be received through a substance, and not just as a natural chemical process in our brains, problematic use becomes increasingly more prevalent.

Internet Gaming Disorder

Internet gaming disorder describes a pattern of spending a prolonged period of time engaging in internet gaming to the point where life responsibilities become neglected. People diagnosed with this disorder must experience at least five of the following symptoms:

- Preoccupation with internet games
- Withdrawal symptoms (irritability, anxiety, or sadness)
- Tolerance, or needing to spend a great deal of time progressing through games
- Loss of interests in previous hobbies

- Continued gaming despite knowledge of problems
- Use of games to relieve a negative mood
- No longer fulfilling roles in a variety of settings

Individuals diagnosed with this disorder are preoccupied with internet gaming to the point where they will not go to work, school, or family events. Considering that the majority of the population of this disorder are pre-pubescent and teenage males, gaming may prevent them from going to school or doing homework that results in poor academic performance. Internet gaming has been categorized as an addiction in other countries and research has shown that internet gaming creates similar bodily and behavioral effects to gambling disorder and substance use disorders.

The lack of data surrounding this disorder prevents psychologists from determining an exact prevalence rate, but there is research supporting that internet gaming disorder is more prevalent among Asian countries. Male adolescents that are twelve to twenty years of age have been the primary demographic for this disorder. In one study conducted in Asia, 8.4% of males and 4.5% of females met the criteria for experiencing preoccupation with internet games, withdrawal symptoms when gaming is removed, tolerance, and loss of interest in hobbies.

Neurobehavioral Disorder Associated with Prenatal Alcohol Exposure

When fetuses become exposed to alcohol and then develop cognitive or behavioral defects, they may be diagnosed with **neurobehavioral disorder associated with prenatal alcohol exposure (ND-PAE)**. When the mother consumes alcohol during the pregnancy, the fetus becomes directly affected on a neurobiological basis. This may include having an intelligence quotient (IQ) below seventy, impairment in executive functioning, impairment in learning, memory deficiency, and issues related to visual-spatial reasoning. On a behavioral scale, people with ND-PAE may display frequent outbursts, irritability, impaired impulse control, or attention deficits. Developmentally, individuals with this condition may also have issues related to communication, social interaction, motor skills, or tasks required for daily living. This disorder is only applicable if the individual was exposed to alcohol during the developmental period of pregnancy and is directly verified through medical records/examinations. When considering the amount of alcohol exposure for this diagnosis, the DSM-5 explains that "light drinking" has the ability to facilitate the development of this disorder. Light drinking is characterized as one to thirteen drinks per month of pregnancy, with the consumption occurring on separate occasions.

ND-PAE is located in this section of the DSM-5 because it serves as a new way to characterize how prenatal alcohol exposure affects development. Other medical conditions related to prenatal alcohol disorder, such as fetal alcohol syndrome (FAS), only require physical abnormalities in order to be diagnosed (limb deformities, smaller head circumference and brain size, heart defects, etc.). ND-PAE addresses how alcohol exposure impairs individuals solely on a cognitive and behavioral level. This disorder encapsulates all aspects and possible results that prenatal alcohol exposure can have on the developing child, although there is still more research to be conducted on whether ND-PAE is necessary to contribute to the DSM-5 as it stems from behavioral and cognitive results from FAS. While the exact prevalence rate for this disorder is undetermined, the prevalence rate for prenatal alcohol exposure is 2%–5% in the United States.

Suicidal Behavior Disorder

If an individual has attempted suicide in the last two years, then they may be diagnosed with **suicidal behavior disorder (SBD)** when in a specific context. If the suicide attempt is driven by a religious act, suicidal ideation due to another mental disorder, or a state of delirium, then they do not meet the criteria for this disorder. Individuals with this disorder are stable in their suicidal behavior, meaning that

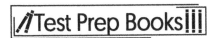

they cannot be persuaded into not attempting suicide by others and are less likely to inform others of their psychological situation before the attempt. Additionally, if the suicidal behavior meets the criteria for nonsuicidal self-injury, then they would not be diagnosed with this disorder.

Suicidal behavior can occur at any time in a person's life, although it is very unlikely for children under the age of five to engage in such acts. Age can be a factor for this diagnosis, considering that young adults ages eighteen to twenty-five and older adults ages forty-five to sixty-four are at higher risk of committing a suicide attempt. Suicidal behavior disorder may be considered for a diagnosis if the individual has a medical condition that occurred as a result of an attempt to end their life. These consequences can be physically seen, like mutilated flesh or skeletal trauma, or more covert as it may affect internal bodily processes (e.g., heart issues from consuming an excessive amount of medication).

Additionally, the symptoms and criteria for this disorder resemble *ataques de nervios* (which means "nervous breakdown"), a culturally specific syndrome present within the Latino community. As always, acknowledging the cultural context of every individual is crucial for a clinical diagnosis, especially when the symptomology may be similar. Suicidal behavior is associated with many other mental disorders, such as major depressive disorder, anxiety disorders, eating disorders, adjustment disorders, and more. SBD can only be applied if the individual has made a suicide attempt, meaning that it can exist simultaneously with the other disorders mentioned.

Nonsuicidal Self-Injury

Nonsuicidal self-injury (NSSI) is defined in the DSM-5 by physically damaging oneself on purpose without the intent of attempting suicide. If the individual has engaged in this behavior for at least five days within the past year, they meet the timeframe criteria for this condition. NSSI can be expressed in a variety of ways; the most common are cutting, scratching, burning, stabbing, hitting, and excessive rubbing. The reasons behind engaging in NSSI must be either to relieve themselves from a negative state, resolve an interpersonal difficulty, or to feel more positive about themselves. The injury must be associated with feelings of distress (depression, anxiety, self-criticism, etc.), a period of being preoccupied by the circumstances of the injury, or frequently thinking about self-injury. Tattoos, body piercings, nail biting, and scab-picking are not forms of NSSI as clarified by the DSM-5. Historically, NSSI has been associated with borderline personality disorder as a symptom. When assessing for borderline personality disorder or NSSI, clinicians must pay attention to other aspects of the individual's behavior. With borderline personality disorder, individuals are more likely to exhibit angry and hostile behaviors. In contrast, those who engage in NSSI feel as though they need to punish themselves and create a problematic behavioral pattern instead of experiencing the emotional instability component as seen in borderline personality disorder.

Case Analysis Practice Simulations

The NCMHCE consists of several case simulations, requiring knowledge on a large body of mental health counseling topics and familiarity with case analysis. This section is provided to give the reader a chance to go through two additional practice simulations, one section at a time, to try to get a feel for the case analysis process. In contrast, the practice test provided at the end of the guide presents ten simulations in the same format as the NCMHCE and is intended to test your knowledge and analysis skills. Read through this section carefully, reading the case provided, the directions, and then the question. After considering the choices, move on to the explanations for that section, focusing on the *why* of the rationale, rather than the *what*. Although it is ideal to arrive at answers while reading through the questions and choices, the main goal here is to get practice early with the case analysis mindset.

Practice Simulation 1

Jade is a twenty-one-year-old college student at Johns Hopkins University. She lives with two roommates in a small apartment, and has been working as a waitress at a local restaurant for six months. Jade has experienced difficulty with body image issues since she was a teenager, but ever since she has started working, she has been exercising rigorously three times a day. She will often show up late to class and work because of her exercise routine. During the day, Jade will not eat at all, but in the evenings consume an exorbitant amount of food to make up for it. After she's finished eating, Jade feels an intense wave of guilt every time because she always consumes more than she originally plans to. When seeing other women that appear to be skinnier than her, Jade feels extremely insecure and depressed. On the weekends, instead of spending time with her friends or studying for exams, Jade maintains her exercise routine and busy work schedule. Concerned with her habits, her roommates encourage Jade to seek assistance from an on-campus clinician. Once there, Jade explains to the clinician that her schedule just does not allow for her to "eat at a normal time" but admits that she is "tired of equating her self-worth" to her body's appearance.

Section A: Initial Information Gathering

Before making a provisional DSM-5 diagnosis, what information is required?

DIRECTIONS: Select AS MANY as you consider correct and necessary.

1. Client's reason(s) for seeking treatment
2. Mood status
3. Marital/Relationship history
4. Client's physiology (height and weight)
5. Amount of food intake
6. History of suicidal attempts
7. History of job-related problems
8. Drug abuse screening test (DAST)
9. History of NSSI

Section A: Relevance of Initial Information Gathering

1. Client's reason(s) for seeking treatment

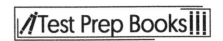

INDICATED (+3)

Understanding how the client feels and the rationale behind her behavior is important when collecting initial data. The clinician should play close attention to the emotions being expressed as the client speaks about her experience. Gauging the level of distress will determine the severity of her condition and the course of treatment.

2. Mood status

INDICATED (+1)

The client's mood status should be regularly evaluated. This allows the clinician to notice if the behaviors or symptoms of mental disorders lessen or worsen depending on mood changes.

3. Marital/Relationship history

NOT INDICATED (-3)

The client's relationship status is not relevant to the presenting issues. Relationship issues have been reported to cause issues related to body image and problematic eating habits. Because Jade does not mention any kind of romantic relationship issues, it would be incorrect to consider this essential to her problems.

4. Client's physiology (height and weight)

INDICATED (+3)

Given that the client's problems appear to be centered around body image and eating habits, knowing the height, weight, and other physiological components of the client is essential when diagnosing certain disorders. This information is generally reviewed before the client interacts with the clinician.

5. Amount of food intake

INDICATED (+2)

The amount of nutrients the client is receiving is vital for the types of problems indicated. This information would allow for the clinician to understand if she is engaging in binge-eating or not.

6. History of suicidal attempts

NOT INDICATED (-2)

The client seems to have experienced mental health issues as a teenager, but there is no indication of suicidal ideation in the information provided.

7. History of job-related problems

INDICATED (+2)

The client's exercise behaviors seem to have started around the time she began working, and causing work-related problems as a result. Knowing if she has engaged in these behaviors in other work environments would provide information about the onset of the behaviors.

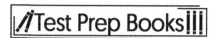

8. Drug abuse screening test (DAST)

NOT INDICATED (-3)

There is no data supporting the presence of problematic drug use. There are specific types of drugs that can be used inhibit hunger, but other symptoms of drug use would be associated with her behavior if that were the case (tolerance, withdrawal, going to great lengths to retrieve substances, etc.)

9. History of NSSI

NOT INDICATED (-1)

The client's behaviors are not representative of NSSI because the behaviors do not result in bleeding, pain, or bruising.

Section B: Identify Potential Issues

Considering the information provided, what are the main issues that need to be addressed?

DIRECTIONS: Select AS MANY as you consider correct and necessary.

1. Financial problems
2. Social anxiety
3. Physical health
4. Concentration problems
5. Eating problems
6. Emotion regulation
7. Academic performance
8. Impulsivity

Section B: Relevance of Identifying Potential Issues

1. Financial problems

INDICATED (+1)

Given the client's living conditions, status as a college student, and heavy work schedule, financial issues may be an area of concern for the clinician to address with the client.

2. Social anxiety

NOT INDICATED (-2)

While the client seems to prefer to engage in activities that do not involve a lot of interpersonal leisure time, the type of work and relationship with her roommates suggest that she has the capability of interacting and forming relationships with others without any indication of anxiety.

3. Physical health

INDICATED (+3)

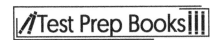

The client's rigorous exercise routine and eating habits can cause significant damage to her physical health. Continuous exercise without rest causes great strain on the body and unbalanced eating may result in severe gastrointestinal issues.

4. Concentration problems

NOT INDICATED (-2)

Concentrating on tasks themselves does not seem to be an issue with this client, as she is able to perform well in areas when she focuses on certain tasks. The issues she is experiencing does not affect her ability to stay on task. What needs to be addressed is where she is directing her attention, not her ability to concentrate in general.

5. Eating problems

INDICATED (+3)

The client presents with problematic compensatory behaviors as well as eating patterns. Given that her main concern is "equating her self-worth" to what her body looks like and the impairment in functioning revolves around this, problems with eating is the issue that resonates the most with this client.

6. Emotion regulation

INDICATED (+2)

The client does associate self-worth with bodily appearance, and feels intense guilt and sadness when eating or when seeing other women that appear to be skinnier than her. By addressing emotion regulation, the clinician will be able to inform Jade with healthy coping mechanisms that can be used when she begins to feel guilty after eating or when being triggered by other women.

7. Academic performance

INDICATED (+1)

Jade mentions that she is often late to class because of her exercise schedule and commits a significant amount of time to exercise rather than preparing for exams. As a result, it appears that her academic performance may have suffered from her behaviors.

8. Impulsivity

INDICATED (+1)

Impulsive behavior can be found in the times that she does allow herself to eat. Because she does not eat during the day, she consumes an excessive amount of food in the evenings.

Section C: Additional Information Gathering

Based on initial intake data, what is the MOST likely provisional DSM-5 diagnosis?

DIRECTIONS: Select as many as you consider correct and necessary.

    1. Obsessive-Compulsive Disorder (OCD)

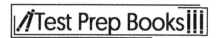

2. Anorexia Nervosa
3. Bulimia Nervosa
4. Rumination Disorder
5. Binge-Eating Disorder

Section C: Relevance of Additional Information Gathering

1. Obsessive-Compulsive Disorder (OCD)

NOT INDICATED (-2)

Upon looking at the synopsis of the client's symptoms, OCD might seem like a reasonable diagnosis. This is because her exercise routine could be considered a compulsion. However, the remaining symptoms are all centered around body image and eating, indicating that the behavior can be better explained by an eating disorder.

2. Anorexia Nervosa

NOT INDICATED (-1)

The client presents thought patterns and behaviors that could resemble a diagnosis of anorexia nervosa. However, there is still information needed about the client in order to meet the criteria for this disorder. Not knowing the weight of the client prevents the clinician from being able to diagnose them with anorexia. Based on how she describes her eating, it can be determined that she engages in binge-eating behavior. While people with this disorder can engage in binge-eating, although it is relatively uncommon, they must attempt to get rid of the food afterward by purging (vomiting, laxatives, diuretics, or enemas). The client does not engage in any purging behaviors.

3. Bulimia Nervosa

INDICATED (+3)

Bulimia nervosa is the most plausible diagnosis that can be given to this individual. She engages in binge-eating, exercises excessively to compensate for the binge, meets the time duration requirements, and evaluates her self-worth based on her weight. What can differentiate this disorder from anorexia is the type of behavior involved as well as the body weight of the individual. The client does not purge; she exercises excessively instead. Additionally, a specific weight requirement is not a criterion of this disorder. Therefore, this diagnosis is still able to be made given the lack of information regarding her actual body weight.

4. Rumination Disorder

NOT INDICATED (-3)

As mentioned before, the client does not engage in any purging behaviors which is the primary indicator of rumination disorder.

5. Binge-Eating Disorder

NOT INDICATED (-2)

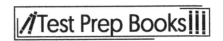

Presence of binge-eating does not necessarily mean the individual has binge-eating disorder. In order to be diagnosed with this disorder, the binge-eating cannot be paired with compensatory behaviors that exist with bulimia nervosa. For this client, binge-eating disorder would be an incorrect diagnosis based on her compensatory behavior of excessive exercise.

Section D: Decision Making

Given the available data and MOST likely provisional DSM-5 diagnosis, what services can you provide that be the MOST beneficial to the client?

DIRECTIONS: Select AS MANY as seem correct and necessary.

1. Cognitive-behavioral therapy (CBT)
2. Group psychotherapy
3. Psychanalysis
4. Applied behavioral analysis (ABA)
5. Expressive therapy

Section D: Relevance of Decision Making

1. Cognitive-behavioral therapy (CBT)

INDICATED (+3)

CBT is the most active and beneficial form of psychotherapy for bulimia. The technique challenges problematic thought patterns and allows the individual to form a new relationship with their body through the reinforcement of new, healthy thought patterns.

2. Group psychotherapy

NOT INDICATED (-1)

Group psychotherapy has been used in the past to alleviate the symptoms and thought patterns associated with bulimia considering it can facilitate connection with people who experience the same problems. However, given the client's tendency to be triggered by other people's weight, it has the potential to interrupt the therapeutic process and may actually worsen symptoms. It might be useful for the clinician to suggest this in the future, but immediate referral to a group program may propose too many risks for the client.

3. Psychoanalysis

NOT INDICATED (-3)

Psychoanalysis is a method of treatment that focuses on unconscious motives surrounding existing behavior. Psychoanalytic therapy may be effective for individuals who have trouble connecting their behavior to their emotions about themselves. For this client, it seems that she is capable of connecting her behavior to how she feels about herself, so psychoanalysis may not be as effective as other treatment methods.

4. Applied behavioral analysis (ABA)

NOT INDICATED (-3)

Applied behavioral analysis is a technique of behavior therapy that focuses on removing and replacing maladaptive behavior traits with more desirable ones. This type of therapy is commonly used on individuals with autism spectrum disorder due to the behavioral difficulties associated with the condition. This client is conscientious with her behavior and understands the complexities behind it, so ABA would not be as successful as other methods.

5. Expressive therapy

NOT INDICATED (-1)

Expressive therapy is a type of therapy that emphasizes emotional expression through exercises that stimulate creativity, such as painting or drawing. While expressing emotions in this way may help the client develop a new hobby, talk-therapy would be more suitable to address the issues at hand.

Section E: Treatment Methods

Based on all the data obtained, what short-term treatment goals might be the MOST beneficial to the client?

DIRECTIONS: Select AS MANY as you consider indicated in this session.

1. Help client to strengthen self-esteem
2. Help client to develop a healthy eating/exercise schedule
3. Help client to explore career goals
4. Help client to strengthen interpersonal relationships

Section E: Relevance of Treatment Methods

1. Help client to strengthen self-esteem

INDICATED (+2)

The client appears to compare herself to others based on physical appearance. By allowing her to strengthen her self-esteem, less emphasis will be placed on physical appearance when regarding self-worth.

2. Help client to develop a healthy eating/exercise schedule

INDICATED (+3)

Implementing a healthy schedule will allow the client's immediate issues to be resolved. The clinician should emphasize the importance of sticking to a healthy schedule and provide nutritional education if needed. This will also work to resolve issues related to punctuality and academic performance, and improve social relationships.

3. Help client to explore career goals

NOT INDICATED (-3)

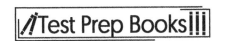

The client's career goals are not of immediate concern. Given that the client is a student at a university, she still has time to consider what her goals will be. The client also has the ability to use the university's resources if that is an area of concern for her.

4. Help client to strengthen interpersonal relationships

NOT INDICATED (-1)

The client appears to have a close group of friends considering that they are the ones that referred her to the clinician. Having the ability to make more time for friends will come with the implementation of a healthy eating/exercise routine as well as strengthened self-esteem for this client.

Section F: Ethical Issues

You receive a call from one of Jade's friends that referred her to you. She is calling to see if Jade has made any progress lately. How do you respond?

DIRECTIONS: Select ONLY ONE answer unless you are instructed to make another selection in this section.

     1. Ask the friend to elaborate because "progress" is too vague.
     2. Explain to the friend that this is a breach of client-therapist confidentiality and no information will be shared.
     3. Answer her friend honestly because she is the one who referred Jade to your services.
     4. Encourage the friend to reach out to Jade herself for that information.
     5. Ask if the friend received consent from Jade to call you about this information before answering.

Section F: Relevance of Ethical Issues

1. Ask the friend to elaborate because "progress" is too vague.

NOT INDICATED (-1)

The friend does not have the right to know about Jade's experience in therapy without her consent.

2. Explain to the friend that this is a breach of client-therapist confidentiality and no information will be shared.

INDICATED (+3)

This situation does not allow for client-therapist confidentiality to be breached. The clinician needs to explain that while the request may be coming from a place of genuine care, information regarding clients is legally bound private by laws and regulations.

3. Answer her friend honestly because she is the one who referred Jade to your services.

NOT INDICATED (-3)

Regardless of who referred the client to the clinician's services, it is unethical for a clinician to share confidential information without the client's consent.

4. Encourage the friend to reach out to Jade herself for that information.

INDICATED (+1)

This response maintains client-therapist confidentiality while also creating the possibility to strengthen the friendship between the two.

5. Ask if the friend received consent from Jade to call you about this information before answering.

NOT INDICATED (-2)

There is no way of knowing if the client gave consent to her friend in this way, as it presents the possibility for false information to be used.

Section G: Termination Phase

Upon successful completion of a predetermined number of counseling sessions, what recommendations would you suggest in order for your client to maintain her ability to minimize her compensatory and eating behaviors?

DIRECTIONS: Select AS MANY as you consider indicated in this section.

1. The client should be encouraged to enter a support group program for individuals with eating disorders.
2. The client should be encouraged to find a new job.
3. The client should take the rest of the year off from school in order to focus on treatment.
4. The client should continue to use the healthy eating/exercise schedule.
5. The client should be encouraged to join an intermural sports league.

Section G: Relevance of Termination Phase

1. The client should be encouraged to enter a support group program for individuals with eating disorders.

INDICATED (+2)

As treatment progresses and both coping mechanisms and thought patterns seem to improve, a support group for this client may prove to be useful in alleviating symptoms related to bulimia.

2. The client should be encouraged to find a new job.

NOT INDICATED (-1)

The symptoms of her mental illness appear to have started around the same time she started working as a waitress, but the nature of the job itself does not seem to intensify the client's symptoms. Taking on less hours at work may be a better recommendation since financial stability is still an important factor to consider.

3. The client should take the rest of the year off from school to focus on treatment.

NOT INDICATED (-2)

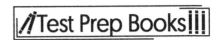

If the client's condition has improved, then delaying educational advancement may just add more stress to the current situation.

4. The client should continue to use the healthy eating/exercise schedule.

INDICATED (+3)

If the schedule has been proven to work for this client, there is no need to discontinue the use of it after treatment. The schedule can be adjusted if more responsibilities appear in the client's life and has the ability to be personalized for the specific client.

5. The client should be encouraged to join an intermural sports league.

INDICATED (+1)

Joining a sports team may benefit this client greatly. With scheduled meetings and practices, the client would be able to incorporate these activities into a structured schedule. Additionally, being active with other people will allow the client to hold herself accountable and have the motivation not to overwork herself physically.

Practice Simulation 2

Kim is a forty-three-year-old woman who is coming to see you for an initial intake interview. Ever since Kim was in her twenties, she has always struggled with anger issues which leads her to having trouble maintaining interpersonal relationships both romantically and platonically. Every time there is a minor inconvenience or conflict with someone, she feels intense anger and takes it very personally; to the point where she initiates intense verbal arguments and does not want to speak to the person ever again. Kim is able to stop herself from being violent with others during her outbursts. She has an extensive history of seeking mental health treatment but has not experienced any improvement. Occasionally, Kim will disappear for days and engage in sex with strangers and spend excessive amounts of money. During the interview, you notice that she has scars and lesions all over her arms. When you inquire about them, she mentions how she recently got into a fight with her sister and reacted by cutting herself so she can "feel something other than anger and emptiness."

Section A: Initial Information Gathering

Before making a provisional DSM-5 diagnosis, what information is required?

DIRECTIONS: Select AS MANY as you consider correct and necessary.

1. History of suicidal attempts
2. Medical history, including current medications
3. Homicidal ideation
4. Childhood experiences
5. History of substance abuse

Section A: Relevance of Initial Information Gathering

1. History of suicidal attempts

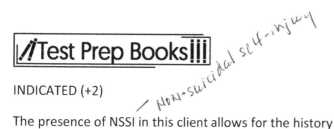

INDICATED (+2)

/ Non-suicidal self-injury

The presence of NSSI in this client allows for the history of suicidal attempts to be explored. She mentions that she has received mental health treatment in the past, meaning that there is a possibility she could have been hospitalized for engaging in suicidal behavior.

2. Medical history, including current medications

INDICATED (+3)

Understanding the client's current medicinal history will provide insight on what symptoms are already being treated and what symptoms are not improving. The clinician would gain more information on the client's overall symptoms than they would receive from briefly meeting with the client for the first time.

3. Homicidal ideation

NOT INDICATED (-2)

Homicidal ideation is commonly evaluated in initial assessments, but based on the client's emotional experience with conflict, she is more inclined to cause harm to herself than others. Assessing homicidal ideation has the potential to damage the therapeutic relationship this early on.

4. Childhood experiences

INDICATED (+1)

The client only mentions symptoms as they presented in adulthood, so having knowledge of childhood experiences will allow the clinician to have an understanding of how pervasive her condition is.

5. History of substance abuse

NOT INDICATED (-3)

The client does not mention any issues related to substance use. This might be a topic to assess later on, but substance abuse does not appear to play a role in her symptomology.

Section B: Level of Functioning

Considering the information collected so far, what information would you need to gather to determine the client's level of functioning?

DIRECTIONS: Select AS MANY as you consider indicated in this session.

1. The client's hobbies
2. The client's weight
3. The quality of the client's relationships
4. The client's ability to perform occupational responsibilities
5. The client's use of television time

Section B: Relevance of Level of Functioning

1. The client's hobbies

NOT INDICATED (-2)

The type of activities the client engages in does not reflect their level of functioning.

2. The client's weight

NOT INDICATED (-3)

This client does not seem to struggle with body image or weight issues, so determining weight should not be prioritized.

3. The quality of the client's relationships

INDICATED (+3)

The client mentions how maintaining interpersonal relationships is a primary issue. Exploring the quality of these relationships even further would help determine the level of functioning as clinically impaired or not.

4. The client's ability to perform occupational responsibilities

INDICATED (+2)

Job performance is a component of level of functioning that is typically assessed during initial intake interviews. Considering the client did not mention what she does for a living, understanding this area of her life and how it is affected would aid in determining level of functioning.

5. The client's use of television time

NOT INDICATED (-3)

Excessive television use is not of concern to this specific client because it was not mentioned during the interview.

Section C: Assessing Client Progress

Considering the information collected so far, what data would be important in tracking the client's progress?

DIRECTIONS: Select AS MANY as you consider indicated in this session.

    1. Interpersonal relations improvement
    2. Use of healthy coping strategies
    3. New friendships gained
    4. Amount of money spent
    5. Drug and alcohol consumption

Section C: Relevance of Assessing Client Progress

1. Interpersonal relations improvement

INDICATED (+3)

The client mentions that her most recent fight has been with her sister. By monitoring the progression of this conflict with the client, the clinician is able to gain an idea of what skills or tools the client has used to resolve the conflict or assess what thinking patterns could be worsening it.

2. Use of healthy coping strategies

INDICATED (+2)

Keeping track of the frequency of coping strategies will hold the client accountable for following the recommendations provided by the clinician.

3. New friendships gained

INDICATED (+1)

Evaluating and processing new friendships with the client can allow for proper reflection and provide preparation for future conflicts if they occur.

4. Amount of money spent

INDICATED (+1)

The client mentions that she will sometimes spend excessive amounts of money when she does not need to, indicating that she is in a state of emotional distress. The clinician may find it helpful to fully understand the frequency of this habit and determine the course of how it should be treated subsequently.

5. Drug and alcohol consumption

NOT INDICATED (-3)

Drug use and alcohol consumption was not mentioned by this client during the initial interview, so this is not an area of the client's life that needs to be regularly assessed.

Section D: Initial Testing

Considering the information collected so far, what initial testing would seem the MOST appropriate in order to formulate a clearer understanding of the client's disorder?

DIRECTIONS: Select ONLY ONE answer unless you are instructed to make another selection in this section.

1. Wechsler Adult Intelligence Scale (WAIS)
2. The Minnesota Multiphasic Personality Inventory (MMPI)
3. Mental Status Examination (MSE)
4. Anger Management Assessment
5. Psycho-Vocational Evaluation (PVE)

Section D: Relevance of Initial Testing

1. Wechsler Adult Intelligence Scale (WAIS)

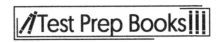

NOT INDICATED (-3)

The WAIS is an assessment used to measure the IQ of adults. The client does not present any neurocognitive or neurodevelopmental deficiencies, so this test would not be relevant for this client.

2. The Minnesota Multiphasic Personality Inventory (MMPI)

INDICATED (+3)

The MMPI is a common assessment used to assist in the diagnosis of personality disorders, depression, anxiety, and other pervasive psychological factors. Given that the client's symptoms have persisted for over twenty years, a personality assessment would serve to be useful in this case to rule out these factors.

3. Mental Status Examination (MSE)

NOT INDICATED (-2)

The MSE is an assessment used to test for psychotic symptoms or difficulties in perceiving the real world. This client does not appear to experience these types of symptoms, so this assessment would not be considered a priority.

4. Anger Management Assessment

INDICATED (+2)

The client's primary issue seems to be related to her anger and the results of her emotional outbursts. Assessing for clinical anger would aid in the diagnosis of several mental disorders.

5. Psycho-Vocational Evaluation (PVE)

NOT INDICATED (-3)

PVEs are assessments conducted by psychologist that evaluate whether or not a physically or cognitively impaired person that has been injured is able to regain full-employment. Level of functioning and decision-making abilities are areas within this assessment. The client's issues do not align with the reasoning for a PVE to be conducted.

Section E: Additional Information Gathering

Identify the LEAST useful information or therapeutic techniques to provide the client with during this intake session.

DIRECTIONS: Select ONLY ONE answer unless you are instructed to make another selection in this section.

   1. Informing the client that confidentiality may be breached if the client presents as a danger to themselves or others.
   2. Explaining how family members can be present in the therapy session and mediated by the clinician under the client's consent.
   3. Empathizing with the client about her symptoms by explaining how you can relate to their situation because you also struggle with self-harm and anger.

4. Initiating a hug with the client after she opens up her symptoms and challenges.

5. Ask the client for her consent to consult with her psychiatrist to gather more information.

Section E: Relevance of Additional Information Gathering

1. Informing the client that confidentiality may be breached if the client presents as a danger to themselves or others.

NOT INDICATED (-3)

Explaining the nuances of confidentiality is imperative to the therapeutic relationship for several reasons. Legally, clinicians are obligated to report if their clients have active suicidal or homicidal ideation. The client's safety, as well as other people's safety, is of primary importance to a clinician that is ethically responsible.

2. Explaining how family members can be present in the therapy session and mediated by the clinician under the client's consent.

NOT INDICATED (-1)

This information may be valuable if the client is interested in resolving interpersonal issues with the therapist present.

3. Empathizing with the client about her symptoms by explaining how you can relate to their situation because you also struggle with self-harm and anger.

INDICATED (+2)

Self-disclosure may be beneficial in some therapeutic contexts, but this manner is not helpful or progressive in this context. By explaining your own personal issues, this takes the attention off of the client and may even force them in an uncomfortable position to comfort you.

4. Initiating a hug with the client after she opens up her symptoms and challenges.

INDICATED (+3)

Physical contact should never be initiated by the clinician. This action resembles a personal relationship rather than a professional one, and may place the client in an uncomfortable position. If a client initiates this kind of action, it is the clinician's decision to either accept or politely reject depending on the existing relationship and the results that would come from it.

5. Ask the client for her consent to consult with her psychiatrist to gather more information.

NOT INDICATED (-2)

Many clinicians consult with client's medical practitioners in order to gather more information about their clients. It also reflects proper ethical behavior to ask for consent from the client.

Section F: Diagnosis

Based on all the data acquired, what seems to be the MOST accurate provisional DSM-5 diagnosis?

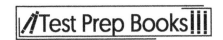

DIRECTIONS: Select ONLY ONE answer unless you are instructed to "Make another selection in this section."

    1. Intermittent Explosive Disorder (IED)
    2. Borderline Personality Disorder (BPD)
    3. Major Depressive Disorder (MDD)
    4. Bipolar I Disorder
    5. Dependent Personality Disorder (DPD)

Section F: Relevance of Diagnosis

1. Intermittent Explosive Disorder (IED)

NOT INDICATED (-1)

This diagnosis is most common in children and adolescents. Without information of the client's childhood, this diagnosis is difficult to make since it rarely develops in adulthood. The onset of symptoms appearing as a young adult suggests that the symptoms are more indicative of a personality disorder rather than a disruptive, impulsive-control, or conduct disorder.

2. Borderline Personality Disorder (BPD)

INDICATED (+3)

This client meets all of the criteria for BPD. Engaging in self-harm, having unstable interpersonal relationships, and experiencing chronic emptiness, intense anger, and marked impulsivity are all indicative of this disorder. Additionally, this disorder encapsulates how pervasive the client's condition truly is.

3. Major Depressive Disorder (MDD)

NOT INDICATED (-3)

The client does not show any indication of depressive episodes in her behavior. Angry outbursts can sometimes manifest as depressive symptoms, but her other actions suggest that her diagnosis has more complex layers than major depression.

4. Bipolar I Disorder

NOT INDICATED (-2)

While the client's anger and impulsivity could be perceived as manic, her other symptoms as well as the time duration suggest that a personality disorder better explains her condition. Depressive episodes are also not present in this particular client's behavior.

5. Dependent Personality Disorder (DPD)

NOT INDICATED (-3)

Individuals with dependent personality disorder have extreme difficulty operating their daily life without the assistance of others. The reason this disorder does not apply to this client is because Kim's behaviors are not indicative of co-dependency to this degree. It is clear that she fears abandonment, however she also initiates the arguments and displays her feelings of betrayal or disagreement in order to please the other person involved. Someone with DPD would not act in this way because they want other people around them no matter what.

Section G: Treatment Methods

Based on all the data obtained, what treatment methods might be the MOST beneficial to the client?

DIRECTIONS: Select AS MANY as you consider indicated in this session.

1. De-escalation exercises
2. Dialectical-behavior therapy (DBT)
3. Family therapy
4. Group psychotherapy
5. Habit reversal training (HRT)

Section G: Relevance of Treatment Methods

1. De-escalation exercises

INDICATED (+2)

De-escalation exercises, such as deep-breathing or other mindfulness techniques, have the ability to be highly successful in those who suffer from anger issues. When a conflict occurs, the client will be able to self-soothe and not be as reactive as she was in the past.

2. Dialectical-behavior therapy (DBT)

INDICATED (+3)

DBT is a style of therapy that was created with the intention to treat BPD. DBT is used to replace maladaptive behaviors with more progressive ones, such as emotion regulation and interpersonal effectiveness. DBT has extensive support from researchers and is highly encouraged for individuals with BPD.

3. Family therapy

INDICATED (+1)

Given that the last altercation occurred with a family member for this client, family therapy may prove to be helpful in resolving future conflicts. The clinician has the ability to mediate the discussion and intervene as necessary.

4. Group psychotherapy

INDICATED (+1)

Research suggests that group psychotherapy has been successful for individuals with BPD, although it is recommended that attending a group program should be encouraged only when progress has been made in individual psychotherapy. This is due to the nature of BPD's symptomology in that progressive group dynamics can be compromised by arguments or other forms of interpersonal conflict.

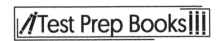

5. Habit reversal training (HRT)

NOT INDICATED (-1)

HRT is a type of behavior therapy that focuses on redirecting problematic behavioral urges. Individuals can be exposed to a stimulus that triggers a behavioral response, and HRT aids in recognizing the trigger and substituting the response with a different behavior. This treatment is commonly used for people diagnosed with Trichotillomania (hair-pulling disorder) or who present other anxiety-related behaviors. The client's tendency to self-harm could be addressed with this treatment, although current research has shown that cognitive-behavioral therapy is the most beneficial treatment for NSSI.

NCMHCE Simulations

Directions: Choose the best answer or answers indicated for each question under the simulation. For each option under the Section questions, the answer explanations will determine whether the option is NOT INDICATED (-1 to -3) or INDICATED (+1 to +3).

Simulation 1

Tamara is a 27-year-old woman from Manhattan, New York. She is newly married and has a newborn girl. Tamara is currently unemployed, and her husband is working two jobs to make ends meet. Tamara has been having difficulty sleeping, which started a few years before the baby was born. She worries every day about the family's finances, retirement, and the baby's well-being, and she can't seem to calm herself down. When asked about going back to work, she immediately begins to cry at the thought of leaving her newborn baby in the care of a stranger. Sometimes her worrying has even gotten in the way of her concentration. Tamara has also been experiencing prolonged muscle tension and bouts of indigestion. At her initial visit, Tamara asked for help getting to sleep at night, staying asleep, and has expressed the desire to just generally "feel better."

Section A: Initial Information Gathering

Before making a provisional DSM-5 diagnosis, what information is required?

DIRECTIONS: Select AS MANY as you consider correct.

1. Client's reason(s) for seeking treatment ✓
2. History of marital problems
3. History of mental illness ✓
4. Educational history
5. Suicidal attempts ✓
6. Mood status ✓
7. History of job-related problems ✓
8. Frequency and severity of symptoms ✓
9. Current stressors ✓
10. Drug abuse screening test (DAST)

Section B: Identify Potential Issues

Considering the information obtained, what are the main issues that need to be addressed?

DIRECTIONS: Select AS MANY as seem correct and necessary.

1. Communication problems
2. Financial problems ✓
3. Parenting problems
4. Trust issues ✓
5. Eating problems
6. Separation anxiety ✓
7. Physical health ✓

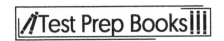

8. Postpartum issues
9. Seasonal mood patterns
10. Concentration problems

Section C: Additional Information Gathering

Based on initial intake data, what is the MOST likely provisional DSM-5 diagnosis?

DIRECTIONS: Select ONLY ONE answer unless you are instructed to "Make another selection in this section."

1. Panic disorder
2. Acute stress disorder
3. Adjustment disorder with anxiety
4. Attention deficit hyperactivity disorder (ADHD)
5. Generalized anxiety disorder (GAD) ✔

Section D: Decision Making

Given the available data and MOST likely provisional DSM-5 diagnosis, what services can you provide that will MOST benefit the client?

DIRECTIONS: Select AS MANY as seem correct and necessary.

1. Family counseling sessions ✔
2. In-home behavioral management plan
3. Healthy eating plan
4. Cognitive-behavioral therapy (CBT) ✔
5. Dream analysis

Section E: Treatment Methods

Based on all the data obtained, what short-term treatment goals might be the MOST beneficial to the client?

DIRECTIONS: Select AS MANY as you consider indicated in this session.

1. Help client to strengthen social relationships
2. Help client to explore career goals
3. Help client to strengthen self-esteem ✔
4. Help client to decrease anxiety ✔
5. Help client search for trustworthy caregivers for her infant ✔

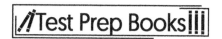

Section F: Decision Making (Ethical Issues)

You receive a call from the client's mother who wishes to know how her daughter is doing and what the specific issues are for which she is being treated. How do you respond?

DIRECTIONS: Select ONLY ONE answer unless you are instructed to "Make another selection in this section."

> 1. Explain to the client's mother that this is a breach of client-therapist confidentiality and no information will be shared. ✔
> 2. Inform the mother that you will speak to your client, and if your client gives her consent to share this information, you will call her back to discuss the details of this case.
> 3. Ask the mother to visit you in order to sign a confidentiality form before you divulge sensitive information.
> 4. Ask that the mother contact her daughter directly for the information she is seeking.
> 5. Ask that the mother and daughter come together for the next counseling session.

Section G: Termination Phase

Upon successful completion of a predetermined number of counseling sessions, what recommendations would you suggest in order for your client to maintain her ability to concentrate and minimize the frequency and level of worry?

DIRECTIONS: Select AS MANY as you consider indicated in this section.

- 1. The client should continue regular individual counseling.
- 2. The client will be encouraged to join a parental support group. ✔
- 3. Prescribed medication and reduction in therapy sessions.
- 4. The client should be referred to a psychiatrist for further evaluation. ✔
- 5. Regular family therapy is recommended for this client. ✔

Simulation 2

Joseph is an elderly man in his mid-80s who, sixteen months ago, lost his wife of almost sixty years. Joseph was reluctant to come to his initial counseling appointment, but finally consented due to his daughter's persistence. He expressed his extreme sadness over the loss of his wife, stating that life has never been the same since this loss. He recently lost his driving license after an at-fault accident, and he doesn't sleep or eat well. He speaks repeatedly of his wife and the way life "used to be," and wishes nothing more than to be with his wife again. When asked why he decided to come to this appointment, he responded that he wants his wife back and he wants his life back.

Section A: Initial Information Gathering

What intake data should be considered in order to determine a provisional DSM-5 diagnosis?

DIRECTIONS: Select AS MANY as you consider correct.

> 1. Traumatic life events
> 2. Duration and intensity of the grieving process
> 3. Religious affiliation

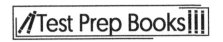

4. Medical history, including current medications

5. Driving record

Section B: Initial Testing

Considering the information collected so far, what initial testing would seem the MOST appropriate in order to formulate a clearer understanding of the client's disorder?

DIRECTIONS: Select ONLY ONE answer unless you are instructed to "Make another selection in this section."

1. Behavioral assessment rating scale
2. The Bender-Gestalt II
3. Mental Status Examination (MSE)
4. Personality Factor Questionnaire
5. Wechsler Adult Intelligence Scale (WAIS)

Section C: Additional Information Gathering

Identify the LEAST useful information to provide the client during this intake session.

DIRECTIONS: Select ONLY ONE answer unless you are instructed to "Make another selection in this section."

1. Information will be kept on file and seen only by the treating counselor.
2. If the client consents, information will be shared with professional colleagues.
3. The treating counselor will consult the DSM-5 in order to help determine a diagnosis.
4. Information will be shared with family members only with the client's express consent.
5. Medical records must be handed over to authorities if ordered by the courts.

Section D: Decision Making

What assessment instruments would be MOST appropriate to help determine a DSM-5 diagnosis?

DIRECTIONS: Select AS MANY as seem correct and necessary.

1. House-tree-person test
2. Self-directed search
3. Rorschach
4. Inventory of complicated grief (ICG)
5. Transactional analysis (TA)

Section E: Diagnosis

Based on all the data acquired, what seems to be the MOST accurate provisional DSM-5 diagnosis?

DIRECTIONS: Select ONLY ONE answer unless you are instructed to "Make another selection in this section."

1. Intermittent explosive disorder
2. Parent-child relational problem

3. Unspecified depressive disorder
4. Phase of life problem
5. Persistent complex bereavement disorder (PCBD)

Section F: Confirming Diagnosis

In order to confirm this diagnosis, which following elements would be the MOST important to consider?

DIRECTIONS: Select AS MANY as seem correct and necessary.

1. Client's prolonged period of grief
2. Client's struggle to focus on anything other than the loss of his wife
3. Excessive longing for the departed
4. Client's level of frustration and anger
5. Client's reluctance to engage in counseling

Section G: Interventions

What interventions would BEST benefit this client?

DIRECTIONS: Select AS MANY as you consider correct.

1. Assistance coping with significant life changes
2. Relaxation/breathing techniques
3. Support groups
4. Exercise
5. Occasional alcohol consumption

Simulation 3

Hana is an 18-year-old female who has just emigrated from Japan to the United States with her parents and older brother. She speaks very little English and presents herself as a very quiet and reserved person. Her brother has enrolled in college classes, but Hana has not yet registered for any classes despite her high academic achievements in high school. She rarely leaves the home, and when prompted to explain why, Hana expressed her great fear at attempting to meet people or take classes in a language she hardly understands. She said that she would prefer to stay in the comfort of her home, where she feels safe, and take care of her parents and brother. She spends a lot of time talking with family and friends back home.

Section A: Initial Information Gathering

Select the MOST appropriate questions to ask this client in order to ascertain the reason/s she is seeking counseling.

DIRECTIONS: Select AS MANY as seem correct and necessary.

1. What was her childhood like growing up in Japan?
2. What is her educational history?
3. How would she describe her social life?
4. What are her career aspirations?

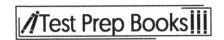

5. How would she describe her relationship with her father?

Section B: Additional Information Gathering

What additional information would be relevant to understanding the client's current mental and emotional well-being?

DIRECTIONS: Select AS MANY as you consider correct.

1. The family's collective income
2. The brother's social life in the United States
3. Cultural sensitivities
4. The client's mental health history
5. The client's relationship with her family members

Section C: Ruling Out Criteria

What would a counselor have to rule out concerning this client before formulating a provisional DSM-5 diagnosis?

DIRECTIONS: Select ONLY ONE answer unless you are instructed to "Make another selection in this section."

1. History of drug use/abuse
2. Sleeping difficulties
3. Currently prescribed medications
4. History of learning disabilities
5. Past hospitalizations

Section D: Diagnosis

After considering all of the initial intake data, what might be the MOST appropriate provisional DSM-5 diagnosis?

DIRECTIONS: Select AS MANY as seem correct and necessary.

1. Conduct disorder, adolescent-onset type
2. Oppositional defiant disorder (ODD)
3. Acute stress disorder
4. Adjustment disorder
5. Acculturation problem

Section E: Interventions

Which of the following interventions may be MOST appropriate to help you monitor the client's progress?

DIRECTIONS: Select AS MANY as you consider indicated in this section.

1. Role play
2. Imagery rehearsal therapy

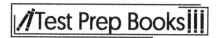

3. Medication

4. Teach back method

5. LEARN mnemonic

Section F: Decision Making

Your client asks if her brother can attend the next session with her. How do you respond?

DIRECTIONS: Select ONLY ONE answer unless you are instructed to "Make another selection in this section."

1. Explain to the client that this would be a breach of client-therapist confidentiality, and that no information should be shared with her brother.

2. Agree to allow the brother to attend the next session.

3. Ask the client to sign a consent form allowing her brother to attend the next session.

4. Explain that you cannot treat other members of your client's family.

5. Suggest that you see the brother separately for a session before you see both brother and sister together.

Section G: Short-Term Goals

Identify the MOST appropriate short-term goals for this client.

DIRECTIONS: Select AS MANY as you consider indicated in this section.

1. Gradually reduce the number of times the client speaks to family and friends in Japan

2. Attend a weekly support group for immigrants

3. Enroll in English-speaking classes

4. Enroll in full-time college as quickly as possible

5. Explore a variety of career paths that interest the client

Simulation 4

Peter is a 24-year-old man who recently graduated from law school but has yet to find employment. His school debts are in the hundreds of thousands of dollars, and he laughs when he talks about this, saying, "This will never get paid off." Peter has openly admitted that he regularly drinks alcohol, which he claims got him through all his years in law school and helps him cope with the stresses of life. He brags about how much he can now drink without feeling any side effects. He tries his best to control the number of drinks he consumes each day, but he finds it difficult. He lives at home with his mom and dad, and there is constant arguing. Peter expresses mild irritation with regard to his mother's insistence that he work harder to find a job and his dad's urging him to "lay off the booze." He admitted that he wants to find work but that he just needs to take a break after so many years in school.

Section A: Initial Information Gathering

What evidence points to possible reasons that this client is seeking counseling?

DIRECTIONS: Select AS MANY as you consider correct.

1. He suspects that he might have a problem with alcohol abuse.

166

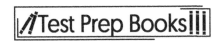

2. He perceives his parents as abusive.

3. He is feeling depressed and overwhelmed by financial debt.

4. He wants assistance with anger management.

5. He is only attending sessions to appease his parents.

Section B: Main Issues

Based on gathered data, what are the MAIN issues that need to be addressed?

DIRECTIONS: Select AS MANY as seem correct and necessary.

1. Anger management
2. Alcohol dependency
3. Alcohol addiction
4. Unemployment
5. Depression

Section C: Decision Making

What is the MOST likely provisional DSM-5 diagnosis based on current information obtained?

DIRECTIONS: Select ONLY ONE answer unless you are instructed to "Make another selection in this section."

1. Social anxiety disorder
2. Depression
3. Alcohol use disorder
4. Anxiety
5. Parent-child relational problem

Section D: Additional Data Gathering

Which of the following would be relevant in exploring further to either confirm or revise the DSM-5 provisional diagnosis?

DIRECTIONS: Select AS MANY as seem correct and necessary.

1. The number of alcoholic drinks the client consumes each day
2. The client's attempt/s to cut down or control his alcohol consumption
3. Job offers that have been declined by the client
4. The number of hours the client sleeps each night
5. His parents' history of alcohol consumption

Section E: Interventions

Based on this provisional diagnosis, which of the following interventions may be MOST effective for this client?

DIRECTIONS: Select AS MANY as you consider indicated in this section.

1. Employment counseling

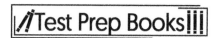

2. Family counseling
3. Behavioral modification
4. Help client to better understand his illness
5. Hypnosis

Section F: Decision Making

Taking into consideration all of the data collected, you feel that one of your colleagues has much more experience in treating clients of this type than do you, but you have made a positive connection with the client. What do you do?

DIRECTIONS: Select ONLY ONE answer unless you are instructed to "Make another selection in this section."

1. Keep the client but consult your colleague for support and advice on treatment options.
2. Refer this client to your colleague who has experience with addictive disorders.
3. Ask the client whom he would rather see—you or the other therapist.
4. Arrange for the client to meet with both you and your colleague on a regular basis.
5. Continue to treat the client and learn as much as you can about his illness.

Section G: Referrals

When considering referral services for this client, which of the following would be MOST appropriate?

DIRECTIONS: Select AS MANY as you consider indicated in this section.

1. Psychiatry
2. 12-step recovery and maintenance program
3. Self-help group
4. Family counseling
5. Legal services

Simulation 5

Derek, a 72-year-old single and very successful businessman from Texas, has been experiencing bouts of low energy over the past eight months, which is interfering with his work and personal affairs. He is known at the office and at home for exploding into rage if people disagree with him, but lately, he has become more withdrawn. His personal physician has suggested that Derek take some time off of work or gradually reduce the number of office hours, but Derek is reluctant. He is the sole owner of his business and explained that he alone has made his fortune, and that without him, the business would collapse. Derek has had two failed marriages, which he claims were directly due to the women's inability to understand him, and that neither of the women were in his intellectual bracket. He has three grown children whom he says are ungrateful for his financial support. On his initial visit, he repeated over a dozen times that he was very successful and that all he needs to keep going is to regain his energy and figure out a way to get his children and his employees to give him more credit and respect for his accomplishments and generosity.

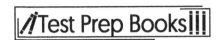

Section A: Initial Information Gathering

Based on this scenario, what is the MOST likely reason or reasons that this client is seeking counseling?

DIRECTIONS: Select AS MANY as you consider correct.

1. Low energy level
2. Work-related stress
3. Financial difficulties
4. Family problems
5. Relationship difficulties

Section B: Additional Information Gathering

What questions might a counselor wish to ask this client during the initial intake session that would help to better understand his illness?

DIRECTIONS: Select AS MANY as you consider correct.

1. What medications is the client taking?
2. Has the client experienced suicidal thoughts?
3. Has the client had a history of heart problems?
4. Has the client experienced any traumatic life events?
5. Does the client have any current or past regrets regarding actions toward or treatment of others?

Section C: Decision Making

Identify the LEAST useful information to provide the client during this intake session.

DIRECTIONS: Select AS MANY as seem correct and necessary.

1. Client-therapist confidentiality rules
2. Obligation to inform law enforcement if you feel threatened by your client
3. Medications that may help to boost his energy levels
4. Techniques on being more self-assertive
5. Effective business management strategies

Section D: Assessment Instruments

What assessment instruments would be MOST appropriate to help determine a DSM-5 diagnosis?

DIRECTIONS: Select AS MANY as seem correct and necessary.

1. Personality Diagnostic Questionnaire
2. Cloninger's Temperament and Character Inventory
3. Beck Depression Inventory–II
4. Mental Status Examination (MSE)
5. Schizophrenia Test and Early Psychosis Indicator

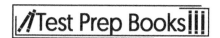

Section E: Diagnosis

Based on all the data acquired, what seems to be the MOST accurate provisional DSM-5 diagnosis?

DIRECTIONS: Select ONLY ONE answer unless you are instructed to "Make another selection in this section."

    1. Narcissistic personality disorder
    2. Social anxiety disorder
    3. Panic disorder
    4. Bipolar disorder
    5. Intermittent explosive disorder

Section F: Diagnosis Confirmation

In order to confirm this diagnosis, which of the following elements would be the MOST important to consider?

DIRECTIONS: Select AS MANY as seem correct and necessary.

    1. History of interpersonal relationships
    2. Client's lack or presence of empathy for others
    3. Client's perceived sense of self-importance
    4. Client's educational history
    5. Client's parental philosophy

Section G: Interventions

Based on the data collected, what treatments or interventions would BEST benefit this client?

DIRECTIONS: Select AS MANY as you consider correct.

    1. Anti-depressant medication
    2. Paradoxical intention
    3. Long-term psychotherapy
    4. Zung self-rating anxiety scale
    5. Exercise

Simulation 6

Over the past year, Lauren, an 8-year-old girl who lives with her mother, father, and newborn baby brother, has been acting out at home and in school. She interrupts her teacher and classmates throughout the day and can't seem to sit still. Her teacher has indicated that she is argumentative and challenges everything that she says. At home, Lauren argues with her parents and doesn't want to sit down long enough to get her homework done. When she does try to complete work, she fidgets while she sits. She loves playing with her baby brother and giggles when she makes him laugh. She has great difficulty calming down at night and is only averaging 8 to 9 hours of sleep each night. Her parents and her teacher are concerned about the changes they've seen in Lauren, but when they ask her what is going on, she seems irritated and refuses to answer any questions.

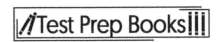

Section A: Initial Information Gathering

Select the MOST appropriate questions to ask this client in order to ascertain the reason/s they are seeking counseling.

DIRECTIONS: Select AS MANY as seem correct and necessary.

1. Can you tell me why your parents brought you here today?
2. Do you love your baby brother and your family?
3. Can you tell me the things you do at school that you love to do/do not like to do, and why?
4. What is your favorite television show?
5. How many friends do you have at school?

Section B: Additional Information Gathering

What additional information would be relevant to understanding the client's current mental and emotional well-being?

DIRECTIONS: Select AS MANY as you consider correct.

1. Client's medical history
2. Family medical history
3. Checklists and other relevant data from the client's school
4. Client's eating habits
5. Family's neighborhood and surrounding area

Section C: Ruling Out Criteria

What would a counselor have to rule out concerning this client before formulating a provisional DSM-5 diagnosis?

DIRECTIONS: Select AS MANY as you consider correct.

1. Depression
2. Oppositional defiant disorder (ODD)
3. Anorexia nervosa
4. Conduct disorder
5. Trouble adjusting to new baby brother

Section D: Diagnosis

After considering all of the initial intake data, what might be the MOST appropriate provisional DSM-5 diagnosis?

DIRECTIONS: Select AS MANY as seem correct and necessary.

1. Conversion disorder
2. Adjustment disorder with depressed mood
3. Separation anxiety disorder
4. ADHD
5. Tourette syndrome

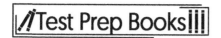

Section E: Decision Making

Which of the following interventions may be MOST appropriate to help you monitor the client's progress?

DIRECTIONS: Select AS MANY as you consider indicated in this section.

1. Behavioral therapy
2. Medication
3. Parent management training
4. Skills-based interventions
5. Journaling

Section F: Ethics

The parents want you to visit the school and observe their daughter in the classroom. How do you respond?

DIRECTIONS: Select ONLY ONE answer unless you are instructed to "Make another selection in this section."

1. Explain that this is against APA ethics guidelines.
2. Explain that this is against your own professional code of ethics.
3. Tell the parents of your client that you will contact the school to arrange a mutually agreeable time and date for a classroom observation.
4. Ask your client if this is OK with her first.
5. Explain that you must get express permission from the school's principal before you can agree to a school observation.

Section G: Short-Term Goals

Identify the MOST appropriate short-term goals for this client.

DIRECTIONS: Select AS MANY as you consider indicated in this section.

1. Sit through one full lesson at a time.
2. Complete her nightly homework.
3. Get a minimum of 10 hours of sleep each night.
4. Spend more time with her baby brother.
5. Follow a checklist at home and school to help her stay organized.

Simulation 7

Abbey is a 50-year-old recently divorced woman who has been experiencing extreme sadness over the past three years. She finds it very difficult to get out of bed every morning and cannot wait to return home from work, so she can lie right back down. She rarely has any energy to do anything other than the general routines of each day—going to work, making dinner, and showering. She rarely exercises, if at all, and complains often about stiffness in her joints and general aches and pains. She will occasionally go on social media sites, but she has admitted that doing so often leads to feelings of isolation. She has

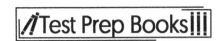

come to her initial visit hoping to receive help in improving her energy levels and her general interest in life, which has all but disappeared.

Section A: Initial Information Gathering

What initial questions might a therapist ask in order to determine a provisional DSM-5 diagnosis?

DIRECTIONS: Select AS MANY as you consider correct.

1. Has the client had suicidal thoughts?
2. Does the client ever experience moments of great joy?
3. What social media sites does the client frequent?
4. What is the client's residential history?
5. What medications is the client taking?

Section B: Additional Information Gathering

Considering the information collected so far, what additional questions would seem the MOST appropriate in order to formulate a clearer understanding of the client's disorder?

DIRECTIONS: Select AS MANY as you consider correct.

1. How well has the client been sleeping?
2. How well is the client eating?
3. Before the symptoms started, what activities did the client find enjoyable?
4. When was the last time the client visited with family?
5. When was the last time a family member visited the client?

Section C: Decision Making

Considering this initial intake data, what assessment instruments would be MOST appropriate to determine a provisional DSM-5 diagnosis?

DIRECTIONS: Select AS MANY as you consider correct.

1. Physical exam
2. CT Scan
3. Patient Health Questionnaire–9
4. Zung Self-Rating Depression Scale
5. Beck Depression Inventory

Section D: Diagnosis

Based on both the intake data and the assessment results, what provisional DSM-5 diagnosis is likely?

DIRECTIONS: Select AS MANY as seem correct and necessary.

1. Atypical depression
2. Persistent depressive disorder (dysthymia)
3. Psychotic Depression
4. Situational depression

173

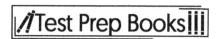

5. Bipolar disorder

Section E: Diagnosis Confirmation

In order to confirm this diagnosis, which of the following would be MOST relevant to consider?

DIRECTIONS: Select AS MANY as seem correct and necessary.

1. The duration of depressive symptoms
2. Prolonged decrease in energy levels
3. Social interactions
4. Personal care
5. Complete disinterest in daily activities

Section F: Treatments and Referrals

Based on this provisional diagnosis, what treatments and referral services would you suggest?

DIRECTIONS: Select AS MANY as seem correct and necessary.

1. Dream analysis
2. Narrative therapy
3. Electroconvulsive therapy (ECT)
4. Talk therapy
5. Selective serotonin reuptake inhibitors (SSRIs)

Section G: Short-Term Goals

Based on the information obtained and the provisional diagnosis established, identify the MOST appropriate short-term treatment goals.

DIRECTIONS: Select AS MANY as you consider correct.

1. The symptoms of depression will be significantly reduced.
2. The client will reenter society with full vigor.
3. The client will begin a moderate self-regulating exercise regime.
4. The client will identify one extracurricular activity of interest and attempt to become involved once per week.
5. The client will learn and apply appropriate coping skills and emotional regulation.

Simulation 8

Samuel is a 9-year-old boy in the fourth grade. Over the past year, his parents and teachers have noticed a shift in Samuel's behavior. Mrs. Edwards, Samuel's teacher, has reported that whenever Samuel is asked to stop doing what he wants to do, or to start doing what he doesn't wish to do, he starts to throw things in the classroom. It started with pencils, but he has also thrown books off of shelves, and has even attempted ripping posters off of walls. At home, Samuel's parents have only noticed this behavior when Samuel's mother asks him to do some chores, start his homework, or brush his teeth. He will attempt to hit his mother or throw clothes, school books, and bathroom items on the ground or directly at his mother. When his father interacts with Samuel, there never seems to be any conflict. The

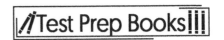

school and his parents are quite concerned and wish for Samuel to receive the help he needs to function in a more socially and emotionally-appropriate manner.

Section A: Initial Information Gathering

What evidence points to possible reasons that this client's parents are seeking counseling?

DIRECTIONS: Select AS MANY as you consider correct.

1. The child's level of aggression at school and at home
2. The child's refusal to apply daily self-care and hygienic practices
3. The child's inability to transition between one task and another
4. The child's obvious preference to his father over his mother
5. The child's refusal to help with household chores

Section B: Main Issues

Based on gathered data, what are the main issues that need to be addressed?

DIRECTIONS: Select AS MANY as seem correct and necessary.

1. Aggressive behavior
2. Opposition to authority
3. Inability to remain calm
4. Incomplete homework assignments
5. Failing grades in school

Section C: Diagnosis

What is the MOST likely provisional DSM-5 diagnosis based on current information obtained?

DIRECTIONS: Select ONLY ONE answer unless you are instructed to "Make another selection in this section."

1. Learning disabilities
2. Antisocial personality disorder
3. Autism
4. Oppositional defiant disorder (ODD)
5. ADHD

Section D: Diagnostic Confirmation

Which of the following would be relevant in exploring further to either confirm or revise the DSM-5 provisional diagnosis?

DIRECTIONS: Select AS MANY as seem correct and necessary.

1. Family dynamics
2. Family history of mental illness
3. School grades

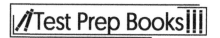

4. Number of friends
5. Involvement in extracurricular activities

Section E: Decision Making

Based on this provisional diagnosis, which of the following interventions may be MOST effective for this client?

DIRECTIONS: Select AS MANY as you consider indicated in this section.

1. Psychotherapy
2. Prescribed medication
3. Play groups
4. Contracts
5. Family therapy

Section F: Treatment Outcomes

Based on this provisional diagnosis, identify the MOST appropriate treatment outcomes for this client.

DIRECTIONS: Select AS MANY as you consider indicated in this section.

1. The child will complete all homework on a daily basis.
2. The child will develop and maintain healthy friendships.
3. The parents will spend more time with their child.
4. The mother will reduce the number of demands on her child.
5. The school will introduce effective behavioral interventions.

Section G: Client Progress

Once a successful course of counseling is complete, which of the following would you consider to be optimal ways to monitor client progress?

DIRECTIONS: Select AS MANY as you consider indicated in this section.

1. Parent management training
2. Continued individual counseling sessions
3. Behavior modification
4. Less frequent family counseling sessions
5. Self-awareness strategies

Simulation 9

Melissa, a 58-year-old school teacher, has recently lost her father and has taken her mother in to live with her and her family. Melissa and her husband have been married for twenty years and have two teenaged sons. Melissa has expressed great sadness over the loss of her father and is finding it very difficult to work all day then return home to manage her family's affairs and care for her mother. She has taken several days off in the last few months as a result. Melissa's mother has diabetes and requires specialized care with regular medical visits. Melissa has expressed the feeling of shortness of breath, a rapid heartbeat, and difficulty concentrating. She can generally fall asleep with little difficulty, but she is often up several times in the night. She and her husband have been bickering a lot lately, and Melissa has expressed the need to "get her life back on track," but doesn't even know where to begin.

Section A: Initial Information Gathering

Before making a provisional DSM-5 diagnosis, what information is required?

DIRECTIONS: Select AS MANY as you consider correct.

1. Client's medical records
2. History of possible mental illness in the family
3. Physical exam
4. Heart monitor evaluation
5. Current medications

Section B: Main Issues

Considering the information obtained, what are the main issues that need to be addressed?

DIRECTIONS: Select AS MANY as seem correct and necessary.

1. Shortness of breath
2. Rapid heartbeat
3. Sleep disturbances
4. The safety of the client's mother
5. The client's relationship with her husband

Section C: Decision Making

Based on initial intake data, what is the MOST likely provisional DSM-5 diagnosis?

DIRECTIONS: Select ONLY ONE answer unless you are instructed to "Make another selection in this section."

1. Persistent complex bereavement disorder (PCBD)
2. Adjustment disorder
3. Acute stress disorder
4. Generalized anxiety disorder (GAD)
5. Panic disorder

Section D: Diagnosis Confirmation

What elements must be present in order to confirm this provisional DSM-5 diagnosis?

DIRECTIONS: Select AS MANY as seem correct and necessary.

1. Identifiable stressors
2. Significant impairment in daily functioning
3. A traumatic event
4. A psychosis
5. High blood pressure

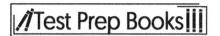

Section E: Treatment

Based on all the data obtained, what treatment modalities might be the MOST beneficial to the client?

DIRECTIONS: Select AS MANY as you consider indicated in this section.

1. Illness insight therapy
2. Guided imagery
3. Medication
4. Psychotherapy
5. Support groups

Section F: Decision Making

You have treated adjustment disorders with anxiety in the past, but it has been a while, and you are forgetting some of the assessment tools and treatment modalities appropriate for this type of diagnosis. What do you do?

DIRECTIONS: Select AS MANY as you consider indicated in this section.

1. Reread current professional literature on adjustment disorders

2. Discontinue treatment and ask that the client seek another professional

3. Attend conferences specific to the diagnosis

4. Secure supervision and/or consultation with informed colleagues to confirm that your treatment approach is both adequate and appropriate

5. Tell the client that it has been a while since you have treated this disorder and let the client decide if she feels comfortable continuing sessions with you

Section G: Referrals

Upon successful completion of a predetermined set number of counseling sessions, what referrals might you suggest for this client?

DIRECTIONS: Select ONLY ONE answer unless you are instructed to "Make another selection in this section."

1. Family counseling
2. Individual grief therapy
3. Independent living education
4. Social skills training
5. Support groups

Simulation 10

Carmen, a 45-year-old woman, came forward two years ago with sexual abuse allegations against a family member after almost thirty years of silence. On her initial visit, she broke down sobbing and said that for the past two years, family members have either refused to speak with her or have told her that

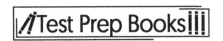

they don't believe her. Carmen has admitted to crying almost every single day and has expressed great hardship in getting out of bed. She is well educated but has had a very unstable work history, having left several professional positions over the years due to extreme stress. She has stated that throughout her life, she has had to fight flashbacks of her abuse and continues to fight these flashbacks to the present day. She has described them as haunting, and no matter how hard she fights, they don't go away. Carmen just wants to feel emotional relief. She wants to feel emotionally stable for once in her life, and she wants to understand why her family has decided to turn their backs on her.

Section A: Initial Information Gathering

What evidence points to possible reasons that this client is seeking counseling?

DIRECTIONS: Select AS MANY as you consider correct.

1. She has recurrent flashbacks of a traumatic event.
2. She does not get along with family members.
3. She struggles with keeping a job.
4. She has trouble sleeping.
5. She seeks assistance in coming to terms with her sexual abuse.

Section B: Main Issues

Based on gathered data, what are the main issues that need to be addressed?

DIRECTIONS: Select AS MANY as seem correct and necessary.

1. Childhood sexual abuse
2. Recurrent flashbacks
3. Emotional instability
4. Work-related issues
5. Family values

Section C: Diagnosis

What is the MOST likely provisional DSM-5 diagnosis based on current information obtained?

DIRECTIONS: Select ONLY ONE answer unless you are instructed to "Make another selection in this section."

1. Paranoid personality disorder
2. Dissociated disorder
3. Bipolar disorder
4. Post-traumatic stress disorder (PTSD)
5. Separation anxiety disorder

Section D: Confirming Diagnosis

Which of the following would be relevant in exploring further to either confirm or revise the DSM-5 provisional diagnosis?

DIRECTIONS: Select AS MANY as seem correct and necessary.

      1. How many marriages—if any—has the client had?
      2. Does the client avoid situations or individuals who could trigger reminders?
      3. Is the client grossly underweight or overweight?
      4. Does the client experience regularly intrusive thoughts?
      5. Has the client reported her abuse to authorities?

Section E: Interventions

Based on this provisional diagnosis, which of the following interventions may be MOST effective for this client?

DIRECTIONS: Select AS MANY as you consider indicated in this section.

      1. Cognitive behavior therapy (CBT)
      2. Positive reinforcement
      3. Medication
      4. Confrontation
      5. Positive self-talk training

Section F: Decision Making

The client asks you if you think acupuncture might help her. How do you respond?

DIRECTIONS: Select ONLY ONE answer unless you are instructed to "Make another selection in this section."

      1. Explain to the client that it is an unproven therapy and it could cause more harm than good.
      2. Ask the client why she feels acupuncture might help her.
      3. Share with the client that acupuncture is an alternative therapy, but it is worth investigating.
      4. Explain to the client that if she chooses any alternative therapy, your sessions will have to be terminated.
      5. Caution the client to explore any alternative therapies in conjunction with the sessions in your office.

Section G: Referrals

When considering ongoing behavioral referral services for this client, which of the following would be MOST appropriate?

DIRECTIONS: Select AS MANY as you consider indicated in this section.

      1. PTSD specialized treatment center
      2. Couples therapy
      3. Psychiatrist
      4. Religious pastor
      5. Certified peer specialist (CPS)

Answer Explanations

Simulation 1

Section A: Relevance of Initial Information Gathering

1. Client's reason(s) for seeking treatment

INDICATED (+3)

The client's insight regarding her mental health challenges and struggles are paramount to initial data collection. The counselor should encourage the client to express herself as openly as she can. The more insight the client has into her own situation and reasons for seeking treatment the better the outcome will be.

2. History of marital problems

NOT INDICATED (-1)

There is no current data to suggest there are marital problems. By the client's own self-reports, her spouse is working two jobs to provide for the family. It appears he is invested in their family unit.

3. History of mental illness

INDICATED (+3)

Ruling out a history of mental illness will provide invaluable information to the therapist and will help to determine an accurate diagnosis along with an appropriate treatment plan. The client described her issues as occurring well before she experienced this life change so any past mental health diagnoses or treatment is useful information for her current treatment.

4. Educational history

NOT INDICATED (-3)

The client's level of education is not relevant to the issues being addressed.

5. Suicidal attempts

INDICATED (+2)

Given that the client has disclosed that she has had issues with her mental health for a long period of time and she is now dealing with post-partum feelings and hormones, it would be useful for a clear mental health history to know if she has ever experienced severe depression or suicide ideation/attempts.

6. Mood status

INDICATED (+2)

The client's mood status should be observed and documented, as this may affect her ability to manage and control the issue.

7. History of job-related problems

NOT INDICATED (-1)

Although the client began to cry at the thought of returning to work, the upset seemed to be more about leaving her daughter in the care of others and less about working. The initial intake data do not indicate any history of job-related problems.

8. Frequency and severity of symptoms

INDICATED (+3)

The frequency and severity of symptoms is highly relevant to the diagnosis and treatment decisions that will ultimately be made for this client.

9. Current stressors

INDICATED (+3)

The client's current stressors have a significant impact on the client's emotional well-being. Gaining a clear picture of all the stressors in the client's daily life will help to establish interventions and techniques that directly address these areas.

10. Drug abuse screening test (DAST)

NOT INDICATED (-3)

There is no data to support any misuse or abuse of prescribed or illicit drugs. This is not only irrelevant but would also be inappropriate to suggest.

Section B: Relevance of Identifying Potential Issues

1. Communication problems

NOT INDICATED (-1)

There is no evidence to support the need for communication strengthening. The client seems to express herself well and has clearly communicated her feelings and concerns in the first intake session.

2. Financial problems

INDICATED (+3)

The client has made repeated comments about the current financial stressors in the family. There is no doubt that this is one of the most significant areas that worries her on a regular basis.

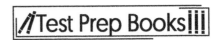

3. Parenting problems

NOT INDICATED (-2)

There is no evidence that supports any concerns relating to parenting problems.

4. Trust issues

NOT INDICATED (-2)

Although the client disclosed issues trusting non-familial care of her newborn, this is more indicative of normal feelings of a new parent who has to leave her child rather than deep rooted trust issues.

5. Eating problems

NOT INDICATED (-3)

There has been no mention of eating problems during the initial information intake phase. This is not relevant here.

6. Separation anxiety

INDICATED (+2)

The client's immediate breakdown at the mention of returning to work and leaving her infant in someone else's care may indicate a separation anxiety issue.

7. Physical health

INDICATED (+2)

During initial information intake, the counselor discovered that the client is presenting with physical health concerns (indigestion, muscle tension, and sleep deprivation). These may all be signs of an underlying medical condition and should be explored further.

8. Postpartum issues

INDICATED (+2)

The client has indicated that the issues all began a few years before her baby was born and have persisted to the present day. However, having a new baby seems to have exacerbated her issues. Having prior mental health issues does make a new mother more likely to develop postpartum issues. These should be explored.

9. Seasonal mood issues

NOT INDICATED (-2)

There is no evidence that would lead to a suspicion of seasonal mood issues.

10. Concentration problems

INDICATED (+2)

The initial intake of information phase revealed that the client struggles regularly with concentration. Based on this information, it would be relevant to investigate this further to rule out any other underlying mental health issues that interfere with concentration.

Section C: Relevance of Additional Information Gathering

1. Panic disorder

NOT INDICATED (-1)

Some of the main signs and symptoms of panic disorder involve difficulty with breathing, a racing heart, feeling weak or faint, and feeling a sense of doom. These symptoms are not relevant in this case.

2. Acute stress disorder

NOT INDICATED (-2)

Almost always involving a direct or indirect traumatic event, acute stress disorder manifests itself when the client feels detached from their surroundings and seems void of an emotional response. Sometimes the client cannot remember a specific moment during a traumatic event. This is not relevant in this case.

3. Adjustment disorder with anxiety

NOT INDICATED (-1)

Although this seems like a possible diagnosis, the client is not suffering from adjustment disorder with anxiety. This disorder is brought on by a major change in life. The client has just had a baby, but her worried behavior was present and had been consistent long before the baby's arrival.

4. ADHD

NOT INDICATED (-3)

Attention deficit hyperactivity disorder is characterized by the inability to pay attention for sustained periods of time, being impulsive, and being extremely hyper. This is not at all relevant here.

5. Generalized anxiety disorder (GAD)

INDICATED (+3)

This seems the most plausible diagnosis for this client. In addition to fatigue and trouble sleeping, GAD manifests as inability to concentrate, excessive worrying over a number of areas in one's life, muscle tension, and even indigestion. When these symptoms have been persistent for prolonged periods of time, GAD may be the cause.

184

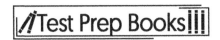

Section D: Relevance of Decision Making

1. Family counseling sessions

NOT INDICATED (-1)

There is no evidence in the initial intake of information to suggest that family counseling would be relevant at this time. The client seems to be more focused and concerned with her own inability to cope with current stressors.

2. In-home behavioral management plan

NOT INDICATED (-2)

Although an in-home behavioral management plan aims to address the emotional, mental, and behavioral needs of a client, it is mainly structured for children and would not be appropriate in this case.

3. Education on healthy eating

NOT INDICATED (-3)

There is no evidence to support the need for educational interventions regarding healthy eating, and no information was collected to suggest the client has an eating disorder.

4. Cognitive behavior therapy (CBT)

INDICATED (+3)

Because CBT is the most widely used and accepted therapy for treating generalized anxiety disorder, this is the best course of treatment for this client. The benefits of CBT for this particular client are great due to the fact that CBT offers clients some control over treatment as they are actively working to create new behaviors surrounding stressors.

5. Dream analysis

NOT INDICATED (-2)

Dream analysis is generally used to uncover a client's repressed feelings and is a controversial form of therapy. It would not be relevant in this case.

Section E: Relevance of Treatment Methods

1. Help client to strengthen social relationships

NOT INDICATED (-2)

There is no evidence to suggest that the counselor should focus on social relationships with this client.

2. Help client to explore career goals

NOT INDICATED (-1)

The client has expressed worry over finances but does not want to leave her infant at home. Although the counselor is not an employment advisor, they may wish to suggest that the client explore work-from-home, contract, and part-time opportunities. This may shift her thought process and give her avenues to explore, which may lead to a reduction in her stress levels and anxiety.

3. Help client to strengthen self-esteem

NOT INDICATED (-1)

There is no evidence to suggest this client has any issues with self-esteem.

4. Help client to decrease anxiety

INDICATED (+3)

From initial intake of information, there is plenty of evidence to suggest that this client suffers from GAD. Practicing techniques and creating a treatment plan to decrease her anxiety is the most appropriate approach to take.

5. Help client search for trustworthy caregivers for her infant

NOT INDICATED (-1)

Although the client has expressed reluctance to leave her infant in the care of strangers, the therapist's role is not to match clients with babysitters or daycare centers. The therapist may however, inform the client that there are agencies she may wish to contact that help families find the right caregiver for their child or children.

Section F: Relevance of Ethical Issues

1. Explain to the client's mother that this is a breach of client-therapist confidentiality and no information will be shared.

INDICATED (+3)

Only under extreme circumstances do mental health professionals have the right—and obligation—to breach client-therapist confidentiality. A mere request from a parent to share information about an adult child will not be obliged. The therapist would need to let the mother know that he/she cannot confirm or deny treatment and would refer the mother to speak to her family member directly with any concerns.

2. Inform the mother that you will speak to your client, and if your client gives her consent to share this information, you will call her back to discuss the details of this case.

NOT INDICATED (-2)

It is not within the scope of a counselor's responsibility to act as the "go-between" with regard to a request for information from a parent about a given client.

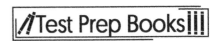

3. Ask the mother to visit you in order to sign a confidentiality form before you divulge sensitive information.

NOT INDICATED (-3)

This would constitute a serious and unethical breach of client-therapist confidentiality.

4. Ask that the mother contact her daughter directly for the information she is seeking.

INDICATED (+1)

It is not within the scope of a counselor's responsibility to intervene between the client and client's family members, but the therapist can simply respond that due to confidentiality he/she cannot confirm or deny that the family member is a patient and redirect them to their family member for such questions.

5. Ask that the mother and daughter come together for the next counseling session.

NOT INDICATED (-3)

The client has established a counselling relationship with the therapist. To break that trust by inviting another member into the counseling sessions without the client's consent would be deemed highly unethical. If, however, the client asks for her mother to attend the next session, that is something that can be discussed and explored.

Section G: Relevance of Termination Phase

1. The client should continue regular individual counseling.

NOT INDICATED (-2)

The predetermined set of counseling sessions has proven successful. The ethical response is to gradually decrease the number of sessions, while monitoring how the client adjusts.

2. The client will be encouraged to join a parental support group.

INDICATED (+2)

The client has expressed a clear concern for leaving her baby in the care of others should she return to work. Parental support groups can provide information on a list of approved daycare centers, possible job leads, and general parental support.

3. Prescribed medication and reduction in therapy sessions.

INDICATED (+3)

GAD is currently treated in two significant ways: antidepressant medication (selective serotonin reuptake inhibitors or SSRIs) and therapy. Currently, medical doctors, psychiatrists, nurse practitioners, PA-C's and in some states, psychologists can prescribe mental health medications. A referral would need to be made for this intervention.

4. The client will be referred to a psychiatrist for further evaluation.

INDICATED (+3)

Currently, medical doctors, psychiatrists, nurse practitioners, PA-C's and in some states, psychologists can prescribe mental health medications. A referral would need to be made for this intervention if the therapist feels that medication would be useful.

5. Regular family therapy is recommended for this client.

NOT INDICATED (-1)

There is no evidence-based reason for beginning family therapy.

Simulation 2

Section A: Relevance of Initial Information Gathering

1. Traumatic life events

INDICATED (+2)

According to the American Psychiatric Association (APA), learning about a loved one's death is considered to be a traumatic life event. Because the client has experienced the death of his spouse, this element needs to be explored.

2. Duration and intensity of the grieving process

INDICATED (+3)

When considering a mental disorder vis à vis grieving the loss of a loved one, the APA differentiates between the duration and intensity of the *natural* grieving process and the grieving process that falls outside the social and/or cultural norms.

3. Religious affiliation

NOT INDICATED (-2)

There is no mention of this client's religious affiliation, nor would this be relevant in considering a DSM-5 diagnosis.

4. Medical history, including current medications

INDICATED (+2)

It is important to determine any underlying causes that might be negatively impacting the well-being of this client. A thorough review of the client's medical history, including any past and current medications, would be advised.

5. Driving Record

NOT INDICATED (-3)

The client's driving record is irrelevant in helping to determine an accurate DSM-5 diagnosis.

Section B: Relevance of Initial Testing

1. Behavioral assessment rating scale

NOT INDICATED (-2)

Primarily used to help diagnose children and adolescents, behavioral assessment rating scales measure a client's problem behaviors in the home, community, and/or school settings. This doesn't apply here.

2. The Bender-Gestalt II

NOT INDICATED (-2)

The Bender-Gestalt II concerns itself with a client's level of visual-motor function, a possible neurological impairment, and/or possible developmental disorders. This doesn't apply here.

3. Mental Status Examination (MSE)

INDICATED (+3)

A mental status exam aims to examine a client's current level of psychological functioning, to determine their mental state. This is relevant in this case. It would be very useful for this particular client to have an understanding of what the baseline for his emotional functioning is at the beginning of treatment. It would be particularly useful, given his impairment, to conduct further MSE's to chart the change in his functioning over time and continually assess his needs.

4. Personality Factor Questionnaire

NOT INDICATED (-3)

Employers may invite an employee or prospective employee to take the Personality Factor Questionnaire in order to determine if the individual is a good fit for a new job assignment or promotion. This primarily attempts to identify an individual's personality traits, how they might act or react in various situations, and how they feel about various topics. This is not relevant here.

5. Wechsler Adult Intelligence Scale (WAIS)

NOT INDICATED (-2)

The WAIS primarily tests an individual's IQ, however new revisions may also be used to rule out possible Alzheimer's disease. This test is not relevant for this case.

Section C: Relevance of Additional Information Gathering

1. Information will be kept on file and seen only by the treating counselor.

NOT INDICATED (-3)

During the initial intake session, treating counselors should establish and make clear all matters involving confidentiality.

2. If the client consents, information will be shared with professional colleagues.

NOT INDICATED (-2)

Should a treating therapist feel that a professional colleague may offer insight and assistance with regard to determining an accurate DSM-5 diagnosis or developing an effective treatment plan, the therapist will only consult this colleague with the express consent of the client.

3. The treating counselor will consult the DSM-5 in order to help determine a diagnosis.

INDICATED (+3)

This is neither a mandatory nor suggested approach to client-therapist communication. While providing informed consent to clients during therapy is part of the process, disclosing that the DSM-IV is the tool being used for diagnoses does not bear any relevance to the client as it is the standard used across the board. It's not useful to disclose this to the client.

4. Information will be shared with family members only with the client's express consent.

NOT INDICATED (-1)

This is part of basic confidentiality and sharing of information that would be explained to the client when treatment begins. This would be most useful as it is standard practice to express to clients that their information will not be shared with family, etc., without their expressed consent.

5. Medical records must be handed over to authorities if ordered by the courts.

NOT INDICATED (-2)

This client was in a recent car accident. If at any time the treating therapist is asked by the courts to share confidential client information, they must comply. Should the treating therapist feel this may be detrimental to the client's well-being, this should be duly noted and shared with the courts.

Section D: Relevance of Decision Making

1. House-tree-person test

NOT INDICATED (-3)

This test is generally used to measure aspects of an individual's personality, possible brain damage, and general mental functioning. It is not a relevant test for this case.

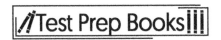

2. Self-directed search

NOT INDICATED (-3)

A self-directed search is an intervention used to support and guide an individual with respect to their career aspirations and is not relevant for this client.

3. Rorschach

NOT INDICATED (-2)

The Rorschach is an assessment instrument that measures aspects of an individual's personality and emotional functioning using a series of inkblots and recording the individual's perceptions of each. This is not relevant here.

4. Inventory of complicated grief (ICG)

INDICATED (+3)

ICG is a self-reporting inventory for clients that aims to measure the level and severity of an individual's grief using a series of grief-related questions impacting one's thoughts and behavior. This is a relevant assessment tool to administer in this case.

5. Transactional analysis (TA)

NOT INDICATED (-1)

Transactional analysis involves the therapist's analysis of the client's social transactions in order to better understand behaviors. A TA also gives the client an opportunity to consider new choices and thought patterns that could lead to different social outcomes. This is not relevant in this case.

Section E: Relevance of Diagnosis

1. Intermittent explosive disorder

NOT INDICATED (-3)

Intermittent Explosive Disorder is the sudden onset of extreme anger and/or violence that is disproportionate to the situation at hand. The client makes no mention of behavioral violence. This is not an appropriate diagnosis in this case.

2. Parent-child relational problem

NOT INDICATED (-3)

Not considered to be a mental health disorder, parent-child relational problems refer to communication and social interactions between parents and their children that negatively impact family dynamics. This is not relevant in this case.

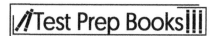

3. Unspecified depressive disorder

NOT INDICATED (-2)

If symptoms of depression cause problems in an individual's relationships or daily activities but the symptoms do not meet the full criteria for a specific type of depression, the individual may be diagnosed with unspecified depressive disorder. Sometimes, after more data has been collected, therapists may be able to diagnose a specific depressive disorder. This is not the most appropriate diagnosis for this case.

4. Phase of life problem

NOT INDICATED (-1)

When an individual enters a new phase of life such as marriage, divorce, retirement, or middle age, they may experience emotional difficulty in coping with these changes. The death of a spouse is not so much a phase of life issue as it is a major life change. The client becoming newly single due to the death of his spouse is a byproduct of this life event. This is not relevant in this situation.

5. Persistent complex bereavement disorder (PCBD)

INDICATED (+3)

Key areas that point to a possible PCBD diagnosis in this case include the extreme sadness in the loss of the client's wife that has persisted more than twelve months, the longing for his wife's return, and his inability to concentrate on little else, other than his sadness over this loss.

Section F: Relevance of Confirming Diagnosis

1. Client's prolonged period of grief

INDICATED (+3)

One of the key elements of PCBD is the prolonged grieving for the loss of a loved one that persists after twelve months. This client lost his wife sixteen months ago.

2. Client's struggle to focus on anything other than the loss of his wife

INDICATED (+2)

The client has indicated to the therapist that he has difficulty concentrating on little else other than the loss of his wife. This is another symptom of PCBD.

3. Excessive longing for the departed

INDICATED (+1)

When asked why his is seeking therapy, the client indicated that he wants his wife and his life back, and that he wants nothing more than to be with this wife again. These are all signs pointing to PCBD.

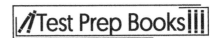

4. Client's level of frustration and anger

NOT INDICATED (-3)

There is no indication of the client having excessive levels of frustration or anger.

5. Client's reluctance to engage in counseling

NOT INDICATED (-2)

Although the client admitted not wanting to initially seek counseling, this is not relevant in determining the DSM-5 diagnosis.

Section G: Relevance of Interventions

1. Assistance coping with significant life changes

INDICATED (+2)

According to the APA's best practices, individuals who are suffering extreme loss are *not* advised to make any significant changes to their way of life until the grieving period has greatly decreased. However, since the client has experienced a significant life change, it is indicated to assist him with coping skills to deal with the life changes he's already experiencing.

2. Relaxation/breathing

INDICATED (+1)

Appropriate relaxation and breathing exercises have been proven to strengthen an individual's level of peace and serenity, and even to counteract their negative response to stress or sadness.

3. Support groups

INDICATED (+2)

Support groups that focus on grief and bereavement may be of particular value to this client and offer empathy, sympathy, and understanding. A support group is also a safe space in which the individual can openly express emotions, build new social bonds, and receive advice on coping with life after the loss of a loved one.

4. Exercise

INDICATED (+1)

Helping the client to begin an exercise regime that is both appropriate for his age and physical limitations can improve his physical and emotional well-being.

5. Occasional alcohol consumption

NOT INDICATED (-3)

Not only is alcohol a depressant, it is also habit forming. It would never be appropriate or ethical for a counselor to recommend alcohol consumption to a client.

Simulation 3

Section A: Relevance of Initial Information Gathering

1. Growing up in Japan

INDICATED (+2)

Knowing more about Hana's cultural experiences and childhood would help the therapist better understand how Hana views herself in the world. This is relevant information to gather in this case.

2. Educational history

INDICATED (+1)

Hana has achieved academic excellence in high school. This indicates a high intelligence and possible motivation to pursue a higher education. It is important for the therapist to learn what the prime reasons are for Hana to have abruptly stopped her educational pursuits.

3. Social life

INDICATED (+3)

Hana has indicated that she rarely leaves the home and spends a lot of time talking with family and friends in Japan. It is important for the therapist to explore what her social life was like in Japan and why she is reluctant to continue a social life in the United States.

4. Career aspirations

INDICATED (+1)

Hana is 18-years-old and so far, has achieved academic excellence. It is very relevant for the therapist to try to ascertain what career avenues Hana is interested in pursuing in order to help guide her down a path toward career readiness.

5. Father-daughter relationship

NOT INDICATED (-3)

There doesn't seem to be any evidence indicating a problem in communication between Hana and her father. This is not relevant here.

Section B: Relevance of Additional Information Gathering

1. Family's collective income

NOT INDICATED (-2)

There is no evidence to suggest that the family's collective income has any bearing on Hana's emotional or mental well-being. This is not relevant in this case.

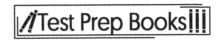

2. Brother's social life in the United States

INDICATED (+1)

Hana and her brother come from the same home and the same country. Hana's brother may therefore have found a social group to which Hana might also relate. It may be beneficial for the therapist to learn what social activities the brother engages in, in order to start a discussion with the client. If there are social settings in which Hana would feel comfortable and safe, the therapist and client might discuss how the client can be included in some of these gatherings.

3. Cultural sensitivities

INDICATED (+3)

When therapists work with clients who come from a different cultural background, it is extremely important to better understand the dynamics and subtleties of that culture and how that culture may be in complete contrast to the culture in the United States. This information may explain a client's difficulty in adjusting to a new—and possibly overwhelming—way of life.

4. Client's mental health history

INDICATED (+2)

It is very important to gather any information from Hana's medical records that may suggest prior mental health concerns, so as to rule out any underlying issues.

5. Client's relationship with her family members

NOT INDICATED (-2)

There is no evidence to suggest that Hana is having communication difficulties with any family member. This is not relevant in this case.

Section C: Relevance of Ruling Out Criteria

1. History of drug use/abuse

NOT INDICATED (-2)

There is no evidence to suggest that this client has any history of drug use or abuse. This is not relevant in this case.

2. Sleeping difficulties

NOT INDICATED (-1)

There is no evidence to suggest that this client is experiencing a disruption in her sleeping patterns. This is not relevant in this case.

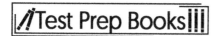

3. Currently prescribed medications

INDICATED (+2)

In order to rule out possible problematic side effects, it would be relevant for the therapist to ascertain a list of currently prescribed medications.

4. History of learning disabilities

NOT INDICATED (-2)

There is no evidence to suggest that this client has ever been diagnosed with any learning disabilities. This is not relevant in this case.

5. Past hospitalizations

NOT INDICATED (-2)

There is no evidence to suggest that this client has had any health-related problems in her past. This is not relevant in this case.

Section D: Relevance of Diagnosis

1. Conduct disorder

NOT INDICATED (-3)

Conduct disorder usually begins to manifest itself in childhood or adolescence. Children and teens may demonstrate difficulty in adhering to rules in school and/or at home and may even demonstrate aggressive behavior. This is not relevant in this case.

2. Oppositional defiant disorder (ODD)

NOT INDICATED (-3)

This client shows no current or past evidence of being frequently angry, easily irritated, defiant, or vindictive—common symptoms in children and teens with ODD. This does not seem to be a plausible diagnosis.

3. Acute stress disorder

NOT INDICATED (-1)

Although women tend to be at greater risk than are men for developing acute stress disorder, this diagnosis does not seem relevant in this case. In order to be diagnosed with acute stress disorder, an individual must have had direct or indirect exposure to a traumatic event, such as witnessing a death or near-death event, or having their life or well-being threatened. This does not apply in this case.

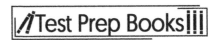

4. Adjustment disorder

NOT INDICATED (-1)

Although a major life change (such as moving from one country and culture to another) can be one of the causes that leads to an adjustment disorder, this doesn't seem to be a plausible diagnosis in this case. Individuals experiencing an adjustment disorder tend to show impulsivity, anxiety, hopelessness, difficulty with concentration, a frequency in bouts of crying and/or great sadness. None of these symptoms seem to apply in this case.

5. Acculturation problem

INDICATED (+3)

When an individual leaves one culture and immigrates to a country with a completely different culture, that individual may experience emotional, social, and even psychological complications. Categorized under "V" codes in the DSM-5 and not a true diagnosis of a mental illness, acculturation problems can interfere with an individual's ability to cope in a new environment. Therapists can assist such individuals with effective coping strategies.

Section E: Relevance of Interventions

1. Role play

INDICATED (+1)

Role playing is often used to help individuals who suffer from extreme fears or social phobias. The therapist and client act out various scenarios that the client finds frightening in order to help develop the skills necessary to overcome these fears. Because this client may be suffering from intense fear of entering a new culture and/or a new academic setting, role playing may be a very effective therapeutic technique.

2. Imagery rehearsal therapy

NOT INDICATED (-3)

Imagery rehearsal therapy is a cognitive-behavioral intervention used primarily to treat clients suffering from chronic PTSD-related nightmares and/or chronic nightmares with no apparent cause. This form of therapy is inappropriate in this case.

3. Medication

NOT INDICATED (-2)

This client does not seem to be having problems with concentration, daily functioning, communication, depression, anxiety, or any other pressing reason to suggest a need for a prescribed medication.

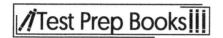

4. Teach back method

INDICATED (+3)

Often used by therapists who are working with individuals whose first language is *not* English, the teach back method allows the client to repeat, in their own words, what the therapist is saying. This helps the therapist to determine the client's level of understanding and also helps the client to better process the information they are being given. Because Hana has indicated that she struggles with the English language, which may account for her fear of entering into social and/or academic settings in the United States, the teach back method may help to build her confidence in communicating in the English language, and therefore, act as a bridge for Hana's eventual reentry into her social and academic life.

5. LEARN mnemonic

INDICATED (+3)

The LEARN mnemonic (Listen, Explain, Acknowledge, Recommend, and Negotiate), has been successfully used by mental health practitioners when working with clients from different cultural and linguistic backgrounds. It involves the therapist's ability to truly listen to the client's cultural experiences and perspectives, while explaining to the client the general perspectives shared by the majority of people in the new environment. It gives the client and the therapist the opportunity to discuss these differences and similarities, which ultimately leads to a recommended treatment plan that both therapist and client can further negotiate, and upon which they can mutually agree.

Section F: Relevance of Decision Making

1. Explain that this would be a breach of client-therapist confidentiality, and that no information should be shared with her brother.

NOT INDICATED (-3)

If the client wishes for a family member to attend a session and the therapist agrees, this does *not* constitute a breach of client-therapist confidentiality.

2. Allow her brother to attend the next session.

INDICATED (+2)

You may wish to ask the client to explain a little bit further why she would like her brother to attend the next session. You may even wish to discuss the limitations of what will be discussed at the session, but if the client wishes for her brother to attend the next session with her and there are no policies prohibiting this, then there is no reason for you to deny the request.

3. Ask that the client sign a consent form.

NOT INDICATED (-1)

Provided that you thoroughly discussed the confidentiality and privacy laws with your client at the onset of your sessions, there would be no reason to insist upon a signed consent form, but you may wish to restate some of the confidentiality obligations to which you adhere.

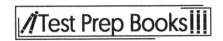

4. Explain that you cannot treat other family members.

NOT INDICATED (-2)

Your client is not asking you to treat her brother. She only wishes that her brother attends the next session with her. This would not be an appropriate response.

5. Ask to meet separately with the brother ahead of a session with brother and sister.

NOT INDICATED (-2)

There is no reason to make this request. This is not an appropriate response.

Section G: Relevance of Short-Term Goals

1. Reduce frequency of calls to and from family and friends in Japan

NOT INDICATED (-3)

The client takes comfort in speaking with friends and family members from her country of birth. To insist upon a lessening of the frequency of contact would not be a responsible course of action and may be detrimental to her emotional well-being.

2. Encourage weekly support groups for immigrants

INDICATED (+3)

There are many support groups for newly-arrived immigrants who feel displaced and overwhelmed by the vast cultural differences they face when moving to the United States. Such a support group could be a great source of comfort to this client and might offer the tools and strategies to overcome cultural differences. Support groups are also a great source of social interaction, in which individuals may find people with similar backgrounds and experiences.

3. Encourage enrollment in English-speaking classes

INDICATED (+3)

English-speaking classes would allow the client to build her confidence in socializing and communicating within her new community. The more proficient she becomes, the more likely she may be to enroll in college classes and connect with people her own age in social settings.

4. Encourage immediate enrolment in full-time college

NOT INDICATED (-2)

This would be an irresponsible course of action because the client does not yet feel proficient enough in the English language, nor confident enough in engaging in an academic setting with her English-speaking peers.

5. Discuss possible career paths that interest the client

INDICATED (+2)

Engaging in a conversation about the client's professional aspirations and interests may motivate her in considering possible career paths that she can take. Exploring different entry-level college courses that cater to these career goals may further encourage the client to step out of her comfort zone and enroll in some beginning classes.

Simulation 4

Section A: Relevance of Initial Information Gathering

1. Suspicion of alcohol abuse

INDICATED (+2)

Although the client hasn't directly stated this suspicion, he has mentioned that his current alcohol consumption bothers his father and that he regularly consumed alcohol to get him through school and manage his stress. He may be hinting that he recognizes this as a problem.

2. Perception of parental abuse

NOT INDICATED (-3)

The client has mentioned his mild irritation with his parents' insisting he look for work and reduce his alcohol consumption. This is not indicative of parental abuse, nor does it indicate that the client is concerned about parental abuse.

3. Depression

INDICATED (+1)

The client's inability to manage his stress without the aid of alcohol, his regular consumption of alcohol, and his need to "take a break" before looking for work, may be indicative of an underlying issue with depression.

4. Anger management

NOT INDICATED (-2)

Although the client has indicated that there is some unrest in the home and frequent arguments with his parents, there is no indication that he requires anger management therapy.

5. Reluctance to attend therapy

NOT INDICATED (-1)

Based on the evidence gathered, there is every indication that the client has freely sought therapy independent of his parents' concerns.

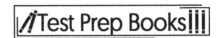

Section B: Relevance of Main Issues

1. Anger management

NOT INDICATED (-2)

Many of the arguments that the client is having with his parents seem to stem from his alcohol consumption and its interference with his living a productive life. Alcohol consumption is the key factor here in dysfunctional living, not anger issues.

2. Alcohol dependency

INDICATED (+3)

The client has openly stated that he relied on alcohol consumption in order to manage his stresses and to get him through law school. This should be a prime focus during therapy sessions.

3. Alcohol use disorder

INDICATED (+3)

The client has demonstrated many signs and symptoms directly related to alcohol use disorder, and this should be of prime focus.

4. Unemployment

INDICATED (-1)

Although the client has mentioned his overwhelming financial debt and his need to take a break before looking for work, his lack of employment doesn't seem to be due to his inability to work or find work, but rather his problem with excessive alcohol consumption.

5. Depression

INDICATED (+2)

Individuals with depression may turn to drugs and/or alcohol as a way of masking the pain. This individual has mounting financial debt, no current source of income, family unrest, and a history of regular alcohol consumption. It would be appropriate for the therapist to further investigate possible depression.

Section C: Relevance of Decision Making

1. Social anxiety disorder

NOT INDICATED (-2)

Although the client has demonstrated a lack of motivation in looking for work, there is no indication that he suffers from excessive fear of either real or perceived social situations—symptoms of social anxiety disorder. This is not relevant in this case.

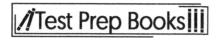

2. Depression

INDICATED (+1)

Although possibly brought on by alcohol consumption, depression may be a possible DSM-5 diagnosis for this individual. It will be necessary to determine if depressive symptoms were present before the individual began to consume alcohol regularly, or whether depressive symptoms have surfaced only after the individual began to regularly consume alcohol.

3. Alcohol use disorder

INDICATED (+2)

According to the DSM-5, a client suffering from alcohol use disorder will likely demonstrate evidence of a physical dependence, a craving for alcohol, increased tolerance, and possible loss of control. Although the client hasn't indicated a loss of control, he has indicated an increased tolerance, and his lifestyle indicates a possible physical dependence. This shouldn't yet be ruled out.

4. Anxiety

NOT INDICATED (-2)

Diagnosing an anxiety disorder is complicated, as it has many symptoms, ranging from sleeping difficulties, an inability to relax, and frequent headaches, to heart palpitations, the feeling of impending doom, and even a shortness of breath. This client, however, doesn't seem to be manifesting any signs or symptoms related to any particular anxiety disorder.

5. Parent-child relational problem

NOT INDICATED (-3)

A parent-child relational problem is not a formal DSM-5 diagnosis, but rather falls into the APA's "V" Codes—issues that are problematic but not necessarily indicative of an actual illness or disorder. Further, a parent-child relational problem generally manifests when a child is an adolescent, not an adult. Some symptoms of a parent-child relational problem may be verbal or physical aggressive behaviors, reluctance to communicate, and constant arguing or interrupting. This is not relevant in this case.

Section D: Relevance of Additional Data Gathering

1. Number of alcoholic drinks consumed each day

INDICATED (+3)

Although there is no set number of daily-consumed alcoholic drinks that meets the criteria for an alcohol-related disorder or illness, the fact that this individual consumes alcohol on a daily basis warrants further investigation.

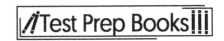

2. Client's attempts to cut down or control his drinking

INDICATED (+3)

An individual who feels the need to limit their alcohol consumption may be suffering from an alcohol-related disorder. This should be further investigated.

3. Declined job offers

NOT INDICATED (-1)

There is no evidence to suggest that this client has declined any job offers. On the contrary, there is evidence to suggest he hasn't even applied for jobs since graduating from law school.

4. Number of hours per night that the client is able to sleep

NOT INDICATED (-2)

There has been no mention of any sleep-related concerns and no evidence gathered to suggest the client has any sleeping difficulties.

5. Parental history of alcohol consumption

INDICATED (+2)

Genetics, environment, and a person's own choices all play a significant role in alcohol-related disorders. It would therefore be very relevant to ascertain the client's parental history and current use of alcohol consumption.

Section E: Relevance of Interventions

1. Employment counseling

NOT INDICATED (-1)

Although the client doesn't seem to be motivated to seek employment despite his mother's insistence that he find work, this seems to be more of a consequence of other primary concerns and will likely improve once the main diagnosis is properly treated.

2. Family counseling

INDICATED (+1)

Because the client still lives at home and there has been significant family upset with regard to the client's alcohol consumption, there may be a need for family counseling once the therapist has had a chance to properly diagnose the client, and the client and therapist have had a chance to discuss this diagnosis along with possible treatment options.

3. Behavioral modification

INDICATED (+3)

One of the most effective interventions for treating alcohol-related illnesses is cognitive behavior therapy (CBT). CBT works to address an individual's thoughts and beliefs regarding alcohol consumption, as well as the individual's alcohol-related choices and overall habits.

4. Help client to better understand his illness

INDICATED (+2)

The more informed an individual is regarding their illness, the more likely that individual is to make more informed decisions regarding their well-being.

5. Hypnosis

INDICATED (+1)

Once regarded as highly controversial, hypnosis is now accepted by most mental health professionals as an effective therapeutic technique used to treat a great many disorders, including addictions.

Section F: Relevance of Decision Making

1. Keep the client but consult your colleague.

NOT INDICATED (-3)

Only in emergency situations (such as a threat to a client's life or well-being, a threat your client has made against the well-being of others, or a pressing court order) do therapists ever share confidential client-therapist information. It would not be appropriate for you to keep your client and share his highly personal information with others.

2. Refer your client to your colleague.

INDICATED (+3)

If you feel that your client's disorder or illness is outside your realm of professional knowledge or experience, it is recommended that you refer the client to a more capable colleague. Your overall goal is to ensure that your client receives the best available counseling and treatment.

3. Ask your client whom he would rather see.

NOT INDICATED (-1)

Although it would be highly recommended that you explain to your client why you are referring him to another therapist, and it will ultimately be the client's decision whether or not to begin therapy with another counselor, it is your sole responsibility to refer the client if you feel you are unqualified to provide appropriate and effective treatment.

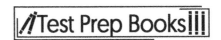

4. Arrange for your client to regularly meet with both you and your colleague.

NOT INDICATED (-3)

If you are unqualified to meet the therapeutic needs of your client, then you must ethically remove yourself from the case and refer him to a colleague or another professional who is both experienced and qualified to treat the client.

5. Continue to treat your client and learn as much as you can about his illness.

NOT INDICATED (-3)

It would be considered highly unethical for you to treat a client if you lack the appropriate experience and qualifications to do so.

Section G: Relevance of Referrals

1. Psychiatry

INDICATED (+3)

If the therapist feels that the client would benefit from further therapeutic techniques, they might refer the client to a psychiatrist. A psychiatrist is particularly equipped to deal with alcohol-related illnesses by providing a number of services. From medically-safe detoxification techniques and testing to rule out any other possible disorders, to prescribing appropriate drugs and even treating affected family members, psychiatrists are well equipped to treating clients with alcohol-related illnesses.

2. 12-step recovery and maintenance program

INDICATED (+3)

A 12-step program such as Alcoholics Anonymous offers services that psychiatry cannot. It provides a safe and confidential environment where recovering alcoholics can gather together to share their stories, 24/7 support when the client connects with a sponsor, and spiritual guidance.

3. Self-help group

INDICATED (+2)

There are several available self-help groups that an individual can join, from groups that deal with addictions to others that focus on physical illnesses, disabilities, depression, anxiety, financial support, and more.

4. Family counseling

INDICATED (+1)

Once the client has a clear understanding of his illness and how it is affecting his family members, family counseling would be an appropriate course of action to consider in order to strengthen his relationship with his parents and include them as support units in his recovery goals.

5. Legal services

NOT INDICATED (-3)

There is no evidence to suggest that this client is in need of legal services of any kind. This is not relevant in this case.

Simulation 5

Section A: Relevance of Initial Information Gathering

1. Low energy levels

INDICATED (+3)

The client has indicated that his low energy levels are interfering with his ability to function in his usual manner, and that he wishes to find a way to feel more energetic.

2. Work-related stress

INDICATED (+1)

Although this client admitted that he tends to become enraged at work when people disagree with him, he stated that lately, he has become withdrawn. He also stated that he wishes that employees would give him the credit that he feels he deserves. These feelings may be causing stress for the client, but don't seem to be his main focus of concern.

3. Financial difficulties

NOT INDICATED (-3)

The client mentioned that without him, his business would collapse. But overall, his business is very financially stable. This is not relevant.

4. Family problems

INDICATED (+1)

The client mentioned that he has three ungrateful, adult children and that he would like them to show more appreciation for his generosity over the years. He is therefore at least somewhat aware of a problem with family dynamics and/or how he and his children may hold different perspectives and wishes for this dynamic to improve albeit only for his benefit.

5. Relationship difficulties

INDICATED (+3)

The client has indicated that he has had two failed marriages and that each wife was to blame for these failures. He doesn't seem to accept any blame here whatsoever and does not seem to be seeking counseling to improve present or future relationships. He also mentions his children and eludes to strained relationships with them as well. Although he does not seem to be seeking help with these

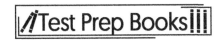

issues, they are worth considering as contributing to this current mental state if he has no real connections in his life.

Section B: Relevance of Additional Information Gathering

1. Current medications

INDICATED (+2)

If the client is taking prescribed medications, consuming excessive amounts of alcohol, or ingesting illicit drugs, this may account for his low energy levels and should be further investigated.

2. Prevalence of suicidal thoughts

NOT INDICATED (-3)

Although the client has indicated that he is more withdrawn than he normally is, and that he is experiencing low energy levels, there is no evidence to suggest he is having suicidal thoughts. This is not relevant in this case.

3. History of heart problems

NOT INDICATED (-2)

There is no evidence to suggest this client is having any heart-related issues. This is not relevant in this case.

4. Traumatic life events

NOT INDICATED (-3)

Traumatic life events (such as a death of a loved one or a personal near-death experience) can cause an individual to have sudden-onset and severe depression, anxiety, excessive fear, chronic nightmares, and the like. This does not apply in this case and is not relevant.

5. Personal regrets

INDICATED (+3)

An astute therapist might recognize that this client is showing signs of emotional detachment from others with a clear lack of empathy and/or sympathy. He accepts no wrongdoing in his professional or personal life and expects a high level of praise and admiration. It would be both reasonable and relevant to find out more about this client's ability to emotionally connect to others.

Section C: Relevance of Decision Making

1. Client-therapist confidentiality rules

NOT INDICATED (-3)

It is always in both the client's and the therapist's best interest to discuss confidentiality rules from the very first session. This is definitely an important area for the therapist to cover.

2. Obligation to inform law enforcement if you feel threatened by your client

NOT INDICATED (-3)

Other than mentioning that he has a tendency to become enraged if things do not go his way, there is no criminal history of physical violence or abuse, nor is he currently showing signs of aggression in his session with the therapist. This would be the least relevant area to discuss with the client and may be counterproductive if specifically brought up outside of the normal package of explaining confidentiality and the reasons why a therapist would need to reach out to law enforcement.

3. Medications that may boost energy levels

NOT INDICATED (-1)

Although this isn't something that should necessarily be discussed at the very first session, there may be a need to eventually consider prescribing medications to boost energy levels.

4. Techniques on being more self-assertive

INDICATED (+2)

There is nothing in the evidence to suggest that this client requires assistance with being more self-assertive. This would be completely irrelevant in this case.

5. Effective business management strategies

INDICATED (+1)

Although he may need some assistance in understanding that his business can operate well in his absence, there is little evidence to suggest this client is in need of business management strategies.

Section D: Relevance of Assessment Instruments

1. Personality Diagnostic Questionnaire

INDICATED (+3)

The Personality Diagnostic Questionnaire is regarded as a very reliable and trustworthy test when screening for various personality disorders. This would be highly relevant in this case.

2. Cloninger's Temperament and Character Inventory

INDICATED (+2)

This is a set of tests used to help the therapist and their client learn more about the client's personality and emotions. It helps clients to become more self-aware, and it helps therapists to develop an appropriate treatment plan for clients living with a variety of personality and emotional disorders. This would be a relevant inventory to administer in this case.

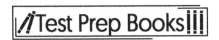

3. Beck Depression Inventory–II

INDICATED (+1)

The Beck Depression Inventory–II is widely used to measure the severity of an individual's depression. Although this client has not demonstrated clear signs of depression, his sudden onset of low energy levels and disengagement from his work life may indicate a depression. This test would at least indicate if depression is present and if so, how severe it is.

4. Mental Status Examination (MSE)

INDICATED (+1)

The MSE might be administered in this case to determine whether or not the client is suffering from depression. The MSE could also reveal an individual's general behavior, mood, attitude, and self-awareness, which will help provide insight to his mental illness and help the therapist to develop an appropriate treatment plan.

5. Schizophrenia Test and Early Psychosis Indicator

NOT INDICATED (-3)

There is no evidence to suggest that this client is suffering from symptoms indirectly or directly related to schizophrenia.

Section E: Relevance of Diagnosis

1. Narcissistic personality disorder

INDICATED (+3)

The client shows many signs of narcissism and may be suffering from narcissistic personality disorder. He lacks empathy for others and accepts no blame for failed relationships and/or communication difficulties. He believes he is the only one capable of running his business, and without him, the business would fall apart. He demands praise from his employees and adult children, and when he doesn't receive it (or he doesn't believe he receives enough praise), he is enraged. He repeats how successful he is at an obsessive level.

2. Social anxiety disorder

NOT INDICATED (-3)

Social anxiety disorder is characterized by an exaggerated fear of being the center of attention in social situations, of meeting strangers, of being teased or ridiculed, and of being in the public eye. The disorder is debilitating to the point where relationships, school, and work can all be negatively affected. This does not apply here.

3. Panic disorder

NOT INDICATED (-3)

When an individual presents with an unnaturally fast heartbeat, excessive sweating, visible shaking, and a shortness of breath, they may be suffering from a panic attack. If these symptoms present often, they may suffer from a panic disorder, but this is not relevant in this case.

4. Bipolar disorder

NOT INDICATED (-2)

When an individual's emotional, cognitive, and behavioral state significantly sway from one extreme to another, the individual may be showing signs of a bipolar disorder. This is not relevant in this case.

5. Intermittent explosive disorder

NOT INDICATED (-1)

Although this client has admitted that he becomes enraged when things do not go his way, there seem to be reasons (albeit irrational ones) associated with his rage. For individuals who suffer from intermittent explosive disorder, the rage is not necessarily linked to any specific trigger and the outbursts are often random. This is not relevant in this case.

Section F: Relevance of Diagnostic Confirmation

1. History of interpersonal relationships

INDICATED (+1)

There is a strong correlation between a continuous history of failed and/or unhealthy relationships and people suffering from narcissistic personality disorder.

2. Client's lack or presence of empathy for others

INDICATED (+2)

Another telltale sign that a person may be suffering from narcissistic personality disorder is their complete lack of empathy for others, even people in their own family.

3. Client's perceived sense of self-importance

INDICATED (+3)

Narcissistic personality disorder is almost always synonymous with a person's inflated sense of self-importance, to the point of obsessing over how important they are and insisting that everyone recognize and agree with this belief.

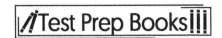

4. Client's educational history

NOT INDICATED (-3)

There is no evidence that suggests there is any correlation between narcissistic personality disorder and a person's level of education.

5. Client's parental philosophy

NOT INDICATED (-2)

Although a person suffering from narcissistic personality disorder may be emotionally detached from their children and unable to nurture them or provide emotional stability, a client's actual parental philosophy does not factor into a narcissistic personality disorder diagnosis.

Section G: Relevance of Interventions

1. Anti-depressant medication

INDICATED (+1)

If it is determined that he is suffering from the effects of depression, which can develop as a consequence of narcissistic personality disorder, it may be beneficial for the individual to take prescribed antidepressants so that his level of functioning does not become impaired.

2. Paradoxical intention

NOT INDICATED (-2)

Somewhat like "reverse psychology," paradoxical intention involves prescribing the exact behavior or action that the client wants to eliminate. This assumes that the client is aware of the behavior that they wish to eliminate, and further suggests that there is one central problematic behavior. This would be an inappropriate technique in this case.

3. Long-term psychotherapy

INDICATED (+3)

Although some therapists may recommend that the client seek family, group, or couples' therapy in addition to individual therapeutic sessions, the most widely used form of therapy for clients with narcissistic personality disorder is a continuation of regular outpatient treatment, coupled with psychotherapy sessions with clearly-defined objectives.

4. Zung Self-Rating Anxiety Scale

NOT INDICATED (-3)

This is a test that screens for both anxiety and depression and is not considered in any way to be a course of treatment.

5. Exercise

INDICATED (+1)

Although there is no evidence to suggest that this client requires a treatment plan that involves an exercise regime, nor is there any evidence to suggest that physical exercise is an appropriate course of treatment for a person suffering from narcissistic personality disorder, his low energy levels may decrease with a regular exercise regime.

Simulation 6

Section A: Relevance of Initial Information Gathering

1. Does the child understand the reason she is visiting a therapist?

INDICATED (+1)

Determining whether or not the child has an awareness of some of the struggles she has been facing will help the therapist formulate an appropriate treatment plan.

2. Does the child demonstrate an age-appropriate emotional bond to her family members?

INDICATED (+1)

Determining the child's emotional state at home will help to rule out any other possible issues or disorders that may be affecting her ability to concentrate and calm down. It may also reveal some other family-related issues that are affecting her overall behavior.

3. Does the child demonstrate an age-appropriate emotional response to school?

INDICATED (+1)

Determining the child's emotional state while in school will also help to rule out any other possible issues or disorders that may be affecting her ability to concentrate and to remain calm during school hours. It may also reveal some other school-related issues that are affecting her overall behavior.

4. Does the child demonstrate an interest in age-appropriate entertainment?

NOT INDICATED (-3)

There is no evidence to suggest that the child is exposed to inappropriate television programs, and there is no relevancy in asking such a question.

5. Does the child demonstrate an ability to make and maintain friendships?

INDICATED (+3)

It is common for a child with ADHD to struggle with making and maintaining friendships and is one of the telltale signs of this disorder.

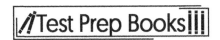

Section B: Relevance of Additional Information Gathering

1. Child's medical history

INDICATED (+2)

Knowledge of the child's medical history will help to rule out any other underlying medical conditions that may be influencing the child's behavior. This is both a relevant and responsible course of action in this case

2. Family medical history

INDICATED (+3)

If one of the child's parents has ADHD or had ADHD as a child, then the child has more than a 50 percent likelihood of having ADHD. It is therefore recommended that the therapist conduct a thorough review of the family's medical history.

3. Checklists and other relevant data from the child's school

INDICATED (+3)

An 8-year-old child spends a minimum of five or more hours each weekday at school surrounded by same-age children in a social and academic setting. Any and all data that the school and the child's teacher can share with the therapist regarding the child's interactions with other children and with staff, as well as her behavior and academic achievements, would help to either determine or rule out the possibility of ADHD.

4. Client's eating habits

INDICATED (+2)

Every child, including children with ADHD, should follow a diet rich in proteins and vitamins. Avoiding fast foods, limiting sugar intake, and ensuring each meal contains appropriate nutrients will help to lessen ADHD symptoms.

5. Family's neighborhood and surrounding area

NOT INDICATED (-3)

There is no evidence to suggest that a child's neighborhood surroundings have a causal relationship with an individual who has ADHD.

Section C: Relevance of Ruling Out Criteria

1. Depression

NOT INDICATED (-1)

Close to 20 percent of children diagnosed with ADHD will also be diagnosed with depression, and although this shouldn't be overlooked, there doesn't seem to be evidence that points to depression in this case.

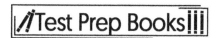

2. Oppositional defiant disorder (ODD)

INDICATED (+3)

Children with ODD tend to be hostile toward authority figures, lose their temper, and show aggressive tendencies. Conduct disorders are among the most common disorders that coexist with ADHD. Because there is evidence to suggest that this child has a tendency to disrupt lessons in class and regularly argues with her teacher, this should be further explored.

3. Anorexia nervosa

NOT INDICATED (-3)

A child's obsession or preoccupation with food and/or with eating may be an early warning sign for anorexia nervosa, gradually followed by a refusal to eat, severe weight loss, and many other complications that negatively affect school and home life. This doesn't apply in this case.

4. Conduct disorder

INDICATED (+3)

The two most common behavioral disorders that coexist with ADHD are ODD and conduct disorder. Both of these disorders show ongoing patterns of aggressive and/or hostile behaviors toward authority figures. As the data collected from the school demonstrates a pattern of defiance and a tendency to argue with authority, this should be further explored.

5. Trouble adjusting to new baby brother

NOT INDICATED (-3)

Although adjusting to a new baby can be difficult for some children and may manifest in behavioral issues at home and at school, this client shows a keen interest in her baby brother and does not demonstrate any signs of maladjustment.

Section D: Relevance of Diagnosis

1. Conversion disorder

NOT INDICATED (-3)

Conversion disorder is characterized by the sudden inability to see, sudden paralysis, or any other sudden onset of neurologic issues that cannot be explained by medical evaluation. This does not apply to this case.

2. Adjustment disorder with depressed mood

NOT INDICATED (-2)

Although the family has had to adjust to the arrival of a new baby, the client is not manifesting any of the signs or symptoms to justify such a diagnosis. Feelings of persistent sadness or hopelessness do not apply here.

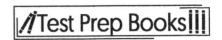

3. Separation anxiety disorder

NOT INDICATED (-2)

It is very common for infants to experience separation anxiety when temporarily separated from either one or both parents, but if a child older than 6 years of age is demonstrating signs of separation anxiety—extreme fear of being separated from a loved one, refusal to leave, refusal to go to school—and the signs and symptoms are consistent over a prolonged period of time, the child may have separation anxiety disorder. This disorder does not apply in this case.

4. ADHD

INDICATED (+3)

Children with attention deficit hyperactivity disorder may present with any number of behavioral issues, from irritability and aggressive behaviors to the inability to calm down or pay attention. This client seems to be showing several signs and symptoms of ADHD—she is fidgety, irritable, acts out in class, is restless, unable to sit long enough to complete assignments—and should be further investigated in order to confirm or rule out this possible DSM-5 diagnosis.

5. Tourette syndrome

NOT INDICATED (-3)

Tourette syndrome is a disorder of the nervous system that involves repetitive, involuntary sounds, words, and/or motions. This does not apply to this case.

Section E: Relevance of Decision Making

1. Behavioral therapy

INDICATED (+3)

For children with ADHD, behavioral therapy is regarded as a very effective intervention. Behavioral therapy teaches children how to cope with stresses and how to act and react in various settings. Behavioral therapy also models respectful, healthy communication.

2. Medication

INDICATED (+1)

If the child's ADHD is significantly interfering with daily functioning in school and at home, medication may be necessary. Adderall and Ritalin are the most commonly used medications to treat ADHD, but there are many others now on the market, from pills to patches. It is important to determine whether or not the child with ADHD requires medication and if so, what the recommended dose would be.

3. Parent management training

INDICATED (+3)

In order for the family to operate and function in a healthy manner, it is very important for parents to learn the best approaches and techniques when communicating with their child who has ADHD. Some of these techniques might involve a checklist for making sure chores and homework are being completed or that personal hygiene isn't neglected. Other techniques include the appropriate use and accurate timing of positive reinforcement and award systems, but it is equally as important for parents to create and maintain a fair and consistent system of consequences for unacceptable behavior.

4. Skills-based interventions

INDICATED (+2)

When appropriately employed and practiced, skills-based interventions will continue to serve individuals throughout their lives. Learning how to organize one's responsibilities and tasks with the use of an agenda, for example, how to pace oneself when working on an assignment for school, or learning basic studying skills, will serve the student well beyond her school years.

5. Journaling

NOT INDICATED (-3)

Although journaling about one's feelings and thoughts may be beneficial to individuals from all walks of life and for those who suffer from a wide variety of illnesses, it doesn't apply here. This client is only 8-years-old and is currently having great difficulty sitting still long enough to complete her homework. It is best to focus on behavioral management, skills-based interventions, and parent management training.

Section F: Relevance of Ethics

1. Against APA ethics guidelines

NOT INDICATED (-3)

There is nothing within the APA ethics guidelines that states a therapist is prohibited from visiting a client's school for observation purposes.

2. Against your own professional code of ethics

NOT INDICATED (-3)

There should be no reason for you to have established a professional code of ethics that prohibits you from visiting a client's school for observation purposes.

3. Agree and contact school to make arrangements

INDICATED (+3)

Agreeing to visit the child's school in order to observe her interactions with her teacher and classmates, as well as how she tackles academic tasks, will help you as the therapist to develop the most effective treatment plan, give parents further insight, and suggest effective strategies that the teacher can employ in the classroom.

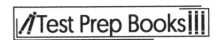

4. Ask the child if she agrees to being observed at school

INDICATED (+1)

Although it isn't necessary for the therapist to ask for the child's opinion, this may be a very effective way to reassure the child that she is part of the process and that her thoughts and opinions matter. It may also improve and strengthen the child's trust in the therapist.

5. Secure the school principal's permission before agreeing to the school visit

NOT INDICATED (-2)

Although it may be seen as courteous to inform the principal regarding the date and time of your observation, this doesn't fall within the therapist's responsibilities. Therapists should ensure that an appropriate date and time for observation has been organized with the child's classroom teacher, and it would likely be the teacher's responsibility to ensure the principal of this arrangement.

Section G: Relevance of Short-Term Goals

1. Sit through one full lesson at a time

INDICATED (+2)

Sitting through one full lesson at a time may be an appropriate short-term goal if there aren't too many other short-term expectations all implemented at the same time. In order for the child to succeed in this goal, it is recommended that she be allowed frequent breaks, but gradually limit the number of breaks until she can sit through the entire lesson. Another technique to help her sit through an entire lesson would be to allow her to use a fidget spinner at her desk or a rubber band on the foot of her chair.

2. Complete her nightly homework

INDICATED (+2)

Again, provided not too many other short-term expectations are placed upon her all at the same time, completing nightly homework may be another appropriate short-term goal. Perhaps using an agenda to ensure all assignments are completed, as well as offering some assistance in pacing herself between assignments, will help her meet this goal.

3. Get a minimum of 10 hours of sleep each night

INDICATED (+2)

It is recommended that children within this age group get a minimum of 10 hours of sleep each night for optimal cognitive, behavioral, and physical development.

4. Spend more time with her baby brother

NOT INDICATED (-1)

There is no evidence to suggest that the child does not spend an appropriate amount of time interacting with her baby brother. This is not relevant as a short-term goal.

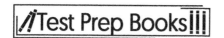

5. Follow a checklist at home and school to help her stay organized

INDICATED (+2)

Checklists can be a very effective tool for children living with ADHD. Checklists can help children organize their tasks and monitor their own accomplishments. Checklists can also be used for home and school responsibilities.

Simulation 7

Section A: Relevance of Initial Information Gathering

1. Suicidal thoughts

INDICATED (+3)

When a client presents with several signs and prolonged symptoms of a possible depressive disorder, it is critical that the therapist rule out suicidal thoughts. If the client indicates that she has had thoughts of suicide, the therapist must take necessary precautions to prevent imminent self-harm.

2. Moments of great joy

NOT INDICATED (-2)

This question would be relevant if the therapist was trying to distinguish between a chronic depressive disorder and a manic-depressive disorder, but this client has already indicated that she barely has enough energy to get through her daily routines and life's joys have all but faded away.

3. Social media sites

NOT INDICATED (-3)

Knowledge of what social media sites the client visits on occasion is not at all relevant in gathering information regarding her mental health status. This does not apply here.

4. Residential history

NOT INDICATED (-2)

Gathering information on where the client has lived over the years will not help the therapist determine an accurate DSM-5 diagnosis. This is irrelevant.

5. Current medications

INDICATED (+2)

It is important for the therapist to have a full list of any and all medications the client is currently taking, to rule out any side effects that may be contributing to or causing some of the client's ongoing symptoms.

218

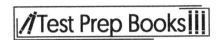

Section B: Relevance of Additional Information Gathering

1. Sleeping patterns

INDICATED (+1)

Individuals who are dealing with depressive disorders often report difficulty with sleeping. This would be relevant information in this case.

2. Eating patterns

INDICATED (+1)

Binge eating, eating too much, too little, or not eating at all can sometimes be signs of a depressive disorder and should be closely monitored.

3. Past extracurricular activities and pastimes

INDICATED (+2)

Learning what the client used to do for enjoyment, and when and why she stopped engaging in that activity, can help the therapist to formulate an appropriate treatment plan to include enjoyable extracurricular activities.

4. Frequency of visits to family home

NOT INDICATED (-2)

The number of visits the client makes to her family home is irrelevant information when trying to determine an accurate diagnosis.

5. Frequency of receiving visits from family members

NOT INDICATED (-2)

The number of visits from family members that the client receives at her home is irrelevant information when trying to determine an accurate diagnosis.

Section C: Relevance of Decision Making

1. Physical exam

INDICATED (+1)

The client is a 50-year-old woman who has mentioned joint stiffness, general aches and pains, and extremely low energy levels. Although only medical doctors can perform physical examinations, it would be prudent for the counselor to consult with the client's doctor to request the client's medical records and/or request a physical exam in order to rule out any other possible illnesses.

2. CT scan

NOT INDICATED (-1)

This would only be prudent if the client is not responding well to therapies and medications used to treat severe depression, but it would not be an initial test to determine a diagnosis. It is important to note that although psychological factors tend to be the root cause of the majority of depressive disorders, it is possible for an individual with a brain tumor to be experiencing depressive symptoms, especially if the individual is over the age of 50, has never before experienced any form of depression, and is not responding well to antidepressants or any other form of therapy.

3. Patient Health Questionnaire–9

INDICATED (+3)

The Patient Health Questionnaire–9 is a widely used test that screens individuals who are presenting with signs and symptoms of depression. It helps mental health professionals screen for both the presence and the severity of depression and is frequently used in order to determine a DSM-5 diagnosis.

4. Zung Self-Rating Depression Scale

NOT INDICATED (-2)

Although the Zung Self-Rating Depression Scale is used to monitor possible changes in the severity of an individual's depressive symptoms, it is not a tool used to diagnose or confirm the diagnosis of a depressive disorder.

5. Beck Depression Inventory

INDICATED (+2)

Used to screen for the presence and severity of depressive symptoms in both adolescents and adults, the Beck Depression Inventory would be an appropriate tool to use in this case.

Section D: Relevance of Diagnosis

1. Atypical depression

NOT INDICATED (-1)

If a person is diagnosed with atypical depression, they are likely experiencing extreme fatigue, sleeping a minimum of 10 hours or more each night, and eating in excess. Although this client has complained of low energy levels, she is not presenting with any issues involving excessive sleeping or eating.

2. Persistent depressive disorder (dysthymia)

INDICATED (+3)

Persistent depressive disorder is characterized by difficulties with concentration, complete loss of interest in daily routines and extracurricular activities, low energy levels, and a lack of interest in social activities, along with other depressive features that have persisted for a minimum of two years. This

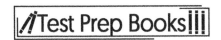

seems the most likely DSM-5 diagnosis for this client, as she has been suffering with depressive symptoms for three years.

3. Psychotic depression

NOT INDICATED (-2)

If an individual is suffering from a major form of depression that coexists with a form of psychosis—a type of "break" from reality—this individual is likely to be diagnosed with psychotic depression. This does not apply in this case.

4. Situational depression

NOT INDICATED (-3)

A type of depression that is directly related to a specific event or situation, situational depression does not apply here as this client has been experiencing depressive symptoms for a few years and nothing indicates that it is due to a specific event or situation in her life.

5. Bipolar disorder

NOT INDICATED (-2)

Individuals with bipolar disorder shift between extreme highs to extreme lows, with each drastic mood swing lasting for short or long periods of time. This does not apply in this case.

Section E: Relevance of Diagnosis Confirmation

1. Duration of depressive symptoms

INDICATED (+2)

A persistent presentation of depressive symptoms for a minimum of two years is one of the main factors that distinguishes persistent depressive disorder from other forms of depression.

2. Prolonged decrease in energy levels

INDICATED (+2)

The fact that this individual has had consistent low energy levels for the past three years is very relevant when considering a diagnosis of persistent depressive disorder.

3. Social interactions

INDICATED (+1)

This client has admitted that she is no longer interested in social events or activities, and that this has been a consistent pattern for the past three years. This too, is indicative of persistent depressive disorder.

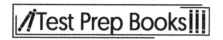

4. Personal care

NOT INDICATED (-3)

Persistent depressive disorder is not characterized by a lack of personal hygiene or personal care. This doesn't apply in this case.

5. Complete disinterest in daily activities

INDICATED (+3)

A major telltale sign that points to a possible persistent depressive disorder diagnosis is evidence of a complete lack of interest in daily routines and activities that has persisted for a minimum of two years.

Section F: Relevance of Treatments and Referrals

1. Dream analysis

NOT INDICATED (-3)

Dream analysis is typically used to reveal a client's repressed feelings and is a controversial form of therapy. It would not be relevant in this case

2. Narrative therapy

NOT INDICATED (-2)

Counsellors may use narrative therapy as a way of helping clients work through specific problems in their lives in order to generate meaningful discussions on the possibility of new, healthy narratives. These new narratives give the client a new avenue—or several new avenues—to explore when confronted with problematic situations. This does not apply here.

3. Electroconvulsive therapy (ECT)

INDICATED (+1) –

ECT is used to treat individuals with major depressive disorders and may be applicable in this case, but only after other less invasive techniques have been used and have proven ineffective.

4. Talk therapy

INDICATED (+3)

Talk therapy is among the most widely used and respected forms of therapy for clients suffering from persistent depressive disorder. Talk therapy allows the client to openly discuss feelings, emotions, past experiences, actions, and reactions to situations. Being able to talk through some of the most vulnerable and personal aspects of a person's life can have dramatic effects on helping them come to terms with their life's challenges, manage their responses to these challenges, and learn coping mechanisms to overcome difficulties.

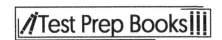

5. Selective serotonin reuptake inhibitors (SSRIs)

INDICATED (+3)

The appropriate use and dosage of SSRIs, coupled with regular talk therapy sessions, has proven to have very positive results for individuals suffering from persistent depressive disorder. SSRIs are antidepressants that are among the most recommended treatments for individuals suffering with a major depressive disorder.

Section G: Relevance of Short-Term Goals

1. Significant reduction in depressive symptoms

NOT INDICATED (-2)

The client has had persistent depressive symptoms for the past three years. It would be unrealistic to assume that in the short term, she will be able to significantly reduce her depressive symptoms. A gradual reduction would be much more appropriate as a short-term goal.

2. Full reentry into society with healthy energy levels

NOT INDICATED (-3)

It is not realistic to assume that a short-term goal for a person suffering from persistent depressive disorder for the past three years will suddenly jump back into social situations with full vigor. Gradual reintroduction to social life should be the focus.

3. Begin a moderate, self-regulating exercise regime

INDICATED (+2)

Exercise has been proven to be extremely therapeutic in the treatment of mental health disorders. Beginning a moderate, self-regulating exercise program to loosen the joints, deal with this client's minor aches and pains, and release some endorphins, which work to reduce the perception of pain and discomfort, would be an appropriate short-term goal.

4. Choose one extracurricular activity of interest and attempt to become involved one day per week

INDICATED (+1)

Another appropriate short-term goal would be to consider extracurricular activities of interest and attempt to become involved in a gradual manner.

5. Learn and apply appropriate skills and emotional regulation

INDICATED (+1)

With the key being "gradual," learning and applying appropriate skills that help to regulate emotions and emotional reactions to her daily life would be an important short-term goal to consider.

Simulation 8

Section A: Relevance of Initial Information Gathering

1. Level of aggressive behavior

INDICATED (+3)

For the parents and the school, the child's regular display of aggressive behavior is a serious concern, as it is interfering with the child's ability to succeed, the well-being of classmates, and health and well-being of the family unit.

2. Unwillingness to apply daily self-care and hygienic practices

NOT INDICATED (-1)

Although this was reported by the parents as a concern, the concern is less about their son's lack of hygienic practices and more about his refusal to practice daily hygiene when he is "told" to do so.

3. Inability to transition between tasks

INDICATED (+1)

The teacher has reported that the child becomes aggressive when "asked" to transition from one task to another. The concern, again, is less about his inability to transition and more about his refusal to do so when asked. However, given that anxiety can present as aggression, if transitions are difficult for this child (due to the request from adults to do so or not) it would be useful to keep this in mind when gathering information.

4. Parental preference

INDICATED (+1)

The parents indicated that their son only shows aggression toward his mother when she asks for him to complete homework or do his chores, but that he interacts well with his father. It may be worth further exploration to determine what types of interaction father and son engage in together, and whether or not the father ever asks or demands anything of his son.

5. Refusal to do household chores

NOT INDICATED (-1)

The concern here is less about the child's inability to complete household chores and more about his refusal when asked.

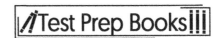

Section B: Relevance of Main Issues

1. Aggressive behavior

INDICATED (+3)

The child's tendency to use aggressive behavior is of particular importance. If he continues to attempt to hit his mother and throw things around the home and classroom, he could potentially harm himself or others. If not addressed effectively, this can worsen over time.

2. Opposition to authority

INDICATED (+3)

It appears as though this child only acts out in fits of aggression when told or asked to perform a task or to stop a particular activity. This warrants further investigation to help determine an accurate DSM-5 diagnosis.

3. Inability to remain calm

NOT INDICATED (-2)

The child is not reported to have issues with hyperactivity. He only seems to react aggressively when he is told to perform—or stop performing—a task.

4. Incomplete homework assignments

NOT INDICATED (-2)

Although not completing homework can negatively impact his grades and his feelings about himself and school, the focus for the counselor should be centered on his aggressive behavior. If the behavior is properly addressed and treated, his homework completion will likely improve.

5. Failing grades in school

NOT INDICATED (-2)

There is no indication that the student is receiving failing grades, but if he continues to refuse to transition from one activity to another and continues to refuse to complete his homework, his grades will in all likelihood begin to suffer. However, if the counselor effectively addresses his aggressive and defiant behavior, and a proper treatment plan is put into practice, his success in school should gradually improve.

Section C: Relevance of Diagnosis

1. Learning disabilities

NOT INDICATED (-2)

Some examples of common learning disabilities are dyspraxia, dyslexia, dysgraphia, dyscalculia, auditory processing disorder, and visual processing disorder. Although children with learning disabilities may act out as a response to their frustration as they try to cope with their learning disabilities, neither the teacher nor the parents have indicated that the child has a learning disability or that they suspect he may have a learning disability.

2. Antisocial personality disorder

NOT INDICATED (-1)

Antisocial personality disorder usually presents itself during adolescence and early teens. Some common signs may be the general lack of concern for other people's rights as well as a general disregard for appropriate social conduct. Teens with antisocial personality disorder may begin to drink in excess, start fights, and engage in irresponsible behavior. This doesn't seem to apply in this case.

3. Autism

NOT INDICATED (-3)

Autism is a spectrum disorder, meaning there are varying degrees of signs and symptoms. However, all degrees of autism do share certain characteristics, such as difficulty with empathy, a preoccupation with certain subjects, extreme need for routines, difficulty forming and maintaining friendships, and a general lack of interest in social activities. This does not apply here.

4. Oppositional defiant disorder (ODD)

INDICATED (+3)

Many children engage in confrontations with authority figures as they grow in age, but if this behavior is continual and aggressive, it may be cause for concern. If a child routinely refuses to follow instructions, disobeys general rules, argues with parents and teachers, and shows acts of aggressive behavior such as starting fights or destroying personal property, the child may be suffering from ODD.

5. ADHD

INDICATED (+1)

ODD and ADHD are often confused when diagnosing a child, as they tend to have some overlapping signs and symptoms, such as difficulty paying attention, difficulty sitting still, and a tendency to interrupt when people are talking. However, what sets these two apart is the tendency for a child with ODD to be extremely argumentative, always challenging authority, and acting out with aggressive behavior. Nonetheless, because they do share similar symptoms, ADHD should be ruled out before a provisional diagnosis of ODD is given.

Section D: Relevance of Diagnostic Confirmation

1. Family dynamics

INDICATED (+2)

Because ODD is believed to be caused by three main types of factors (genetic, biological, and environment), it would be prudent for the counselor to collect information on how the family operates. Do the parents have consistent and fair consequences in place for misbehavior? Do the parents argue in front of their child? Is time spent regularly enjoying activities as a family? Who is the disciplinarian? A

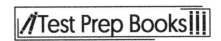

better understanding of the family dynamics will give the counselor a better insight into what is happening with the child

2. Family history of mental illness

INDICATED (+3)

In addition to having a possible environmental cause, ODD is also believed to be both genetic and biological. It is therefore very relevant to ascertain a complete history of any family mental illness, especially if it relates to ODD.

3. School grades

NOT INDICATED (-2)

Although school grades are likely a byproduct of this client's aggressive behavior, as is the refusal to complete tasks that are asked of him, the school grades themselves would not factor into confirming or revising a DSM-5 diagnosis of ODD.

4. Number of friends

NOT INDICATED (-3)

Children living with ODD often have difficulty developing and maintaining healthy friendships, but the number of friends does not have any bearing on a DSM-5 diagnosis of ODD.

5. Involvement in extracurricular activities

NOT INDICATED (-2)

A child with ODD can be involved or uninvolved with extracurricular activities. A child's involvement in extracurricular activities is not relevant to a DSM-5 diagnosis of ODD.

Section E: Relevance of Decision Making

1. Psychotherapy

INDICATED (+3)

Psychotherapy, better known as counseling, can help a child with ODD to develop effective techniques for managing anger, expressing feelings, and rethinking how they perceive authority.

2. Prescribed medication

INDICATED (-2)

There is no current medication that specifically treats children with ODD.

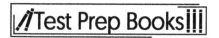

3. Play groups

NOT INDICATED (-1)

Play groups may be an eventual treatment outcome once the child has learned to better manage his anger and can follow instructions and requests without becoming aggressive.

4. Contracts

INDICATED (+2)

School and family contracts are often used to help a child begin to take responsibility for their actions. Often built in with rewards and consequences, contracts encourage a child to be aware of negative behavior and puts them in the driver's seat to work on self-control techniques.

5. Family therapy

INDICATED (+2)

Because ODD can be rooted in environment, it may be beneficial to conduct family therapy sessions in order to work on how each family member interacts with one another and how they communicate as a family. During family therapy sessions, contracts can also be established to help set up a system of rewards and consequences for behavior.

Section F: Relevance of Treatment Outcomes

1. Daily homework completion

INDICATED (+1)

After successfully establishing contracts at school and at home, and after working on anger management techniques, one reasonable treatment outcome would be that the child begins to complete his daily homework assignments.

2. Build and maintain healthy friendships

INDICATED (+1)

This may take a while, but another reasonable treatment outcome, once the child learns to control his aggressive behavior, would be to start to build and maintain friendships with his peers.

3. Increased parent-child bonding

INDICATED (+2)

With an established family contract in place, along with a better parental understanding of what ODD is and how the parents can help their son to overcome his difficulties, a closer family bond is very likely to occur.

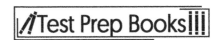

4. Reduction on the number of demands that mother places on child

NOT INDICATED (-2)

There is no indication in any of the data to suggest that the mother places an unreasonable number of demands or expectations on her son. She expects him to do his part in household chores, to practice proper hygiene, and complete his homework. This is not a relevant treatment outcome, but the therapist may suggest that the mother and father equally share in the responsibility of establishing and managing expectations.

5. Introduction of a school-based behavioral intervention strategy

INDICATED (+2)

One possible treatment outcome is the partnership with the classroom teacher to develop a behavioral intervention strategy that will help the child transition from task to task, complete assignments, and communicate respectfully with his teacher and peers.

Section G: Relevance of Client Progress

1. Feedback on parent management training

INDICATED (+2)

Following successful completion of parent management training, the counselor will likely request feedback from the parents to monitor the overall efficacy of the training.

2. Continued individual counseling sessions

NOT INDICATED (-2)

A gradual decrease in the number of individual sessions would be an appropriate way to encourage the child to independently use his newly acquired self-regulation techniques while still scheduling the occasional visit to monitor his progress.

3. Behavioral modification

INDICATED (+3)

The expectation is that the parents and the classroom teacher have already introduced the behavioral modification approach and are tracking its efficacy based on the child's behavior. The counselor should request feedback to monitor how well this approach is working for the child.

4. Continued family counseling sessions

NOT INDICATED (-2)

Family counseling sessions should gradually decrease once the family has had a number of sessions to address effective communication and work on a family contract.

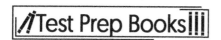

5. Self-awareness strategies

INDICATED (+3)

The best indication that the child is progressing is the monitoring of how well he is able to demonstrate self-awareness. True progress is being made if the child demonstrates an awareness of his aggressive behavior, his anger, and his tendency to argue, along with an awareness that he has the freedom to make choices and use self-regulating techniques to control his aggression.

Simulation 9

Section A: Relevance of Initial Information Gathering

1. Client's medical records

INDICATED (+3)

This client has indicated a shortness of breath, rapid heartbeat, and difficulties with her sleeping patterns. It would be very important to consult her medical records to rule out any underlying conditions.

2. History of possible mental illness in the family

INDICATED (+2)

If there is a history of mental illness in the family, this would be very relevant information that would assist the counselor in formulating a provisionary DSM-5 diagnosis.

3. Physical exam

INDICATED (+2)

A shortness of breath and a rapid heartbeat can be signs of a serious heart condition. With the client's consent, it would be very prudent for the counselor to request a physical exam via the client's family doctor.

4. Heart monitor evaluation

NOT INDICATED (-1)

As the counselor is not the treating medical physician, they would not be authorized to order a heart monitor evaluation. The request for a physical exam, however, might lead to this precautionary measure by the treating physician.

5. Current medications

INDICATED (+1)

Certain medications can interfere with a person's emotions and can cause heightened anxiety levels. It would be extremely relevant for the counselor to inquire about medications that this client is currently taking, including the dose and frequency of use.

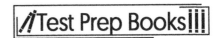

Section B: Relevance of Main Issues

1. Shortness of breath

INDICATED (+3)

Shortness of breath should be immediately addressed in order to rule out any serious health issues.

2. Rapid heartbeat

INDICATED (+3)

A continuously rapid heartbeat can be signs of a serious health issue and can be life threatening. This should be immediately addressed.

3. Sleep disturbances

INDICATED (+2)

There are many reasons that individuals experience difficulty with sleeping, from sleep apnea and allergies, to excessive worrying, chronic pain, and even hyperthyroidism. Not only is it important to discover the root cause of sleeping difficulties, but the fact that the client is not getting enough sleep is, in itself, a health concern and should be investigated.

4. The safety of the client's mother

NOT INDICATED (-3)

There is no evidence to suggest that the client's mother isn't being properly cared for or is in an unsafe environment. This is not relevant in this case.

5. The client's relationship with her husband

INDICATED (+1)

The client has indicated that she has been married for twenty years and just recently, the couple has been bickering quite a bit. Upon further discussion and inquiry, the counselor may wish to suggest couples' therapy.

Section C: Relevance of Decision Making

1. Persistent complex bereavement disorder (PCBD)

NOT INDICATED (-2)

PCBD is the presence of extreme grief over the loss of a loved one that lasts beyond six months. Individuals with PCBD demonstrate a preoccupation with the loved one's death, an unwillingness to accept the loss, or even a desire to join the departed person. This does not apply in this case.

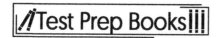

2. Adjustment disorder

INDICATED (+3)

According to the DSM-5, adjustment disorders are characterized by the onset of either behavioral or emotional symptoms that can be directly attributed to one or more specific stressors. Individuals suffering from an adjustment disorder will also experience complications at home, work, or in otherwise daily functioning as a result of their condition, but once the stressor or stressors are eliminated, the symptoms should greatly diminish and disappear within a six-month window. This diagnosis seems very relevant given the initial intake data.

3. Acute stress disorder

NOT INDICATED (-3)

Acute stress disorder is defined as a severe emotional response to a traumatic event, such as a direct or perceived physical or sexual assault. This is not relevant in this case.

4. Generalized anxiety disorder (GAD)

NOT INDICATED (-1)

Adjustment disorder can sometimes be mistaken for GAD, as the two diagnoses share similar symptoms such as an impairment with concentration, sleeping difficulties, and excessive worrying that negatively impacts daily functioning. However, a person suffering from GAD can be worried about any number of events that have or haven't even happened, or their worrying cannot be associated with anything in particular. This doesn't apply in this case.

5. Panic disorder

NOT INDICATED (-2)

If an individual experiences recurrent, unexpected panic attacks, followed by periods of unrest as the individual "awaits" the next attack, they might be suffering from a panic disorder. Other significant signs and symptoms of a panic disorder involve an interference with daily functioning, or the modification of daily routines or behavior directly due to these attacks. This does not apply in this case.

Section D: Relevance of Diagnosis Confirmation

1. Identifiable stressors

INDICATED (+2)

According to the DSM-5, adjustment disorders are characterized by the onset of either behavioral or emotional symptoms that can be directly attributed to one or more specific stressors. The client is dealing with two stressors: the recent loss of her father and adjusting to caring for her mother in the family home.

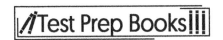

2. Significant impairment in daily functioning

INDICATED (+3)

The client has admitted that she has been frequently absent from work, is arguing with her spouse, and is having difficulty with concentration and sleeping. This signifies significant impairment in daily functioning, which is one of the requirements for an adjustment disorder diagnosis.

3. A traumatic event

NOT INDICATED (-3)

A traumatic event is defined as a direct or perceived physical or sexual assault, or the witnessing of a violent, life-threatening act. This is not a requirement for an adjustment disorder diagnosis.

4. A psychosis

NOT INDICATED (-3)

A psychosis refers to a condition in which an individual may see objects, people, or events that aren't real, hear sounds that don't exist, or experience delusions—unfounded and often absurd beliefs that are caused by the disorder. This is not a requirement for an adjustment disorder diagnosis.

5. High blood pressure

NOT INDICATED (-1)

Although the client's rapid heartbeat and shortness of breath may be indicative of elevated blood pressure, it is not a requirement for an adjustment disorder diagnosis.

Section E: Relevance of Treatment

1. Insight therapy

NOT INDICATED (-2)

Some individuals act and react to events in their lives in ways that they may not understand. This is because their actions and reactions may be triggered at a subconscious level. Insight therapy helps these individuals to recognize how events from their past—parental relationships, school experiences, friendships—may be responsible for controlling how they act and react in their present lives. This is not an appropriate form of therapy for this client.

2. Guided imagery

INDICATED (+1)

Guided imagery aims to engage any combination of all five senses and has been well documented for decades as an established therapeutic practice. Guided imagery is used to assist the individual in using imagination to overcome difficulties or obstacles in their life. It has been proven to reduce stress and lower blood pressure and anxiety levels. This may be an effective therapy to apply in this case.

3. Medication

INDICATED (+2)

Adjustment disorders often involve bouts of insomnia, depression, and anxiety. There are effective and clinically-proven medications to lessen these symptoms, such as antianxiety drugs and antidepressants.

4. Psychotherapy

INDICATED (+3)

Psychotherapy, or talk therapy, can be very beneficial to clients with adjustment disorders. Psychotherapy sessions help individuals to focus on the stressors causing the disorder and assist in the development of self-regulation skills to help restore a healthy emotional and behavioral response to the stressors.

5. Support groups

INDICATED (+1)

Once the client has had a chance to work with the counselor and has started to develop healthy coping strategies to deal with her disorder, support groups would be a very beneficial next step, especially support groups that deal specifically with bereavement and aging parents.

Section F: Relevance of Decision Making

1. Read up on current professional literature regarding adjustment disorders.

INDICATED (+2)

It is perfectly reasonable and ethical to continue treating this client if you feel confident enough that you have the experience and skillset to treat this disorder. However, if it has been a while since you've treated anyone with an adjustment disorder, it would be wise to read up on the most current professional literature.

2. Discontinue treatment and ask that the client seek the services of another professional.

NOT INDICATED (-3)

In a legal sense, this may be seen as "abandonment" and could land you in serious legal jeopardy. Patient abandonment should be avoided to the extent possible, but if you feel you do not have an adequate knowledge and skillset to effectively treat this client, your responsibility is to seek out a colleague who can confidently treat the client and refer her to that colleague.

3. Attend conferences specific to the diagnosis.

INDICATED (+2)

If you have both the expertise and the skillset to offer services to this client, but you would like to learn whether or not there have been advances in treatment options, find out if there are any current or upcoming conferences that deal with this diagnosis and attend the conferences. Staying current with the most up-to-date treatment modalities is always a wise and ethical practice.

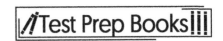

4. Secure supervision with, and/or consult with informed colleagues to confirm that your treatment approach is both adequate and appropriate.

INDICATED (+2)

If you have received the client's express consent to share her personal health information (PHI) with other colleagues, it is perfectly reasonable to consult with other mental health professionals or ask for their supervision to ensure your treatment approach is both adequate and appropriate.

5. Let the client decide whether or not she wishes to continue based on your limitations.

NOT INDICATED (-3)

The client has come to *you* to seek professional treatment for her mental health concerns. It is both unethical and inappropriate for you to ask for *her* professional opinion on whether or not to continue sessions with you based on your feelings of inadequacy.

Section G: Relevance of Referrals

1. Family counseling

NOT INDICATED (-1)

Family counseling would only be appropriate if the individual sessions were not proving beneficial and the client specifically requested that family members be brought into the sessions. Assuming that the individual sessions have been successful, there would be no need for family counseling at this time.

2. Individual grief therapy

NOT INDICATED (-2)

Although the client is grieving the loss of her father, the predetermined number of sessions has proved successful and the client is applying self-monitoring and regulating techniques to help control her anxiety and maintain a healthy family balance. Individual grief therapy would not be necessary at this stage.

3. Independent living education

NOT INDICATED (-3)

Independent living education is designed to assist young adults in the transition from family life to living on their own. In an independent living environment, young adults may receive treatment, as well as lessons in life skills that include healthy eating habits, an introduction to a well-balanced exercise regime, establishing positive relationships, and if necessary, assistance with combatting addictions and managing mental illness disorders. This does not apply in this case.

4. Social skills training

NOT INDICATED (-3)

Simply put, social skills training works with individuals who have great difficulty relating to others either in the family home, at school, or in the workplace. Social skills training helps these individuals to develop the skills necessary to establish and maintain healthy relationships. This is not relevant here.

5. Support groups

INDICATED (+3)

This client has recently experienced the death of her father and is currently caring for her mother in her family home while trying to work full-time and care for her other family members. A support group, especially one that focuses on bereavement and/or aging parents, would be of particular benefit to this client.

Simulation 10

Section A: Relevance and Initial Information Gathering

1. Recurrent flashbacks

INDICATED (+3)

The client has indicated that she has experienced recurrent flashbacks throughout her life and that these flashbacks are haunting. Flashbacks of traumatic events can be extremely debilitating in a person's life and can potentially interfere with emotional, behavioral, and cognitive functioning.

2. Family problems

INDICATED (+2)

Through tears, this client has expressed the desire to understand why some family members refuse to speak to her, and why others choose not to believe her allegations of sexual abuse. This is clearly an emotionally painful issue and requires attention.

3. Difficulty keeping a job

INDICATED (+1)

Initial intake data demonstrate a very poor work history and the inability to stay with one job for extended periods of time. There is a strong correlation between mental health issues and work-related problems. This is an area that requires further attention.

4. Sleeping difficulties

NOT INDICATED (-2)

There is no evidence to suggest that the client is having any sleeping difficulties.

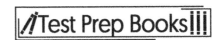

5. Sexual abuse counseling

INDICATED (+3)

The client has admitted that two years ago she came forward with allegations of sexual abuse that she experienced thirty years ago. This has led to a family crisis in which some members refuse to believe her, while others have all but abandoned her, leaving her in great distress.

Section B: Relevance of Main Issues

1. Childhood sexual abuse

INDICATED (+3)

Adult survivors of childhood sexual abuse can experience a wide variety of emotional, physical, social, and cognitive difficulties. These difficulties can range from mild to severe and can be very debilitating.

2. Recurrent flashbacks

INDICATED (+2)

Recurrent flashbacks are indicative of extreme stress and are most commonly connected to a past traumatic event in an individual's life. If the recurrent flashbacks interfere with daily functioning, they can complicate an individual's ability to concentrate at work and at home and can negatively impact the individual's overall well-being.

3. Emotional instability

INDICATED (+2)

The client has expressed the desire to feel "emotional relief" and "emotional stability," and has admitted that she believes at least one of the reasons for her poor work history is her high level of stress.

4. Work-related issues

NOT INDICATED (-1)

Although the client has admitted to having a very poor work history, specific work-related concerns were not discussed. There seems to be more of an issue with the client's ability to cope with the stresses of any particular job than with specific job-related issues.

5. Family values

NOT INDICATED (-1)

The "family systems theory" focuses on how members within a system—in this case, a family—interact with one another and affect one another. Decades ago, some family therapists even advocated for a "family affair model," which argued that, in cases of sexual abuse within the family, all members of the family were at least in some part responsible for the abuse.

Even though in this particular case, certain members of the client's family have either expressed a disbelief in the client's allegations or have stopped communicating with her altogether, this has more to do with how individuals and families cope with sexual abuse allegations and less about a particular family's set of values, traditions, or belief systems.

Section C: Relevance of Diagnosis

1. Paranoid personality disorder

NOT INDICATED (-3)

Characterized by an individual's heightened suspicion of others, an exaggerated level of anger, a belief that people are out to get them, and increased social isolation, paranoid personality disorder is irrelevant in this case.

2. Dissociative disorder

NOT INDICATED (-2)

Although one of the symptoms of dissociative disorder is the presence of depression, as well as interpersonal and work-related coping difficulties, in order to be diagnosed with dissociative disorder, an individual must demonstrate a certain level of detachment from oneself and one's emotions, as well as a blurred sense of reality or significant shifts in personality. This is not an appropriate diagnosis.

3. Bipolar disorder

NOT INDICATED (-3)

Bipolar disorders are characterized by extreme "mood episodes" that can be depressive, manic, or even hypomanic in nature. As this client indicates a relatively consistent depressive mood, this diagnosis would not be appropriate.

4. Post-Traumatic Stress Disorder (PTSD)

INDICATED (+3)

PTSD is a disorder associated with people who have directly experienced or have witnessed a traumatic event, such as sexual assault, a near-death experience, or a violent death. Individuals diagnosed with PTSD can experience recurrent, intrusive flashbacks of the traumatic event and a persistent heightened level of sadness.

5. Separation anxiety disorder

NOT INDICATED (-2)

Individuals suffering from separation anxiety disorder experience a heightened level of distress associated with the suggestion of being separated from a significant person in their lives. Among other telltale signs, they also tend to have an extreme and unwarranted fear that harm will come to their loved one/s if they are not with them at all times. These symptoms are not relevant in this case.

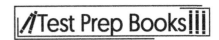

Section D: Relevance of Confirming Diagnosis

1. Number of marriages

NOT INDICATED (-3)

The number of marriages in the client's life is completely irrelevant to a revision or confirmation in the diagnosis of PTSD.

2. Avoidance of people or situations that trigger reminders

INDICATED (+1)

One of the criteria in the DSM-5 for a PTSD diagnosis is the avoidance of people or situations that trigger a reminder of the traumatic event/s. This is a very important data indicator.

3. Grossly underweight/overweight

NOT INDICATED (-3)

A person's weight is not at all a factor in the diagnosis of PTSD and is therefore irrelevant.

4. Regular, intrusive thoughts

INDICATED (+2)

Another sign of possible PTSD is the presence of persistent, intrusive thoughts that negatively impact an individual's life. This is highly relevant data that will help to either confirm or revise a provisional PTSD diagnosis.

5. Abuse reported to authorities

NOT INDICATED (-3)

Statistics have shown that on average, two-thirds of sexual assault incidents go unreported to authorities. This is a staggering statistic, but whether or not this client reported her sexual assault to authorities does not factor into a diagnosis of PTSD. This is completely irrelevant when considering a revision or confirmation of a diagnosis.

Section E: Relevance of Interventions

1. Cognitive behavior therapy (CBT)

INDICATED (+3)

CBT is regarded as the best form of therapy for clients with PTSD. From relationship-building techniques and client empowerment, to teaching a client to increase his/her sense of self advocacy and learn to set healthy boundaries, CBT can help a person with PTSD regain control of their everyday functioning. Some forms of CBT include prolonged exposure (PE), eye movement desensitization and reprocessing (EMDR), and cognitive processing therapy (CPT).

2. Positive reinforcement

NOT INDICATED (-2)

Positive reinforcement is primarily used to encourage children and adolescents to respond respectfully and in socially-acceptable ways at home, in school, and in social settings. This is not an appropriate technique to use in this case.

3. Medication

INDICATED (+2)

The vast majority of mental health practitioners agree that CBT should be the first approach to treating a person diagnosed with PTSD. However, some cases may warrant the use of medications that can help to reduce and/or eliminate intrusive thoughts, avoidance issues, and mood alterations. Currently, the only FDA-approved medications to treat the symptoms of PTSD include sertraline (Zoloft) and paroxetine (Paxil).

4. Confrontation

NOT INDICATED (-2)

Although some victims of sexual abuse may have the desire to confront the perpetrator, whether or not to confront is a personal choice and is not a treatment approach that counselors use when treating sexual abuse victims or individuals suffering with PTSD.

5. Positive self-talk training

INDICATED (+2)

Positive self-talk training is one of many PTSD management techniques that show promising results. Positive self-talk, coupled with learning calming, breathing, and relaxation exercises, grounding techniques, and even writing about the traumatic experience/s, can work to increase an individual's sense of self-control and help the individual to self-regulate and manage their PTSD symptoms.

Section F: Relevance of Decision Making

1. Unproven therapies can cause more harm than good

NOT INDICATED (-3)

Complimentary alternative medicines (CAMs) can refer to herbal medicines as well as alternative therapies, including meditation, yoga, and acupuncture. Although the jury is still out on the overall efficacy of CAMs, there is some evidence to suggest that they can be beneficial for individuals living with PTSD. Although a counselor's obligation is to educate the client on the fact that CAMs are not *proven* methods of treatment, for a counselor to suggest to a client that CAMs may cause more harm than good would be inappropriate.

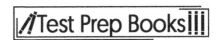

2. Further explanation and justification from client is required

INDICATED (+1)

It would be prudent for a counselor to ask the client why she feels acupuncture may help her and should educate the client regarding the need for more scientific research to determine its overall efficacy.

3. Alternative therapies are worth exploring

INDICATED (+1)

There is some current evidence to suggest that acupuncture, animal-assisted therapy, and other CAMs are beneficial in treating people with PTSD. Alternative therapies can be worth exploring as long as the counselor also educates the client regarding the lack of scientific data regarding their overall efficacy.

4. Should the client choose an alternative therapy, your sessions would be terminated

NOT INDICATED (-3)

Terminating therapy should only occur if the counselor does not have the experience and/or the skillset to offer appropriate treatment (in which case, the counselor should refer the client to a professional colleague who specializes in the specific disorder), when it is evident the client no longer requires counseling, or when the client is no longer benefiting from the counseling service. It would be completely unethical to refuse service to this client, should she choose to also pursue a CAM such as acupuncture.

5. Caution alternative therapies in conjunction with counseling sessions

INDICATED (+3)

The most appropriate response would be for the counselor to educate the client on the lack of scientific evidence regarding the efficacy of CAMs, while continuing to offer regular counseling sessions that directly address symptoms of PTSD.

Section G: Relevance of Referrals

1. PTSD specialized treatment center

INDICATED (+2)

There are outpatient and inpatient therapeutic centers that specialize in helping individuals with PTSD. PTSD specialized treatment centers provide a safe environment for individuals to freely discuss their experiences and learn coping techniques to effectively deal with triggers, flashbacks, and depression, which can often lead to breakthroughs in long-term management of PTSD.

2. Couples therapy

INDICATED (+2)

Referring the client to couple's therapy is definitely in the best interest of the client. PTSD can negatively impact an individual's level of intimacy, especially if the PTSD is a direct result of sexual assault or abuse.

Couples therapy helps to educate both the client and the client's partner on what PTSD is, recognize the signs and symptoms, and build a healthy level of respect and trust.

3. Psychiatrist

NOT INDICATED (-2)

Gone are the days that a patient sees a psychiatrist for talk therapy. The main role of a psychiatrist is to partner with psychologists and other mental health practitioners in order to prescribe necessary medication. In order for this client to continue with behavioral therapy, referral to a psychiatrist would not be appropriate.

4. A religious pastor

NOT INDICATED (-2)

There is no evidence to suggest that this client has a religious affiliation, nor does a pastor necessarily have a degree or expertise in dealing with PTSD disorders. This would be an inappropriate referral.

5. Certified peer specialist (CPS)

INDICATED (+3)

Certified peer specialists are individuals with real-life experience who have successfully recovered or are role models for successful management of their mental health disorder. CPSs must have successfully passed an occupational health exam allowing them to work directly with individuals living with the same or similar mental health disorder. A CPS helps individuals to develop a personal recovery plan for long-term management of their mental health disorder. This would be an appropriate referral for this client.

Dear NCMHCE Test Taker,

We would like to start by thanking you for purchasing this study guide for your NCMHCE exam. We hope that we exceeded your expectations.

Our goal in creating this study guide was to cover all of the topics that you will see on the test. We also strove to make our practice questions as similar as possible to what you will encounter on test day. With that being said, if you found something that you feel was not up to your standards, please send us an email and let us know.

We would also like to let you know about another book in our catalog that may interest you.

NCE

This can be found on Amazon: amazon.com/dp/1628458615

We have study guides in a wide variety of fields. If the one you are looking for isn't listed above, then try searching for it on Amazon or send us an email.

Thanks Again and Happy Testing!
Product Development Team
info@studyguideteam.com

FREE Test Taking Tips DVD Offer

To help us better serve you, we have developed a Test Taking Tips DVD that we would like to give you for FREE. **This DVD covers world-class test taking tips that you can use to be even more successful when you are taking your test.**

All that we ask is that you email us your feedback about your study guide. Please let us know what you thought about it – whether that is good, bad or indifferent.

To get your **FREE Test Taking Tips DVD**, email freedvd@studyguideteam.com with "FREE DVD" in the subject line and the following information in the body of the email:

   a. The title of your study guide.

   b. Your product rating on a scale of 1-5, with 5 being the highest rating.

   c. Your feedback about the study guide. What did you think of it?

   d. Your full name and shipping address to send your free DVD.

If you have any questions or concerns, please don't hesitate to contact us at freedvd@studyguideteam.com.

Thanks again!

Made in the USA
Monee, IL
10 April 2021